HALO IN THE SKY

HALO IN THE SKY

*Observations on Anality
and Defense*

LEONARD SHENGOLD, M.D.

Foreword by Edward M. Weinshel, M.D.

YALE UNIVERSITY PRESS
New Haven and London

First published 1988 by The Guilford Press.
Paperbound edition published 1992 by Yale University Press.

Printed in the United States of America.

Library of Congress Catalog Card Number: 91-67589
ISBN: 0-300-05710-5 (pbk.)

The paper in this book meets the guidelines for permanence and durability of the Committee on
Production Guidelines for Book Longevity of the Council on Library Resources.

Grateful acknowledgment is made to the following for permission to reprint previously published
material:

International Journal of Psychoanalysis: Revised version of "Defensive Anality and Anal Narcissism" (1985), 66:47-73. Revised version of "Anal Erogeneity: The Goose and the Rat" (1982),
63:331-345. International Review of Psychoanalysis: Revised version of "Kaspar Hauser and
Soul Murder: A Study of Deprivation" (1978), 5:457-476.

Random House: "The Geography of the House." Copyright © 1965 by W. H. Auden. Reprinted
from *W. H. Auden: Collected Poems* by W. H. Auden, edited by Edward Mendelson, by
permission of Random House, Inc.

10   9   8   7   6   5   4   3   2   1

But human nature is not my invention. I am convinced that the most raging material appetites express themselves unwittingly in outbursts of idealism, just as the most obscene carnal excesses are engendered by pure desire for the impossible, ethereal aspiration toward supreme bliss. Besides, neither I nor anyone else knows the meaning of those two words: "soul" and "body"—nor where one leaves off and the other begins. We are aware of certain *drives*, and that is all. Materialism and spiritualism still weigh too heavily on the study of man to permit an impartial investigation of all these phenomena. The anatomy of the human heart is as yet uncharted. So how can you expect it to be cured? To have embarked on such studies will remain the nineteenth century's sole claim to fame.

 Gustave Flaubert, 1857–1880 (p. 16)

The ego . . . is first and foremost a body ego.

 Sigmund Freud, 1923 (pp. 26–27)

In a typical case the anal ring was phantasied as a kind of halo suspended in the sky.

 Edward Glover, 1938 (p. 294)

Contents

Foreword

It's been said, in one way or another, that psychoanalysis is a way of rationally studying the irrational; and, certainly, there is great interest among psychoanalysts in trying to understand how a given irrational psychic product can be converted into a rational one. In a related and more general way, psychoanalysts have always been fascinated with the still mysterious process in which the "infant mewling and puking" becomes transformed into a civilized human being. Similarly, psychoanalysts have been intrigued with the even more enigmatic questions of the evolution of human civilization—long before Freud's charge in his 1930 *Civilization and Its Discontents* that "we must ask ourselves to what influences the development of civilization owes its origins, how it arose, and by what its course has been determined."

Actually Freud had already indicated his interest in the development of civilization in his 1893 paper "On the Psychical Mechanism of Hysterical Phenomena," in which he paid homage to the English writer who "has wittily remarked, the man who first flung a word of abuse at his enemy instead of a spear was the founder of civilization." In his 1905 monograph *Jokes and Their Relation to the Unconscious*, Freud offers another observation (this time by a certain G. C. von Lichtenberg) in which a "higher personal civilization" is acquired by the suppression of aggression. Von Lichtenberg's remark was "Where we now say 'Excuse me!' we used to give a box on the ears."

In the 1914 "Moses of Michelangelo," Freud takes a further step in his conceptualization of the civilizing process. Freud, as you will remember, rejects the then-prevailing theory that Michelangelo's masterpiece portrayed the enraged Moses just as he was about to hurl down the Tables. Says Freud: "But Michelangelo has placed a different Moses on the tomb of the Pope, one superior to the historical or traditional Moses. He has modified the theme of the broken Tables; he does not let Moses break them in his wrath, but makes him be influenced by the danger that they will be broken and makes him calm that wrath, or at any rate prevent it from becoming an act. In this way he has added something new and more than human to the figure of Moses; so that the giant frame with its tremendous physical power becomes only a concrete expression *of the highest mental achievement that is possible in a man*, that of struggling successfully against an inward passion for the sake of a cause to which he has devoted himself" (my italics).

In *Beyond the Pleasure Principle*, Freud discusses his well-known observations of the 18-month-old little boy with his game of the reel and string. The little boy's game was, Freud concluded, a way of coping with his mother's absence, an absence which he accepted without crying or other disturbance. Freud stresses that the game "was related to the child's *great cultural achievement*—the instinctual renunciation (that is, the renunciation of instinctual satisfaction) which he had made in allowing his mother to go away without protesting" (my italics).

Freud tackled the whole issue of how man became civilized head-on in the above-mentioned *Civilization and Its Discontents*; and while he was not altogether successful or satisfied with his quest for the definitive answers to the questions concerning the origins and development of civilization, Freud made it clear he felt that the gradual and effective taming of the instinctual drives—both sexual and aggressive—and their derivatives was the key to those achievements. It is no surprise that Freud made the resolution of the Oedipus complex and the emergence of the superego with its powerful sense of guilt the central and, to some extent, superordinate determinants for the colossal achievement which permitted man to become civilized. What has evolved for the human race phylogenetically is recapitulated ontogenetically in the development of the individual, considerable evidence for which we encounter in our clinical work.

In *Civilization and Its Discontents* Freud does deal briefly with the fact that, by and large, cleanliness is a necessity in a civilized society; and, as a result, a man had to surrender his freedom and his pleasure in being dirty (or at least not being clean) if he were to participate in such a society. Freud speaks of the repression of anal erotism associated with the emergence of civilization; and we are all familiar with the dilemma of the young child in his struggle to maintain his anal pleasures and gratifications while simultaneously trying to maintain his good relationships with the important people in his immediate society. Yet this was not a topic Freud pursued in his considerations of the emergence of human civilization; he did not, for instance, raise any questions about the status of the 18-month-old boy's toilet training as a possible causal factor of the child's exemplary behavior.

In a sense this is what Leonard Shengold's *Halo in The Sky: Observations on Anality and Defense* is all about. I have summarized in some detail what Freud has told us about man's becoming civilized, because Shengold's point of departure in his fascinating account—I should say "story—of how the human animal becomes civilized *and* humanized is, as he states in his opening sentence, "devoted to the clinical viability of Freud's drive theory, part of which is Freud's concept of the body ego." Shengold is an unabashed Freudian, albeit a very independent one—"classical" in an adherence to the basic concepts but of considerable flexibility in the elaboration and application of those concepts. One might characterize his approach as that of "new ideas in old bottles"; and, as such, Shengold has provided us with a necessary complement to what Freud contributed to our understanding of these issues.

The term *anality* encompasses the psychological, biological, and interpersonal phenomena of the period in the child's development between 1½ and 3½ years of age. It is the phase during which the child (and the parents) must cope with the challenges of toilet training, must adapt to his own burgeoning capacity for motility and the concomitant expanding universe, and must accommodate to the dramatic unfolding of his ability to think. Internally the child is exposed to the impact of powerful destructive, even murderous, archaic impulses for which his still tenuous defensive structures are ill-prepared; but it is also a stage of marked growth of psychological structure, including those structures which subserve the defensive apparatus. The outcome of these momentous internal conflicts and external struggles is truly decisive for the child's ongoing development and for the future of his psychological health and for his potential as a human being.

As Shengold examines and unravels the manifold and many-faceted components of this complex drama, he never lets the reader forget the "body," the body ego, the body feelings, and the ever-menacing primitive affects which can disrupt the course of normal development. In the center of all of this are the urethral and anal sphincters—especially the latter—whose mastery constitutes the pivotal task and most difficult challenge of the anal stage. The core and the linchpin of the anal–narcissistic defensive structure is "modeled on the prototype of bodily mastery of the sphincters" together with the mastery of locomotion and the acquisition of the power of effective thinking. Shengold declares that "metaphorically," the anal–narcissistic defensive system operates as a sphincter "door" which must be able to close in order to control and to permit the toleration of unpleasure that follows the frustration of instinctual needs. This capacity for "controlling closure" is the prerequisite for the modulation of the powerful emotional and sensory needs of infancy; and it is equally crucial for that metaphorical sphincter to be capable of a comparable opening which allows for the appropriate discharge of the whole repertoire of formidable impulses and primitive affects.

The extent to which the child can negotiate effectively and with reasonable safety these redoubtable conflicts and struggles will determine the functional balance between the forces of defense and of impulse. The resultant capacity for modulating these forces will determine the individual's ability to hold back and to retain as well as the ability to release and to give. The resulting comfortable confidence in the capacity for such control facilitates the modulation of the affective expression that is necessary for the integration of a "whole" human being and for stable and fulfilling human relationships. The achievement of a well-balanced "controlled closure," to put it too concisely, represents the "rational" outcome of anal stage development; if that control is too great or if the control is irresolute and uncertain, the outcome will be an "irrational" one.

This summary hardly does justice either to the substance or the elegance of Shengold's careful exposition. He presents his evidence on three levels: first, a thorough and thoughtful presentation of the theoretical underpinnings for the anal–narcissistic defensive apparatus; second, a series of rich clinical case extracts which illustrate convincingly each of the theoretical arguments he advances; and third, a minicollection of representative "case histories" from literary classics. We are treated to discussions from the works of literary (and psychological) masters such as Flaubert, Proust, Rabelais, Shakespeare, Auden, Trilling, Swift, Kundera, Yeats, Wordsworth, Chekhov, and von Feuerbach (whose history of Kaspar Hauser is a poignant, chilling, and repulsive account of dehumanization and soul murder); and the reader can share the insights of these authors in regard to the vicissitudes of anality. And, somehow, Shengold has managed to provide us with scattered "hors d'oeuvres" of items such as certainty and uncertainty, idealization and devaluation, fascination, caricature, autohypnosis, scotomization, and the role of anality in the perversions. Shengold has the knack of writing as a poet while eschewing all of the poetic licenses which might undermine his scientific position. Above all, what shines through his writing is an uncompromising respect for the individual human being and that human being's humanity.

Shengold has amply demonstrated that it is possible to turn feces into gold. *Halo in the Sky* will provide every reader valuable insights not only into the mind of the civilized human being—but also into mind of each individual reader.

Edward M. Weinshel, M.D.
October 1987

Acknowledgments

I have written elsewhere about the basic importance of metaphor for mental development and for psychoanalysis (Shengold, 1981) and I have dealt specifically with the metaphor of a journey (Shengold, 1966). The reader will find this latter interest made manifest in my meandering, peripatetic style. I think (or rationalize) that there is method in it, and that it is, at the least, relevant to proper and inevitable psychoanalytic method. Many of my ideas are achieved by way of association and discursively attached to the main narrative. Looking back at the writing I have done as a psychoanalyst, I see definite thematic paths winding through and connecting most of my papers. I have therefore absorbed transformed versions of several previously published works into the making of this book. I hope my wandering has made for connected and coherent psychic travel.

Acknowledgments and gratitude begin with my patients from whom I have learned so much. For the sake of keeping confidentiality I have changed and transposed minor descriptive "facts" (and at least once have conflated two people with similar character pathology into one). I have done my best—an unavoidable, inadequate best (see Spence, 1982)—to present the details of the clinical encounters as I remember them (generally they were noted down on the day they occurred); I have aimed for emotional "truth."

I want to thank four wonderful teachers: Lionel Trilling, Robert Fliess, Jacob Arlow, and Mark Kanzer. I am blessed with a number of good friends who read and criticize my work regularly: Sam Abrams, Roy Lilleskov, Austin Silber, and, especially for this book, Shelley Orgel, Vann Spruiell (who suggested the title), and Ed Weinshel. In these latter years the friendship and advice of the late Vic Calef and Leo Rangell have meant much to me. For several specific suggestions about this work I am grateful to the following discussants of various presentations of parts of it: Erna Furman, Allan Jong, Mark Kanzer, Ed Knight, and Brian Robertson; I acknowledge some of their comments in the text. I appreciate the general guidance of Bob Wallerstein. I was directed to relevant literature by Ron Baker, Eric Gann, Jeffrey Masson, Brian Robertson, and Arnold Rothstein. Finally, I cannot sufficiently thank my wife who reads everything I write with loving discrimination and does her best (against considerable resistance) to keep my prose spare, grammatical, and germane.

1

Introduction

PURPOSE AND GENERAL PRINCIPLES

This book is devoted to the clinical viability of Freud's drive ["*Triebe*"] theory, part of which is Freud's concept of the body ego. These beleaguered ideas provide mysterious, ill-defined, but indispensable links between body and mind—links central not only to Freudian theory, but to any developmental thinking based on common sense. Psychology cannot disregard the body: "Behold! the Body includes and is the meaning, the main concern—and includes and is the Soul" (Whitman, 1855, p. 25). Whitman says, "I sing the body electric" (p. 107). I would like to say, "I sing the body ego electric."

Freud defines "*Triebe*" (perhaps best but nonetheless awkwardly translated as "instinctual drives"; Strachey usually simply uses the overconnotative "instincts") as:

> a concept on the frontier between the mental and the somatic, as the psychical representative of the stimuli originating from within the organism and reaching the mind, as a measure of the demand made upon the mind of work in consequence of its connection with the body. (Freud, 1915, p. 121)

Biological energies, then, influence the mind by way of the instinctual drives. Freud (1933) said, "the theory of the instincts is so to say our mythology. Instincts [instinctual drives] are mythical entities, magnificent in their indefiniteness. In our work we cannot for a moment disregard them, yet we are never sure that we are seeing them clearly" (p. 95). There are currently many psychological theorists who feel that

1

they can and should "disregard" them—disregard not only the drives but any connection between the psychological and the biological. They make a part of our nature into the whole. Man is presented as purely psychological, or social, or as a computer, or as a linguistic construct. (There are also those who want to reduce everything to the biological.) I believe we need our magnificently indefinite mythology, which often contains more wisdom than do naively aspiring efforts toward pure, quantifiable science.

We also cannot isolate the mind from energies (Freud's economic point of view) or from the biological without abandoning our humanistic legacy of the knowledge of man's nature. Trilling reminds us that "the interaction of biology and culture in the fate of man is not a matter which we have yet begun to understand" (1955, p. 116). Trilling believes that Freud's emphasis on biology is "actually, a liberating idea. It proposes to us that culture is not all-powerful. It suggests that there is a residue of human quality beyond the reach of cultural control" (p. 113)—a ray of hope in this century of totalitarianism.[1] Of course we have to differentiate as well as to connect the biological and the psychological, but the mind must deal with the biological as well as with the interpersonal ("object-relations"), the social, and the cultural. The analyst should include rather than exclude in his vain but necessary attempt to reconstruct the actuality of an individual's past and present.

In contrast to the developmental continuity envisioned by Freud and Anna Freud, many recent psychoanalytic papers on the instinctual drives have presented or implied a dichotomy between preoedipal and oedipal drives, sometimes as if the two were in contest for pathogenic primacy rather than designating a developmental sequence of infinite individual variety. (See Blum, 1977, for a similar view.) Further, the preoedipal has frequently been equated with the earliest psychic development ("oral" in libidinal terms)—to a comparative neglect of the equally important "anal" developmental phase.

I am not saying much that is new in my emphasis on anality. Anality was the heart of the preoedipal in early psychoanalytical theorizing; restoring proper perspective does not mean downgrading the impact of the first year and a half of life or of the oedipal phase. We should think in terms of a continuity of development (transformations and regressions that make for confluences and confusions) without asserting any kind of pathogenic priority. Anal libido (sexual energy) and erogeneity (excitement of anal and perianal parts) as part of that phase of instinctual drive development which we call "anal–sadistic," represent an ontogenetically repeated part of human phylogenetic heritage that continues to operate in the maturing individual's mind alongside earlier and later manifestations and transformations (see Abrams, 1977). Anal phenomena are familiar to every student of the psyche who works with people, but they have somehow receded into the background (I am using an anal metaphor here) of our theory in recent years. I concentrate on two primal defensive modes that begin in the narcissistic period of ontogenetic primeval time: These are idealization and devaluation (or debasement), which develop out of the infant's first "yes" and "no." They come to maturity and flourish, as defensive operations of the ego, during the anal developmental phase.[2]

My central concept, anal–narcissistic defensiveness, concerns the use of anal drive-derived energy and mental structure for defensive purposes. This is a new emphasis (although not a new discovery). I am trying in this book to contribute something toward the basic psychoanalytic concept of defense, which I see as an aspect of the even more basic concept of body ego.

To this purpose, I stress the defensive aspects of anality in the concept of anal-narcissistic regression. In my discussion of the growth of the mind's defensive system, I have not correlated primal or archaic affect with the evolution of unpleasure into anxiety and depressive affect, ignoring not only Freud but the basic papers of Rangell (1955, 1968, 1978), Brenner (1974, 1975, 1976, 1981) and others (this would take another book, and not by me). And I restrict my clinical material to male cases, so as not to overburden my discussion with an analysis of the differences relating to anality in the two sexes. (I believe that these differences have to do with the admixture of sphincter defensiveness with aspects of later development such as the female castration complex—but this requires a separate publication.) My emphasis has precluded the use of more clinical material illustrating the expressive and creative aspects of anality—the range and the contradictory richness of the anal–narcissistic world where opposites coexist and reversals abound. Although greyness and caricature and dehumanization are part of anality, along with the congealed rage that I do stress, so also is concentrated vitality, as evidenced by my quotations from Flaubert. I should, however, like to echo Freud's qualified apology regarding the subject of this book. Freud (1917) says, referring to problems involving "anal erotic instinctual impulses" (p. 127):

> Yet the material is so obscure, the abundance of ever-recurring impulses
> so confusing, that even now I am unable to solve the [problems] fully and
> can do no more than make some contribution to [their] solution. (p. 128)

Furthermore, there is much (although not enough) in the psychoanalytic literature which reflects the aspects of anality not included
here, especially in the work of Karl Abraham. In fact, the work of
Abraham has been relatively neglected, along with anality. Karl Abraham was one of the greatest psychoanalysts—perhaps the most
talented after Freud—and he has written so much about anality. In my
travels to various institutes where psychoanalysis is taught, I have
often found that this master of clinical phenomenology is no longer
being read. Despite his premature death (1925) and consequent inadequate absorption of Freud's later theories, Abraham is a master: He
was an early proponent of the integration of psychic fields of reference
(drives, object-relations, defenses, character—see Hanly, 1982). Abraham also appears only rarely in current bibliographies. (This is unfor-
tunately true also of so many of the gifted analysts of the 1920s through
the 1950s.[3]) I hope this book will promote the reading or rereading of
Abraham's brilliant and clinically relevant papers.

Certainty and Uncertainty

Freud declared that psychoanalysis is not a *Weltanschauung*—does
not give a view of the universe, a key to the mysteries of Nature. But
psychoanalysis does, or at least should, provide an approach to a
Weltanschauung, since the work of analysis evokes man's eternal
philosophic questions: who am I? where have I been? where am I
going? what do I know? Freud, so aware of his intellectual forebears,
was insistent on trying to delineate the limits of knowledge: this I
know; this I don't know; this I think I know; this I cannot know. His
mind was able to contain contradictions—to set the relatively certain
beside the hypothetical and the inherently unknowable. Freud's metaphor for analytic work was a most concrete one derived from archaeol-
ogy and architecture (and based on his "scientific" materialist determinism): "Wir setzen doch Stein auf Stein" [we set stone upon stone]
(see Fliess, 1956, p. xiii). Yet, more than anything else, it was dreams,
so insubstantial and mysterious, that made him sure of the rightness of
his observations and assumptions. Freud had his own powerfully

influential blend of 19th-century determinism and philosophic humanism. Trilling (1947) says:

> man, as Freud conceives him, is not to be understood by any simple formula . . . but is rather an inextricable tangle of culture and biology . . . [Freud's] desire for man is only that he should be human, and to that end his science is devoted . . . the poetic qualities of Freud's own principles, which are so clearly in the line of the classic tragic realism, suggest that this is a view which does not narrow the world . . . but on the contrary opens and complicates it. (p. 57)

Freud followed the intellectual tradition of the broadest philosophical inquiry that centers on questioning one's own grasp of one's self and of the universe, and yet permits working with deep conviction (a tradition starting with the Greeks, and so manifest in Montaigne and Pascal). This dichotomy is inherent in the clinical work that provided Freud and still provides his followers with the means to revise and to add to Freud's original ideas.

Optimal clinical work demands a flexible ability to balance an awareness of the limitations of knowledge with a transient certainty. For Trilling this quality of mind is contained in Coleridge's prescription for the poet: to be able to "suspend disbelief." (Trilling suggests that the essence of moral life is "making a willing suspension of disbelief in the selfhood of someone else" [1955, p. 94].) This *not disbelieving* makes it possible to be convinced that something must be so, must be true—for a particular human being, and even (sometimes) for all human beings—while being simultaneously aware of the danger of false conviction and even of delusion (*cf.* E. Kris, 1956). Friedman (1982) shows that the ideas of some present-day psychoanalytic theorists (who are consciously trying to correct, broaden, or abandon what they consider to be Freud's narrow, materialistic-deterministic assumptions with the aim of being all-encompassing and "humanistic") can, paradoxically, lead to oversimplification and denial of aspects of the human condition. Freud's empiric scientific bent, together with his artistic "nightside" (the tragic awareness of the unknowable and the unknown) made for a precarious but salutary balance between certainty and humility.[4] His follower, Karl Abraham, was an inveterate schematizer and classifier (he had the zeal of an embryologist), but he was always aware of, and his papers are pervaded with, the complexity of clinical material. These two men, whose writings form the foundation of the psychoanalytic concept of "anal ity" which is the subject of this book, responded to human beings with a fullness and a multifariousness that shows in (although it occasionally seems to be there in spite of) their theoretical ideas.

A healthy equilibrium between certainty and doubt is hard to attain and hard to maintain. Such balance offends our narcissism by frustrating our earliest need for absolute certainty; yet being too certain can also threaten our narcissism by setting up rigid limitations that belie omnipotence—that interfere with our wish to be able to do anything. (This is one of those double-edged traps that makes the continuation of early narcissism untenable without resorting to denial.) Some part of our mind must always assume that of course the breast will be there if we need it; and that we can always get it back if we lose it; so there is a continual temptation to abandon the risky and inconstant dynamic tension of wisdom—a wisdom that involves the giving up and the letting go of our "intimations of immortality."

Complexity and Diagnosis

In this book I want to stress something that everyone knows, but which can easily be neglected by those who strive for novelty, or more legitimately, for fresh therapeutic approaches: that however exciting a clinical discovery, we must remember how infinitely complicated psychic events are. It follows that most of our theoretical concepts, or metaphors, are inherently inadequate, despite their considerable (and sometimes seemingly indispensable) heuristic value. The fact of the infinite complexity of human (and therefore of clinical) events is not controversial. Freud's comparison of analytic work to the peeling away of the layers of an onion is much too simple, although it might fit a retrospective view; and there are (short, happy) periods of a psychoanalysis during which the homely analogy seems appropriate enough. Psychoanalytic work is the revelation and the exploration of complexities.[5]

Neurosis has turned out to be human nature and not just the result of "seduction by the father" (Freud, 1896, p. 239). Analysts quickly learn to distrust diagnostic categories (even those designed by national committees working for many years). The basic clinical phenomena that involve an individual's whole personality, such as transference and defense, are not satisfactorily communicated by stating that a person is an hysteric, a schizophrenic, or is suffering from

Generalized Anxiety Disorder (300.2, *DSM-III-R*). There are two relative exceptions to this generalization about diagnostic labels: the severe obsessive–compulsive character, and the paranoid personality, which designations can evoke at least a descriptive approximation of the human beings so diagnosed. Both (and they are frequently confluent, as Freud and Abraham have demonstrated) do, loosely but definitely, characterize the three hypothetical parts of the mental personality: id, ego, and superego. Even so, of course, no two obsessional characters or paranoid personalities can be quite the same. Yet the human beings conjured up by these diagnostic tags actually do (at least in many aspects of their existence) resemble caricatures—"flat" characters like those of Dickens (immutable, predictable), rather than "round" ones like those of Tolstoy (changeable, unpredictable). (I am using the terms and examples of E. M. Forster [1927].) Those who suffer from obsessive–compulsive character disorders and from the various forms of paranoia are entangled in conflicts over anal erogeneity and anal–sadistic libido, and analysts have traced both illnesses to fixations that include and feature the anal period of development. Why should there be this link with anality? Is there a quality of oversimplification and caricature, inherent in the anal period? I think that there is, and will return to this question.

Outside of our theory there are no separate lines of human development, although we can, to gain perspective and with profit (as Anna Freud has shown), abstract such lines for learning purposes from the multidimensional, uncircumscribable reticulum of development. My ornate reticulum metaphor is still pitifully deficient, but it serves to complicate the words "separate" and "lines" as I used them in the first sentence of this paragraph. Freud was instinctively attuned to complexities and distrustful of simplifications and absolutes. One can tell this from his prose style. He rarely uses the word "always" in a generalization, and when he does there is often a note of defensive negation that denotes some weakness or incompleteness in his thinking.[6] Guttman's *Concordance* (1981) lists over a thousand (1,023) uses of "always" in Freud's works, but many of these are either modified— that is, "not always" or "almost always"—or are tied to specific individual or concrete observations. There are relatively few general dicta qualified by "always."

In my observations, I hope to avoid certainties and to honor complexities. My ideas are illustrated by material from both applied analysis and clinical analytic work. The clinically based evidence is of course the more reliable, since the analyst's understanding of what the patient is saying can be confirmed (or belied) by seeing whether, as Freud (1937) was fond of quoting from the popular Viennese playwright, Nestroy, "It will all become clear in the course of future developments" (p. 265). What creative artists write (often about themselves) can teach so much, even if it does not furnish the observer with the personal responsibility for relative reliability that comes with direct clinical contact. However, some of the greatest artists are master psychologists; I make most use in this book of Flaubert, Proust, Rabelais, and Shakespeare, all of whom are, to use an expression of Flaubert's, "triple thinkers." This happy phrase refers, I believe, to the ability to work consistently and simultaneously on more than one mental level. Such artists can tap the unconscious with happy results; they are humanity's best *Menschenkenner* who in their creative work can present us with even more than they are aware that they know.

DEFINITIONS AND ORIENTATIONS

The word "anal" has specific psychoanalytic meanings that complement its everyday connotations. The Oxford English Dictionary (Vol. 1, p. 33) defines "anal" as: "1. of or pertaining to the anus, or excretory opening. 2. situated near, or in the region of the anus." If these two definitions (which involve *place*) are combined, one gets the popular concept and term "ass" (in England, "arse") or, more polite, "bottom." These slang terms denote a condensation of anus, perianal region, rectum, and buttocks; and such reference can include the genitals, especially the vagina (here conceived of anally or cloacally, as denoted by the coarse expression "piece of ass" for a sexually available female). Psychoanalytic meanings include these *place* references, but they also indicate *time* and *energy*. Here "anal" signifies: (1) a period of psychic development following the "oral" phase, in which the anus and perianal region ("ass") become the predominant erogenous zone (*i.e.*, the source of anal feelings, or anal erogeneity); (2) a specific quality of (hypothetical) psychic energy originally conceived of as *libido*. (This "economic" concept is part of Freud's developmental theory of instinctual drives.) Anal libido was understood both to supplement and to some extent to change the quality of oral libido (which continues to operate beside it). As Freud's theory evolved, the admixture of aggressive energy with erotic drive energy was called by

Freud and by Abraham "anal–sadistic libido." (It is undoubtedly this instinctual mixture which gives "anal" the emotional connotations of *morally bad* and *dirty* which are so obvious in anal slang and curses.) There is little precision about the timing of this period of predominant anal phenomena, but it is usually described as extending from about age one to age three and a half. (Of course, anal phenomena start earlier and continue afterwards.) The timing of the anal phase varies from person to person, partly on the basis of inner maturational differences, and partly due to each individual's unique environmental stimuli and experiences. Moreover, the anal stage is at some point overtaken by (although it also continues alongside, as had the previous oral stage) the newly predominant phallic and genital erogeneity (sensations, source, and place) and libido (mixture of drive energies).

The "anal phase of development" as used in contemporary psychoanalysis would refer to everything that takes place in the dynamic play of the mind from ages one to three and a half: conflict; progression (maturation) and regression involving instinctual drives; the establishment of ego and superego structure and functions; and object relations (narcissism, separation, individuation). Using the anal drive terminology would indicate an adherence to the concept of the continuing centrality of the body and of the validity of drive theory; these beliefs are the subject of much current controversy.

"Anal" is a word that usually carries an emotional *charge* based on its body-ego "geography," an "economic" (in Freudian metapsychological terms) geography that makes for an "economic–geographic" determinism: the drive force of part of the body ego, which comes "first and foremost." Preoccupation and fascination[7] with the anal product, feelings, and functioning start in the first year of life. To quote Jones (1918):

> Perhaps the most astonishing of all Freud's findings—and certainly the one that has evoked the liveliest incredulity, repugnance, and opposition—was his discovery that certain traits of character may become profoundly modified as the result of sexual excitations experienced by the infant in the region of the anal canal. . . . There are, however, two biological considerations, relating respectively to the ontogenetic and phylogenetic antiquity of the physiological process concerned, that should render the statement made above a little less unthinkable . . . One is that the act of defaecation constitutes one of the two greatest personal interests of the infant during the first year of life . . . [This is related to] the circumstance that the alimentary function in general is the most constant preoccupation of all animals other than man. The other consid-

eration is that many of the sexual processes and organs have been derived from the excretory ones, in both the individual and the race. (p. 413)

For adults, the conscious emotional charge evoked by "anal" is a combination of good and bad feelings: body feelings—pleasure and "unpleasure" with some (and potentially much) sexual excitement—attached to emotion-laden value judgments that are usually predominantly involved with qualities of dirtiness and badness. (It is probably the maturationally early admixture of the aggressive drive with anal erogeneity and libido that makes for a corresponding admixture of moral badness [evil] with aesthetic badness [dirt].) The anal "bad" means both "dirty" and "evil." For the child, there is an initial "good" feeling of predominant pleasure and sexual gratification (if all has gone well) in the experience of passing feces through the anal sphincter (and in playing with and smearing feces); this is accompanied by what appear to be feelings of pride, ownership, and creative power. In later development, varying proportions of these "good" or "healthy" feelings persist in every person alongside (and in dynamic relationship to) the "bad." This mixture, partly conscious and partly unconscious, together with different proportions of excitement and a sense of danger, makes up for each of us the individually variable equation in later life of *anal* equals *good-and-bad*. For most children, usually during the second year of life, it is parental training (which both carries and expresses the unconscious power—ascribed in psychoanalytic theory to the superego—of the parents' emotional biases as well as society's injunctions) plus the crucially timed concurrent enhancement of the aggressive drive (hence the term "anal–sadistic") that makes for the developmental *transition* from *anal* equals *predominantly good* to *anal* equals *predominantly bad*. (Freud considered this partly inherited, partly environmentally conditioned change to be defensive. He understood it to be a result of phylogenetically determined "organic repression" of anality, which (he speculated) had something to do with man's assumption of the erect posture and the consequent diminution in the evolutionarily primal important power of the sense of smell and of excretions to determine behavior (a power still so manifest in many animals—as Jones reminds us).) This notion would supply a corresponding "organic" defensive prototype for my idea of anal defensiveness, which follows.

The anus in the higher animals has developed in the course of evolution from the more primitive and undifferentiated cloaca, which functions both as an excretory and a sexual passage, combining expulsion and reception. I believe there is some continuing biological, phylogenetically derived basis for the psychological resonances and importance of the anus and the anal sphincter, which can be linked to the cloacal coalescence of excretion and sexual receptiveness; this evolutionary remnant involves a current of primal bisexuality that continues to influence both sexes. For both sexes, the anal region ("ass") appears to function in some confluent contradictory fashion—combining passivity and reception with activity and expulsion; surrender and submission with hostile attack. The world that is dominated by anal psychology is full of opposites, reversals, and contradictions. Following the advent of sphincter action (which is superimposed on the previous coexistence of peristaltic and quiescent alternations), bodily (and reflective psychic) effects are marked by mixtures of control and loss of control; closure and openness; repulsion and receptivity. Anal rituals of surrender and submission in the higher animals have been documented in many species by ethologists; and slang and curses in most cultures feature expressions combining aggressive attack and genital and copulatory allusions (such as "Fuck you!") that have a basic, regressive, excremental–destructive quality.

HISTORICAL REVIEW:
FREUD'S FACTS AND THEORIES

Body Ego

Psychoanalysis is based on a mixture of "facts" and theory. In the face of an unexpected phenomenon, Freud was wont to quote his old teacher Charcot's *mot: La théorie, c'est bon, mais ça n'empêche pas d'exister* [Theory is good, but that doesn't prevent the facts from existing.] Our "facts" (the limitations of what is certain in the realm of psychology make the quotation marks desirable) are based on what can be observed about people and what we can get them to tell us about themselves. These observations consist of those available to anyone (which have been especially productive for students of the developing child); and those made from the privileged position of the analyst, who listens in a special way when the patient tries to say everything that comes into his or her mind. How the analyst listens can be influenced by theoretical and personal prejudices that might distort what is heard. To try to avoid this, analysts need constant disciplined awareness; it takes experience and skill to be able to hear and see the new, the unexpected, the individual, and the idiosyncratic in patients; one must resist premature theoretical ordering of the clinical "facts" gleaned from ideas and feelings the patient expresses while trying to follow the rules of analysis.

Freud began his observations of psychopathology with a focus on the traumatic as it gives rise to the pathogenic repressed. With increasing clinical experience evoking his innate intellectual daring and his insight, he soon began to acquire a developmental point of view as part of a formulation of a general psychology: The deprived and deficient and traumatized patients—*they*, more and more, came to reflect for him the human condition; they became *we*.

The assumptions with which Freud began his search for "facts" were related to his heritage as a child of the 19th century, but they brought about a revolutionary attitude toward the mentally ill. The first assumption was that all psychic phenomena are meaningful; this was the principle of psychic determinism: Any psychic event can be put into a cause-and-effect sequence. Whatever the philosophical weaknesses of this, it remains a basic working assumption for any intelligent psychological observer. The second assumption, an explanatory ground for the first, was the existence of unconscious mental functioning—or, to use the metaphor of a space or place as Freud did in his early theory, the existence of "The Unconscious." What was revolutionary in this was Freud's insistence that the unconscious part of the mind is dynamic and omnipresent, basic (both in the sense of first and in the sense of most important) to all psychic functioning. The third assumption was the fact of psychic conflict—opposing forces in the mind operating in impelling dialectic.

For Freud, it was a "fact" that the mind evolves from the body and that the body and its functions continue throughout life to influence how we feel and how we think. In his later theory, the id, a hypothetical psychic structure, is the repository of the instinctual drives; out of the id are differentiated the ego and the superego.

Freud centered first on the sexual drives[8] in his study of the interplay of his basic assumptions. He focused on their hypothetical energy (libido) and on their maturational spread over the body's orifices and its surface (erogeneity). The emphasis on the instinctual continued throughout Freud's life, and was maintained by his daughter, Anna. Ritvo (1984) writes:

The role of the body and its functions in the psychic life of the individual consistently occupied a central place in the psychoanalytic thinking and writing of Anna Freud. The centrality of the body and its functions in her thinking is clearly evident in her concept of developmental lines. (p. 449)

Anna Freud (1949) herself reminds us that Freudian psychology:

ascribes to the innate instincts the main role in shaping the personality. It is the claim of the instinctual urges on the mind which results in the development of new functions, the so-called ego functions. (p. 37)

Freud's belief that drive development is primarily important to the establishment of ego[9] was expressed in the well-known dictum: "The ego . . . is first and foremost [*vor allem*] a body ego" (1923, pp. 26–27). Freud added a note about the body ego to *The Ego and the Id* in 1927 (to the English edition only):

i.e., the ego is ultimately derived from bodily sensations chiefly from those springing from the surface of the body. It may thus be regarded as a mental projection of the surface of the body. . . . (1923, p. 26)

It is the drive-derived erogeneity that (organizing and combining with external perception) charges up the surface. Willi Hoffer (1952) attributes the genesis of the body ego directly to the drives:

The developmental aspect of the drives expressed in their progress through the different stages of pregenitality to genitality has steered us to a new mental structure, the body ego. (p. 32)

It follows that the body ego and the sense of self (of "I-ness") change as the drives develop and change—as the center of erogeneity shifts from oral to anal to phallic to genital. During the time of pregenitality developing toward genitality, the ego and the superego are formed— from "islands of functioning" through "pre-stages." Hoffer continues:

the ontogenesis of the ego is [a mystery] . . . We can, however, see a little light if we conceive the body as the first object *in* which and *through* which an instinct not only seeks gratification but which lends itself in an instinct-regulating manner to this function. (p. 32)

In the course of drive and ego maturation, and also as a result of concurrent physical contacts between the child and the parent, the erogenous zones become the omphali of body sensation, centers of body ego. The erogenous zones concentrate intensity; they are situated at the orifices connecting skin and mucous membrane. The existence of these intensities has a special relationship to the differentiation between the inside and the outside of the body, connecting perceptions from the surface with perceptions from within. These connections make possible the correlation and the differentiation needed to establish body ego and ego boundaries. Because what occurs in the mind in relation to these bodily foci of sensation and "cathexis" influences the emerging ego and superego, there is interrelation of drive and structure from the beginning of psychological birth. It is the laying down of memory traces of what is experienced at the oral and then the anal centers of erogeneity that would contribute to the body ego as a psychic structure. And, to elaborate on Hoffer, there would be a model of "instinct-regulation" for the body ego patterned after the functioning of each libidinal zone. The oral pattern would in part continue to function and in part would subsequently become transformed; so would the anal in its turn; and then the phallic/genital.

Ritvo (1984), following Hoffer, sees body representation as continuing throughout life to be central to ego functioning:

> [In the adolescent] the image and functions of the body are all too readily available for the representation and experiencing of inner conflicts on the externalized screen of the body in the efforts at discharge, *defense*, and mastery. The mouth and eating offer rich possibilities because the oral cavity and its activities have a long history in the individual as both interoceptor and exteroceptor, facilitating both internalization and externalization in the mental processes that serve detoured discharge and *defense* in psychic conflict. (my italics, p. 468–469)

In his paper, Ritvo emphasizes orality, but his remarks could easily be transposed to anality, with anal mechanisms and processes giving rise to anal defenses as part of body-ego defensive functioning.

Aspects of Defense

DEFENSE AND DEFENSES

Defense is a psychoanalytic concept that follows from one of Freud's three initial basic assumptions, that of psychic conflict. (As stated earlier, the other two basic assumptions are psychic determinism and the existence of a dynamic unconscious part of the mind.) Defense refers to the responses and activities of the mind in relation to situations of danger. Some prior establishment of body ego and psychic ego is implied, since psychoanalytic theory posits defense as an ego function. Psychic danger can arise from the two worlds external to the mind: from the body, and from the world outside the body. As both these external realms come to be represented inside the mind in the course of development, intrapsychic conflict (which involves those psychic representations) will evoke danger. The mind in conflict, then, means that one part of it is defending itself against another part. Freud first studied the effects of the drives (mental forces stemming from the body) as they give rise to intensities that evoke the need for control and discharge: id drives against ego defenses (as we would now call them).

Psychoanalysis has developed a rather vague developmental sequence of defense[10], which starts with quasi-physiological processes that are conceived of as existing before the consolidation of ego structure. (I think our vagueness is a virtue, because, as Freud wrote to Jung, "anyone who gives more than he has is a rogue" [McGuire, 1974, p. 40].[11])

As a kind of somatic prototype for ego defensive functioning, psychoanalysts postulate the existence in early infancy of a stimulus barrier of some sort that makes for physiologically based resistance to pain and other excessive intensities. The stimulus barrier is an aggregate of the physiologically derived processes that operate against trauma (or too-much-ness, Freud's primal situation of danger for the infant). Defense in later development assumes the prior establishment of mind—first the body ego, then the psychic ego. That is, the ego must be differentiated from the id and a concept of the self must be differentiated from that of the parents and the external world. When the ego begins to mature and function, we picture it making use of its *defense mechanisms*—specific ways of averting danger, such as repression, projection, and introjection. For the operation of *repression* (*i.e.*, the expelling of an idea from consciousness), the ego must have emerged; for the psychic use of *introjection* (the taking in from the outside) and *projection* (the casting out to the outside), there must be boundaries to the self that make possible the establishment of a sense of inside and outside (see A. Freud, 1936). Anna Freud warns of the confusion that can follow from shifts in psychoanalytic theory (she is alluding to, and opposing, the Kleinian conceptions of projection and introjection at a period prior to the existence of ego), stating that "the chronology of psychic processes is still one of the most obscure fields of analytic theory" (1936, p. 53).

After the early acquisition of the quasi-physiological stimulus barrier, there arise the most primitive psychic defense mechanisms. These are:

> regression; reversal, or turning round upon the self [and they] are proba-
> bly independent of the stage which psychic structure has reached and as
> old as the instincts themselves. (A. Freud, 1936, p. 52)

Indeed, Freud called "reversal into its opposite [and] turning round upon the subject's own self . . . [*instinctual*] *vicissitudes* [that operate as] modes of defense against the instincts" (my italics; 1915, pp. 126–127). Regression can also be an instinctual vicissitude. (I view the idea of an instinctual vicissitude operating as a defense against the instincts as foreshadowing my conception of anal defense, which follows.)

The core of the early defensive functioning is the establishment of body ego, a body-centered, physiologically and drive-derived precursor of the psychic ego. I will subsequently refer to and try to illustrate what might be called body-ego early defenses: negation (I spit it out, which leads to *projection*) and affirmation (I swallow it, which leads to *introjection*); these are expressed in the body-narcissistic early defensive modes of *devaluation* and *idealization* (see Chapter 6, section entitled "Digression on Defenses: Primary and Secondary Idealization and Devaluation").

ORGANIC REPRESSION

Freud also played with the idea of somatic and inherited prototypes of defense that involve anality and would, it follows, become active in the anal phase of individual development. As mentioned earlier, he was speculating about the phylogenetic impact of the evolution of man's assumption of erect posture and the consequent diminution of the primacy of the sense of smell for the sense of sight. The resultant so-called "organic repression" featured for him a depreciation of anal eroticism: "the organic defence of the new form of life achieved with man's erect gait against his earlier animal existence" (1930, p. 106). He wrote of this idea first to Fliess in 1897, at a time when he did not clearly differentiate the psychic mechanism of repression from somatic prototypes, and he repeatedly returned in his writings to the idea of an inherited "organic" defense derived from the development of the human species (1909, p. 247–248; 1912, p. 189; 1930 pp. 99–100, 106). His last statement on the subject:

Anal erotism, therefore, succumbs in the first instance to the "organic repression" which paved the way for civilization . . . with the assumption of an erect posture by man and with the depreciation of his sense of smell, it was not only his anal erotism which threatened to fall a victim to organic repression, but the whole of his sexuality; so that since this, the sexual function has been accompanied by a repugnance which cannot further be accounted for. . . . Thus we find that the deepest root of the sexual repression which advances along with civilization is the organic defence of the new form of life achieved with man's erect gait against his earlier animal existence. (1930, pp. 100, 106)

Freud's hypotheses are no doubt too simple, but (with our evolving theories of evolution) they cannot be dismissed. We are familiar with the greater-than-human importance of the sense of smell in most mammals, and with the anal rituals of submission in relation to aggressive and sexual rivalry in many animals.

REGRESSION

In psychic development, "regression" refers to a partial or full return to earlier modes of functioning and organization of functioning (e.g., psychic structure). Freud wrote of temporal, formal, and topographical (from the motor to the sensory end of the topographic picture of the mind) regressions (in a 1914 note added to Freud, 1900). Anna Freud tells us:

> that regression can occur in all three parts of the personality structure, in the id as well as in the ego and superego; and that it can concern psychic content as well as methods of functioning; that *temporal* regression happens in regard to aim-directed impulses, object relations and fantasy content; *topographical* and *formal* regression in the ego functions, the secondary thought processes, the reality principle etc. (1965, p. 95)

She views temporary regressions in the child as part of normal psychic development. Regressions can range from the transient and easily reversible to relatively long-lasting or even fixed. The mind's kaleidoscopic dynamism probably includes constant reversible short-term regressions as well as some regressions that are retained by the individual throughout life. In a late paper, Freud (1937) speaks of partial transformations achieved in ordinary expectable psychic development (and also those brought about in the course of a successful psychoanalysis): ". . . portions of the old mechanisms remain untouched. . . ." He exemplifies this by referring to drive—specifically to libidinal—development:

Our first account of the development of the libido was that an original oral phase gave way to a sadistic-anal phase and that this was in turn succeeded by a phallic-genital one. Later research has not contradicted this view, but it has corrected it by adding that these replacements do not take place all of a sudden but gradually, so that portions of the earlier organization always persist alongside of the more recent one, and even in normal development the transformation is never complete and residues of earlier libidinal fixations may still be retained in the final configuration. The same thing is to be seen in quite other fields. (1937, p. 229)

We would rarely now think of "final" configurations, but rather would see evolving predominant, repetitive, dynamic patterns that feature continual regressions and progressions—patterns consistent with having achieved relatively stable "transformations" of psychic functioning. Aspects of our more primitive selves are always emerging: The benevolent philanthropist can suddenly become the miser; the loving father transiently gives way to a selfish, intemperate rival to his child.

For theoretical and heuristic purposes, we have artificially isolated three broad areas of development: the libidinal and aggressive drives; ego and superego; and object relationships. Regression can affect any of these. Anna Freud has worked out a more discrete system of "developmental lines" that shows the interaction of these broad developmental areas (see Neubauer, 1984); for example, developmental lines: (1) from dependency to emotional self-reliance and adult object relationships; (2) toward body independence (from drinking to rational eating; from wetting and soiling to bladder and bowel control); (3) from irresponsibility to responsibility; (4) toward body management; (5) from egocentricity to companionship; (6) from the body to the toy, and from play to work.

Of course, if regression pushes far enough backwards, all these "lines" and areas converge as the individual approaches the stages of early narcissism with their emotional extremes and everything-or-nothing values. The convergence can reach the primal undifferentiation of autism.

The earliest developmental stages are dominated by the body ego and by first oral and then the supplementary anal islands of consciousness and control. The child's narcissistic regression is conceived of experientially as a return to the feeling that the universe is reduced to the equivalent of the nursery, then to the limits of one's own body, and eventually to states of fusion with the parent and to undifferentiation.

This backwards traversal revives predominant feelings of omnipotence and grandiosity; magical thinking pervades the mental representations of the self and of the parents. With the shutting down of the world to the limits of the body, the earliest primitive defenses return.

Our concept of established mechanisms of defense is too general to do justice to the infinitely varied dynamic jumble of defensive operations that each of us evolves; (and Brenner [1981] reminds us that defenses serve many psychic ends).[12] During the period of their evolution there are qualities conferred onto the defenses by the changing nature of the drives as well as by the differentiation of ego functions. There is a high point of defensive activity during the anal period. The defenses gain in intensity during the anal–sadistic period—probably in relation to the concomitant maturational increase in the aggressive drives. (Phylogenetically, there may be some connection with the need for repression of the preponderant anality of what Freud calls our "earlier animal existence.") The ego's mechanisms of defense take on specifically anal qualities. *Displacement* (top to bottom, front to back) and *reversal* may be so important, in part, because of the developmental shifts between the mouth and the anus as organizing psychic centers. Reversal into the opposites is one of the oldest mechanisms, "as old as the instincts themselves," and it flowers during this developmental time of extreme ambivalence and of concentration on the reversed, the back side. (There is some physiological understructure here, in that the anus both expels and can be penetrated.) In the second and third year of life, an easy reversibility (of aim, object, role, affect, etc.) can approach a cancelling out of meaning: If hate quickly turns to love, and love back to hate, neither need count. Feces, and fecal equivalents, such as money, can connote either good or bad, with sometimes bewildering coexistence and reversals.

Many of the "anal" defense mechanisms are related to the developmental achievement of thought—a separating out of a realm for "trial action" (*e.g.*, intellectualization). If the separation is exaggerated, there can be a defensive disconnection between psychic representations and what they represent; or, as Freud might put it, between word-presentations and thing-presentations. Just as the anal sphincter separates and disconnects the fecal column, so there can be imposed a defensive discontinuity in chains of thought, both between ideas; and between ideas, feelings, and action. These inevitable discontinuities we call *isolation*. Isolation is involved in all kinds of psychic *splitting*—vertical and horizontal splits in psychic structure that operate in the service of defense. Anal introjection and anal projection are both continuations and transformations of their oral prototypes. The opposed (and reversible) defensive pair of idealization and degradation flourishes during the anal developmental period.

The complicated interconnected use of all of these defense mechanisms (and more that must be delineated and added to those I have listed) can make for defensive operations that culminate in the power of *denial*: various ways of disregarding, disowning, or negating external and psychic reality; of treating events (realistic and psychological) as not having happened—as *non-arrivée* as Freud often put it. By using one or many of these defensive mechanisms cast in an anal mode, feelings as well as facts can be disposed of in an effective, massive way; everything meaningful—everything associated with feeling, conviction, and value—can be reduced to nothing, to shit.

CLINICAL ILLUSTRATIONS OF DEFENSIVE ANALITY

Patient X.: Reducing the Bad by Establishing a Mental Fortress of Shit

Patient X was a young unmarried heterosexual who had entered analysis to overcome inhibitions in his professional and sexual life. He was not a pervert, but like all human beings had certain perverse fantasies and practices. These appeared mostly in relation to masturbatory fantasy. Acknowledging feeling, especially anger, was very difficult for him.

Shortly after an agreed-on raise in his analytic fee, he had been driving his car past my office and had nearly collided with another automobile. (There had recently been a well-publicized hit-and-run accident in the neighborhood, in which a psychiatrist had been killed.) The near-accident had clearly been my patient's fault. He was most upset, but immediately felt relief that no one was hurt. Then he noticed an elderly man crossing the street and had the frightening thought that he might have run him down and killed him. Associations in the session that followed convinced me that the action (and the fantasies of getting rid of someone of his parents' and his analyst's generation) represented an outbreak of anal–sadistic impulses. That night he had a confirmatory dream:

> He is fully grown up, but finds himself all alone in the large public bathroom in the basement of the primary school he attended as a boy. He feels an urgent need to defecate and is glad as he enters a small toilet booth that no one else is around. As he sits on the W.C., he notes (at first with alarm and disgust) that the walls of the cubicle he has chosen are covered with feces. The shit is mostly dry and hard, but some of it is fresh and oozing. It is not only foul, but poisonous—dangerous, as if it contains a malodorous corrosive. But then it occurs to him that the odor seems familiar, and his anxiety subsides with the realization that it is actually his own shit. He is used to it and he really doesn't mind it. Now he feels safe and comfortable and can defecate and urinate in peace.

In X's associations to the dream, it became intellectually clear to him that the car's near-collision was connected with the idea of the death of his analyst, toward whom, he said, he was "probably" angry: "You would say it's because I am paying a higher fee." He went on to tell me that the first time he had experienced death was when he was five—a beloved but feared grandmother had suddenly died. He couldn't understand why his parents were crying and what all the fuss was about. He remembered having said to himself when he was alone sitting on the toilet, "I'm glad that old shitty grandma is dead." When he repeated this to me, it was voiced in a peculiar expressionless hypnotic tone that he characteristically used when expressing feelings he had trouble being responsible for.

It would be metaphorically valid to state that this man had grown up with the isolated toilet cubicle-walled-in-shit as a constantly present, potentially usable compartment of his mind. This projection of his own anus and rectum became a psychic place for defensive retreat where he felt he could control his dangerous (partly anal–sadistic) murderous feelings, fantasies, and impulses. With a further projection onto external reality accompanied by disguising and isolating idealization, the shit-lined room became the solitary wonderful bathroom to which he retreated (from adolescence on), usually in response to a situation of psychic danger or of narcissistic injury; this had been the site for restorative masturbation accompanied by grandiose, polymorphous perverse fantasies.

The vulnerability of a fortress of shit is obvious.

Patient Y.: Turning Everything (Bad and Good) into Shit

Here is the outline of an ordinary resistance-session that took place when I was about to go away for several weeks. This young man had been ignoring the impending separation. During the previous session there had been references to a beloved nurse who had been dismissed when the patient was a child.

The patient entered the office; uncharacteristically he did not respond to my "hello" at the door.[13] He lay down on the couch, was silent for several minutes, and finally said, "I feel angry." After about five more minutes of silence, I asked, "Is this angry silence?" "I suppose so," the patient responded. "You'll say that I'm angry with you. But I feel angry with everyone. I am always angry. I was furious with my wife this morning when I woke up. And with the taxi driver on the way here. There is nothing special about *you*. There is nothing special about me either; everyone seems to be angry these days—just read the morning paper." The patient then proceeded to tell a series of anecdotes illustrating his anger with people at work, and their anger at him or at others. These complaints and charges all concerned money, and (paradoxically) the more details he provided, the more he became vague and circumstantial. His tone of voice became a drone. He was producing a list, obscured in a kind of hypnotic, petty, obsessive financial miasma, that seemed aimed at demonstrating that "everyone" was angry. At the end of the hour he suppressed a yawn and seemed a bit wistful. Then, with some satisfaction appearing in his voice, he added, "I managed to turn this whole session to shit, didn't I?"

I realized that there was a sense in which he had done just that. At the start he had been angry with the analyst, as he had been with the nurse who left him and with the parents who had dismissed her. Impinging on his consciousness was the longing for the lost nurse, a feeling that could be repeated toward the departing analyst. But the longing was obscured by his anger. The anger, in turn, had been defused by attributing it to "everyone." By generalizing his emotions, the patient was trying to escape responsibility for them, and for focusing them on the analyst. If "everyone" is angry with "everyone," there is indeed "nothing special" about the patient's anger; anger so universal does not count. His defensive generalization was aimed mainly at affects, but it also expressed affects. To equate "everyone" and "everything" with "shit" is hostile and degrading. The too-important analyst (like the nurse from long ago) was reduced to "nothing special," to "shit," which could then be actively eliminated. (This activity denies the passive experience of being deserted.) He could also try and hold on to the "shit," for in the looking-glass world of anality opposites coexist. And, excrement, alongside its devaluation, is felt (at least in the unconscious) to be all-important, a part of one's body.

The patient's feeling that there was "nothing special" about himself or his analyst concealed the enhanced and exigent specialness inherent in narcissistic regression—here an anal–narcissistic regression. Emotions and body-feeling involved with other people can be reduced to feces that can be controlled by the psychic counterpart of the anal sphincter. At the beginning of the session the patient was relatively "open" about his anger; that feeling state already represented a narrowing of the range of affect with the elimination of the yearning of the previous day. By the end of the hour, the anger had disappeared—after he had produced what he considered to be a mass of undifferentiated "stuff." There were still feelings at the end of the session—wistfulness, mild discontent, a hint of triumph—but they were unfocused and attenuated. Predominantly he was safe: Life's intensities, and precious people like his nurse, had been transformed into the indifferent and the trivial; he was in control and he needed no other. Beneath this indeterminate, "anal–narcissistic" defensive surface, the observer can glimpse the congealed and concealed passionate dynamic complexities. Even if we take account only of the defenses, we note that the patient isolates, projects, becomes hypnotic, inhibits, generalizes, negates, obfuscates, regresses. Although the predominant beginning feeling tone was anger, which was expressed directly (and seemingly responsibly) at one point, one can discern other emotions and other instinctual derivatives that the patient was not aware of communicating. His silence alone can express confluent oral, anal, phallic, and genital passive and aggressive wishes toward the analyst.

The details of the session would make clearer the presence here (as in any piece of human discourse) of feelings and impulses that stem from every phase of instinctual development, that evoke all the psychic danger situations, that involve all levels of object relationship—feelings and impulses expressed and defended against in stormy kaleidoscopic, conflictive counterpoint. By and large the patient's obscuring, reductive defensive effort had been successful. By the end of the session the patient had effectively deprived both himself and the analyst of variety, vibrancy, and value. The exciting, mysterious, chaotic universe had, transiently but characteristically, become simplified, controlled, and certain. Life, and specifically this bit of it ardently related to the analyst, consisted not of making love or making war but of making stool and making lists.

Anal–Narcissistic Defense

My idea is that there is a panoply of near-somatic body-ego defenses that children develop during the anal phase—that is, between the very early existence of the (most likely physiologically based) stimulus barrier and the later formation of the repression barrier during the oedipal period. Anal–narcissistic defense (as I call it) acts as a kind of emotional and sensory closeable door that serves to control the largely murderous and cannibalistic primal affects derived from the destructive and from the perverse sexual drives of early life. This "door" operates along the body-ego model, as it were, of the control of the anal sphincter. Anal-narcissistic defense represents an amalgam of (1) anal impulses (resorted to defensively in later life by way of regression); (2) anal symptoms; and above all (3) anal defense mechanisms (such as X's isolation and intellectualization). The specific anal defense mechanisms arise in response to an anal phase developmental surge of aggressive instinctual drive, which presents the child with the task of mastering inner forces that threaten to be beyond his capacity. The anal defensive complex is returned to in subsequent psychic danger situations as a concomitant of a defensive regression toward narcissism, as in my patient's dream of toilet solitude. The sphincter-like defensive power of reducing intensities enables the individual to modulate unpleasure and pain, to avoid *over*stimulation, and to diminish and evade conflict-ridden feelings associated with object-ties. If the defense goes too far (as it had with my patients X and Y), everything that evokes value and meaning can become undifferentiated *stuff*, and turn to excretable shit. In his dream image, X became clean and safe, but his bad shit had been projected onto a defensive wall of indifference[14]—a metaphor for the anal character structure of both patients that isolated them from the world of others, and from the contradictory emotions that make for our humanity.

I will now proceed to develop my concept of anal–narcissistic defensiveness slowly—continuing with the perhaps dull but necessary area of theory and then proceeding once again to the more exciting and involving clinical and literary examples of what I am asserting.

FURTHER HISTORICAL DEVELOPMENT:
ANALITY IN THE ANALYTIC LITERATURE

Freud expressed his views on human sexual development in his 1905 book, *Three Essays on the Theory of Sexuality.* What shocked his limited audience (and eventually, as Freud in his Copernicus/Darwin role predicted, the world) was his emphasis on the sexuality of infants and children. Freud equated elements of perverse sex—found in the compulsive sexual actions of perverts and in the fantasies and sexual foreplay of neurotics (*i.e.*, everyone)—with aspects of infantile sexuality as it develops in everyone. Because the genital equipment of children only functions properly after puberty, Freud declared that childhood sexuality was polymorphously perverse. In his 1905 book, Freud described his concepts of erogeneity (source and place of excitation in the body) and of libido (sexual drive energy); and he defined the source, aim, and object of the sexual drives. In this book, Freud began his "most astonishing" (see Jones, 1918, quoted above) systematic exploration (random observations had been made earlier) of the nature of anality. In later papers he linked anality and feces with symbolic equivalents: things, especially dirt, money, babies. He stressed how important the aggressive drive is to anality; and he indicated connections between anal impulses and specific character traits in adults.

Abraham, in a 1921 paper, outlined the history of the "theory of anal character" (p. 370) up to that point. Freud's short 1908 paper, "Character and Anal Erotism," had noted "three particularly pronounced character traits, namely, a love of orderliness which often develops into pedantry, a parsimony which easily turns to miserliness, and an obstinacy which may become an angry defiance" (Abraham, 1921, p. 371). These traits, normal or pathological, Freud connected with intense anal feelings—pleasures involved with emptying the bowel, with retaining its contents, and in the anal product, feces. Freud said that such anal strivings could be expressed in sublimation (for example through painting and sculpting) and/or be defended against in reaction formation (with a resulting inclination for orderliness and cleanliness).

After Jones (1913) observed that hatred is engendered by the educative interference with the child's anal–erotic pleasures, Freud (1913) stated his conviction that sadism is regularly combined with anal strivings (determined by the unfolding of the instincts as well as by environmental intervention). In this paper, Freud formulated the idea of the "sadistic–anal pregenital organization," which, he postulated, integrates the anal phase. Abraham also mentions the contributions of Sadger (1910), Ferenczi (1914), and especially of Jones' 1918 paper.

Jones (1918) pointed out the possibly different vicissitudes of conflicts concerning excretory *functions* and excretory *products*. Character traits could be derived from either or both. Jones observed that the child who is being toilet trained has to be taught to give up both the pleasure of soiling his body and handling his feces, and the pleasure of the process of excretion when the parents insist that he perform his elimination functions at regular times. These parental demands make the child angry. Abraham pointed out that they also interfere with the child's narcissism. The parents' demands and attitudes are internalized by the child to form psychic structure.

Pregenital Sexual Organizations

Freud conceived of the interrelation and integration of drive and psychic structure as taking place under the aegis of the interlocking "pregenital sexual organizations" (1905, p. 198). This concept, first spelled out in 1913 (and then added in a later edition of the 1905 book), implies that at some point in the formation of psychic structure there is an expansion into a synthesizing *system*; and one might speak, following Freud, of oral, anal, phallic, and genital *organizations*— hypothetical mental structures that actively blend what is arbitrarily envisioned as "lines of development." Freud's subsequent structural theory would not make use of the term "pregenital sexual organizations,"[15] but would shift the metaphor of psychic anatomy during the early phases of libidinal development to pre-stages of the ego and superego.

Most attention was paid by Freud and his followers (especially Abraham and Jones) to the anal (Freud later called it the "sadistic-anal") pregenital sexual organization. In a 1917 paper, *On Transformations of Instinct as Exemplified by Anal Erotism*, Freud wrote that the "genital organization [is] preceded by a 'pregenital organization' in which sadism and anal erotism play leading parts" (p. 127). The "sadistic anal pregenital sexual organization" is a loosely conceived structural entity that exerts a synthesizing and integrating function over a specific maturational period following the earliest "oral" developmental phase in which psychic differentiation begins.

This period not only is marked by an upsurge of anal erogeneity but also, as Freud (1913) and Jones (1913) indicated, is one that poses the problem of taming the admixture of preponderantly aggressive drives (whose first appearance, of course, comes earlier). The unfused mixture of aggressive and libidinal drives comprehended in Freud's idea of "sadistic–anal libido" threatens to overwhelm the child's nascent psychic structures. This phase presided over by the "anal organization" is one of general unfolding psychic development, of the acquisition of mastery of the inner and the outer worlds. It is also the time of transformations (see Abrams, 1977)—transformations of instinct (fusion, neutralization) and of evolving psychic structure (the pre-stages of ego and superego that guide the transformations). Speaking generally and metaphorically, one could say that once the aggressively charged instinctual mixture can be contained, there is an increasing transformation of somatic into psychic energy. Due to sufficient body ego and then ego development, the flourishing anal erogeneity is experientially registrable. All this anal phase development takes place during and after the establishment of what Mahler calls psychological birth. (For more on Mahler, see Chapter 5.)

Abraham's Phase Division

Abraham, whose papers (1921, 1924) catalog the clinical manifestations of anality, divides the anal period into two sub-phases. The differentiation he describes supplied the concept of transformations in the psychic resonances of anal erogeneity and libido—transformations that emphasize the need for the control of destructiveness. Abraham implies a developmental change in the child's conception of his anus, which at first is felt as a body part that expels and destroys, reflected in the psychic mechanisms of externalization and projection of the bad *not-me*. (This anal destructiveness is an elaboration of oral cannibalistic devouring.) In the second anal phase, the anus becomes an instrument that is also used to hold on with and to contain. (The biting sphincter becomes the controlling sphincter.) The registration of the transient experience of the anus holding on and closing down makes the registration of a closed (or a closeable) system possible; the child can now know what it is like to feel his body as an entity, with boundaries, and with "doors" that shut. Concurrent psychic ego development has made registration possible by the time of anal predominance—and this registration of controllable closure and opening makes subsequent (body and psychic) ego development possible: Being able to feel that one has boundaries is necessary for achieving separation from the parent and for acquiring full individuation, which involves attaining the working concept of "self" and the spontaneous feeling of "I." (Fliess [1961] points out that it is in the anal period that the child characteristically begins to talk of himself in the first rather than in the third person.)

Notes to Chapter One

1. Compare Rappaport (1958), who furnishes a more jargon-ridden version of Trilling: "man's constitutionally given drive-equipment appears to be the ultimate primary guarantee of the ego's autonomy from the environment, that is its safeguard against stimulus–response slavery" (quoted by Curtis, 1985, p. 341).

2. The Early Christian Fathers' *inter urinas et faeces nascimur* (we are born between urine and feces) clings to sexual life and cannot be detached from it in spite of every effort at idealization (Freud, 1905a, p. 31).

3. For example, Edward Glover's paper *A Developmental Study of the Obsessional Neurosis* (1935) anticipates some of my conclusions about anal defensiveness. (I am grateful to Dr. Erik Gann for pointing this out to me after I had presented some of the material in this book).

4. In his lecture (1933) The Question of a *Weltanschauung*, Freud uses a favorite rhetorical device: He first presents arguments against the scientific view of the world, then criticizes those arguments, and finally comes to a compromise. He puts forth what he says is the "religious" point of view about scientific "certainty":

> [Science] collects observations of uniformities in the course of events which it dignifies with the name of laws and submits to its risky interpretations. And consider the small degree of *certainty* which it attaches to its findings! Everything it teaches is only provisionally true: what is praised to-day as the highest wisdom will be rejected to-morrow and replaced by something else, though once more only tentatively. (my italics; p. 172-173)

Freud goes on to defend Science but states:

> We must admit to some extent the correctness of [these] criticisms. The path of science is indeed slow, hesitating, laborious. This fact cannot be denied or altered. No wonder the gentlemen in the other camp are dissatisfied. They are spoilt: *revelation* gave them an easier time. (my italics; p. 174)

Freud's doubting and inner dialectic about certainty are obvious. But he is clearly as much against scientific as he is against religious "revelation."

5. Compare two contemporary masters of analysis (and a third, recently departed): Rangell (1961) speaks of the fashionable "selective elaboration" of one area of psychic functioning that is said to play a central role "in all neurosogenesis . . . what is neglected as a result are the wider implications of multiple components and multiple functions . . . the theory of object relations is used to displace the more inclusive theory of the libido which embraces and takes into account the source, aim and object of the instinctual drive rather than considering only the object involved" (p. 599). Weinshel (1970) praises the complexity of Hartmann's concepts:

> [He] has skillfully demonstrated that optimal psychic functioning does not necessarily depend on the most highly differentiated, highest level psychic processes and activities. On the contrary, he has shown that such optimal functioning is dependent on a scrupulous blending of the archaic with the highly developed, the irrational and the rational, the primary process with the secondary, the undifferentiated with the differentiated. (p. 688)

6. For example, Freud (1926b, 1926c) writes: "The correct reconstruction, *you must know*, of such forgotten experiences of childhood *always* has great therapeutic effect whether they permit objective confirmation or not" (my italics; p. 216). The "you must know" [*Sie müssen wissen* (*G. W.*, 14, p. 245)] seems to insist that Freud's imaginary dialogue partner (is it unconsciously his old "only audience," Fliess, that he is addressing here?) has already agreed to the establishment of the very questionable assumption which is purportedly "always" [*immer*] true—an assumption based on circular reasoning: If the reconstruction has "great therapeutic effect," it is correct; and if "correct," it has "great therapeutic effect." In this instance, Freud's projected quasicertainty seems to me to reveal his suppressed unsureness about his generalization.

7. I define "fascination" as the narcissistic absorption in the sexual parts of the self or of another (or in a displacement of a symbol for such body parts). This is discussed fully in Chapter 6.

8. For a review of the development of drive theory see Bibring (1941).

9. Ego is Strachey's translation throughout the *Standard Edition* for Freud's *"Das Ich"*: Bettelheim is right in asserting that the direct translation "the I" is to be preferred.

10. See Abend (1981) for an excellent succinct critical review of the psychoanalytic literature on defense.

11. This statement epitomizes Freud as champion of indicating precisely what remains *uncertain* (see section "Certainty and Uncertainty," this chapter). Compare this statement from Freud's letter with a similar one from a letter of Chekhov (1888) in which the latter defended himself against the charge that the psychology in one of his short stories was unclear. (Chekhov was a physician as well as a "triple thinker" writer, and in both callings a master psychologist):

> It is not the psychologist's job to understand things that he in fact does not understand. Let us not be charlatans and let us state openly that you can't figure out [everything] in this world. Only fools and charlatans know and understand everything. (quoted in Karlinsky & Heim, 1973, p. 106)

12. Compare Abend (1981) on Anna Freud's list of mechanisms of defense:

> analytic scrutiny . . . made it clear that these simple mechanisms were neither simple nor mechanisms, but appeared instead more like complex structures which served other purposes beside defensive ones and were themselves the product of compromise formation. . . . Gradually it became apparent that all behavior, normal as well as pathological, includes in its composition some aspects of defense. (p. 74)

13. Note how often the door to the analyst's office figures in the clinical material of this book. Later in this chapter in the section entitled "Abraham's Phase Division," I bring in my view of the anal sphincter as a "closeable door" for the body ego.

14. Compare this quote from the letters of Gustave Flaubert. (Flaubert was a great letter writer; his letters are full of free and vibrant body imagery. Oral, and especially anal and phallic, metaphors abound):

> I feel, against the stupidity of my time, *floods of hatred* which choke me. Shit rises to my mouth as in the case of a strangulated hernia. [Gustave's father and brother were physicians.] *But I want to keep it, fix it, harden it; I want to concoct a paste with it with which I will cover the nineteenth century,* in the same way they paint Indian pagodas with cow dung. (my italics; quoted in Barnes, 1984, pp. 15–16)

15. But see Peller (1965) who viewed the concept of the "pregenital sexual organization . . . as the framework for all aspects of development" (p. 732). The varying and evolving constellation of drives in the successive preoedipal "phases of organization [influences] the child's relationship to libidinal objects, his cognitive efforts, the organization of his affects and his experiences, or the pre-stages of these" (pp. 732–733).

2

Defensive Anality, Sphincter Defense, and Anal Narcissism

INTRODUCTION

The change, described by Abraham (1924), from the feeling of an initially sadomasochistically predominant crushing destructiveness to that of anal containment and control, represents a prevailing change in psychic function from discharge to defense. My key to understanding here is Fliess's idea of the unconscious basic involvement of the anal sphincter in the defensive mastery of "regressive . . . archaic," primal (basically aggressive murderous cannibalistic) affect:

> It is often as though the anal sphincter were charged with the mastery of regressive and archaic affect, *intrinsic to whatever phase of development*, because it is the strongest [sphincter]; and as though the ego chose *anal-erotic elaboration upon instinctual strivings of whatever nature* as the most reliable means of preserving its organization. (my italics; 1956, p. 124)

For me this implies what I have called *defensive anality*: a mobilization of anal erogeneity, defense mechanisms, and symptoms—that is, "anal-erotic elaboration"—by danger situations at all levels (including the developmentally advanced castration threat which flourishes during the oedipal development that follows the period of anality).

Mastery of the urethral sphincter, which is usually attained first and during the period dominated by the "anal organization," plays its important, although lesser, defensive part alongside anal sphincter control. Bedwetting, a frequent childhood response to neglect and/or overstimulation (a response that expresses an unconscious cry for help), probably also involves a regressive enhancement of the anal organization and of reliance on the defensive power of the stronger anal sphincter. This would account for the terror of loss of integrity of the anal sphincter (frequently associated with fear of rats) seen in some sufferers from eneuresis: for example, Freud's Rat Man (see Freud, 1909, p. 284) and George Orwell, a bedwetter with a lifelong hatred and fear of rats (see Shengold, 1985a). (Two of the patients described in this book had been bedwetters as children.)

Of course, responses (fantasies, erogeneities, adaptive and defensive mechanisms, symptoms) from *all* developmental levels are evoked by psychic danger situations. I am giving a primacy to the anal level. I believe that anal defensiveness (sphincter defensiveness is an alternate term) is the most important part of body-ego defensive functioning. Being able to control the anal and urethral sphincters—a control involving both voluntary holding on and voluntary letting go—is conceived of here as inherent to the mastery of preponderantly aggressively charged, "unneutralized," relatively un- or defused instinctual output: what Fliess calls "archaic affect." This crucial sphincteric mastery, or, rather, struggle for mastery, makes for a possible anal fixation point for everyone—one that is usually consistent with enough flexibility to permit further instinctual (and especially libidinal, "neutralizing") and structural (ego and superego enhancing) development toward future transformational periods.

What I have been outlining amounts to the metaphorical view of the psychological birth of the human being as an *anal* birth.

BEGINNINGS OF OBJECT RELATIONSHIPS

The anal period is a time of crucially important developmental interaction between mind and body, whose point of arrival is the firm establishment of ego boundaries and the sense of a separate self. This separation is accomplished (under conditions of at least adequate parenting and parental "letting go") by the continuing and now differentiated psychic registration of what is outside the body and the mind—first the parents and then the rest of the external environment. The worlds outside and inside the body have become mental representations:

> The environment proper becomes reflected in "object-representations" to which the ego opposes itself; and the body in "organ representations," elemental to a body ego, from which the rest of the ego is distinguishable as psychic ego. (Fliess,[1] 1956, p. 128)

Mahler, quoting Anna Freud, refers to the importance of "the negativistic behavior of the anal phase" (1968, p. 20) for intrapsychic separation and self boundary formation. Mahler has been careful to place her contributions within the entire developmental nexus as conceived of by Freud:

> Early psychoanalytic writings showed the development of object relationships was dependent on the drives . . . concepts such as narcissism (primary and secondary), ambivalence, sado-masochism, oral and anal character, and the oedipal triangle relate simultaneously to problems of drive and of object development. Our contribution should be seen as supplemental to this in showing the growth of object relationship from narcissism in parallel with the early life history of the ego, set in the context of current libidinal development. (Mahler, Pine, & Bergman, 1975, p. 6)

The establishment of reliable mental representations that constitute the basis for object relationships (*reliable* meaning possessing "object constancy") is made possible by yet another kind of transformation that bursts into flower during the period of anality: the revolutionary transformation of body feeling into thought.

Anna Freud outlines the symptomatic and characterological conversion—conversion from the body to the mind—of what she reminds us are chiefly "anal–sadistic impulses" in her description of obsessional neurosis:[2] "Obsessional neurosis is hard to unravel not in spite of but because of the pathology being located in the thought processes themselves, thereby attacking the patient's very means of communication with us as well" (1966, p. 116). I would stress that what is primarily attacked and compromised in this conversion of anal–sadistic impulses is the patient's own intrapsychic communication—the patient's own journeys within the mind. And, in the same sense that we are all neurotics, we have all been to some extent "converted" into obsessive-compulsives, although proportions and qualities exist in infinite variety. Not only do we all need to develop the capacity to "delay . . . instinctual gratification through the interpolation of thought-yielding judgment" (Fliess, 1956, p. 123), but this capacity is to some extent always deficient, a result of the inevitable continuation of intrapsychic conflict.

The now registrable cloacal and perigenital (anal) sensations are correlated with awareness of, and the active involvement of, the body's musculature, which discharges aggressive energy and contributes to the establishment of the sense of inside-and-outside the body by making possible the exploration of the environment. Locomotion supplies a way to distance oneself from objects, and also the active *experience* of being in control of closeness and distance (at the time of Mahler's "rapprochement subphase"). Locomotion provides a sense of and a beginning mastery of physical perspective; locomotion's correlate, thinking, provides emotional distance and mental perpective (*cf.* Freud's "thinking . . . is essentially an experimental kind of acting" [1911a, p. 221]).

Anal Narcissism

Locomotion and the freedom to travel in the mind are both involved in the child's developmentally determined and environmentally enforced struggle over the autonomous use and mastery of his excretory "movements"—a struggle over who will control his anal and urethral sphincters. Freud and Abraham have described how important toilet training is in the *unseparable* line of development from narcissism to object love:

> Defaecation affords the first occasion in which the child must decide between a narcissistic and an object-loving attitude. He either parts obediently with his faeces, "sacrifices" them to his love, or else retains them with the purpose of auto-erotic satisfaction and later as a means of asserting his own will. If he makes the latter choice we are in the presence of defiance (obstinancy) which, accordingly, springs from a *narcissistic clinging to anal erotism*. (Freud, 1917, my italics; p. 130)

Abraham was especially interested in the psychic consequences of the *renunciation* of narcissism demanded by toilet training. He noted that the child's physical pleasures in feces and in excreting are accompanied by:

> a psychical gratification which is based on the achievement [of the excretory act]. Now in that the child's [toilet] training demands strict regularity in its excretions as well as cleanliness it exposes the child's narcissism to a first severe test. (1921, p. 373)

The child must give up its narcissistic gratification in its excretory achievement and creation, and substitute for this the object-related pleasure of gaining parental approval, praise, and love. And of course children are not all equally able to make this renunciation and substitution. (Today we would feel that the renunciation and substitution are inherently unsatisfactory, leaving every child with some degree of conflict and frustration.) Abraham sounds a warning as significant now as it was in 1921; he bids us take note of:

> the effect of early injuries to infantile narcissism [due to toilet training], especially if those injuries are of a persistent and systematic nature, and force a habit prematurely upon the child before it is psychically ready for it. (p. 374)

The psychological readiness depends on the child having developed some capacity to relate to others. "This psychic preparedness only appears when the child begins to transfer on to an object (the mother etc.) the feelings which are originally bound narcissistically" (p. 374). Once the child can relate to the mother, the narcissistic anal gratifications can be given up out of love. Before this, the renunciation is motivated by fear and will leave psychological resistances to the training along with a narcissistic fixation; "a permanent disturbance of the capacity to love will result" (p. 374). Today this last statement appears too strong; much would depend both on the overall mother–child (or, better, parent–child) relationship—loving or unloving, empathic or unempathic, etc.—and its many and complicated specific interfaces.

Abraham was constructing complex, interweaving developmental lines that connect narcissism with the capacity to relate to and care for others through the nodal point of anal development modified by experiences of toilet training.

Freud and Abraham have described and illustrated character traits that arise from the conflict over anal impulses in toilet training. Traits such as obstinacy are "transitional" (in Winnicott's sense): They spring "from a narcissistic clinging to anal erotism" (Freud, 1917, p. 130), but also provide a path toward object relationship—a means of holding onto the parents by hostile provocation. The internalization of the parents who take part in the toilet-training struggles changes the quality of both the self and the object representation. There is no separable line for narcissism here.

ANAL OBJECT RELATIONS: PRECURSORS OF
THE SUPEREGO AND THE EGO IDEAL; VALUES

During this time of the firm establishment of object representations there also begins the appreciation of the meaning and value of other people. This implies ego modification and the onset of the organization of the superego and the ego ideal. These begin, Freud (1940) said, with "parental influence . . . which as a precursor of the superego, restricts the ego's activities by prohibitions and punishments, and encourages or compels the setting up of repression" (p. 185). These partly internalized parental prohibitions and rewards center around toilet training; the transformation of narcissism into object relationship and then into character and superego takes place in relation to what Ferenczi (1925) called "sphincter morality":

> The anal and urethral identification with the parents . . . appears to build up in the child's mind a sort of physiological forerunner of the ego-ideal or superego . . . a severe sphincter-morality[3] is set up which can only be contravened at the cost of bitter self reproaches and punishment by conscience. (p. 267)

The precursor of the superego can be conceived of as existing partly outside the mind (parental influence) and partly within it (internalized parental prohibitions and encouragements that bring about an "adjusting alteration within the ego" [Fenichel, 1945, p. 103]).

The child assumes not only the parents' punitive and restrictive attitudes, but also the accepting and permissive parental influences. (Both these contrary internalizations are transformed in relation to the ambivalent but predominantly aggressively charged instinctual psychic climate.) The positive influences contribute to the structure of the ego-ideal. As filtered through the ego, these internalizations function for the child in the mechanisms of idealization and its opposite, devaluation. The child's toilet training has been accomplished both out of love and out of fear of the parents. Idealization is reflected in the wish to master the sphincters in order to be like the idealized parents; it is more connected with libido. The internalized prohibitions are associated with devaluation (of self and of parents) and are more implicated with aggression. These mechanisms contribute to the two aspects of the child's conscience: the ego ideal (idealization) and the primitive superego (devaluation). Both a going toward the parents (fusion, love) and a moving away from the parents (differentiation, hate) are inevitable and necessary; a flexible and proper balance of both directions is crucial for optimal continuing development.

Regression to Anality

Anna Freud (1952) points out that many ego achievements such as the:

> ability to speak . . . after approximately six to twelve months from its establishment . . . remain immune [to regression] except in the case of grave psychotic disorders . . . In the case of walking, this function is already independent of instinctual upheavals a few weeks after its beginning . . . bowel and bladder control, on the other hand, may remain susceptible to id disturbance, i.e., reversible, during the whole period of early childhood. (p. 243)

And, one might add, reversible to a lesser degree throughout life. For what has been postulated about the defensive need for anal control would make understandable the frequent evocation of anal symptoms and mechanisms (or, as Fliess puts it, "anal-erotic elaboration upon instinctual strivings" [1956, p. 124]) on any occasion that might give rise to any of the major danger situations outlined by Freud: loss of love, castration, the guilt of conscience, and above all the traumatic situation of overstimulation, which is the basis for all the others. The so regularly observed regression to anality (a state already pervaded by pre-existent oral elements) is then expressed in the complex interplay involved in psychic conflict: defense and gratification and compromise-formation marked by expressions derived predominantly from the anal phase.

Values and the Full Emotional Life

I have stated that the mastery of the anal sphincter is paramount in the establishment of mental representations of the body and of the self as closed systems. And yet a concomitant of the need to achieve an illusion of closure, fixity, and stability (without which there might be no feeling of identity) is the danger of fixation at the level of anal organization (and, later, of regression to an anal fixation point). Paradoxically, unless in the course of maturation the illusion of closure becomes subject to doubt, full humanity will not be achieved. (Certainty is for the compulsives and the gods.) If there is an inordinate continuing need for completeness and rigidity, the whole character structure can become involved—the anal fixation can have unfortunate lifelong consequences. The individual who is by turns literally and emotionally bent on "keeping a tight asshole" (I am quoting the patient (Y) whom I described at the beginning of this book) and in the throes of the opposite—emotional diarrhea—can become (in part, or in large part) a caricature: two-dimensional; embroiled in possessions (fecal equivalents); lacking the perspective, the sense of transiency and self-doubt, and the flexibility of full humanity. "Death destroys a man," says E. M. Forster, "but the idea of death saves him" (1921, p. 324). Death is *the* open door. Anality, the involvement with *things*, denies death as it scants life in its insistence on the fixed and the eternal. There are several ways in which this incomplete humanity can become manifest: Massive isolating defenses can result in *as-if* or *false-self* functioning; there can be a deadening of affect (including anxiety), sometimes effected by way of alterations of consciousness (autohypnosis); the feeling of identity can be fragmented and compartmentalized. The predominating obsessive–compulsive character that expresses the continuing sway of the too-powerful "preoedipal anal–sadistic organization" (which can exist beneath and beside the subsequent oedipal one) involves varying combinations of too much defense against, and too much letting go of, archaic affect. Character traits result that encompass an infinite variety of contradictory variables (contradictions and reversals are the stuff of anality, which is made up of coexistent defensive and expressive components): the entirely predictable (life as caricature) alongside occasional unpredictability; dullness interspersed with violence; being emotionally dead yet also subject to outbursts of affect. There is an enormous range of degrees and varieties of too-much anal defensiveness, but also a common monolithic imago, a dead weight that haunts the soul and threatens to come to life: a zombie who wants to kill.

The compulsion to restrict, control, and constrict can influence mind and body, making for interferences in psychic continuity as well as separation of feeling and idea. These disconnections can amount to vertical splits in the ego—splits, that is, in the individual's *sense* of *I*—which isolate what can be *owned* as part of the self. They disrupt memory, perception, apperception, and will; the mind's metaphor-making central activity is compromised. Even in so-called normal development, there is some mysterious maturational amnesia—a major and striking and complicated disturbance of the memory function that seems to take place somewhere in the advance from the anal through the oedipal period. For example, one sees in children who are anally fixated a special exaggeration of the ordinarily encountered recession of the poetry and creativity of the child's early verbal expression. Seemingly artistic children can become inhibited; for all children, in varying degrees, it is as if there develops a reduced availability of access to primary process. With overwhelming stimulation or breakdown of functioning in subsequent development, there is regression to the fixation period, made imperative by the need to recathect the psychic cluster of representations attached to the anal sphincter— representations so necessary for the control of "archaic affect" and therefore of the automatic anxiety involved in traumatic experiences.[4]

DENIAL AND AS-IF FUNCTIONING; SPLITTING

The intrapsychic elaborative "counterpart-use" of the anal sphincter as reflected in the splitting of connected ideas, and of ideas from affect (isolation), and in the expulsion of "bad" psychic products from the mind (projection), can culminate in denial—a quasi-delusional break with reality; a break with the registration of, and the responsibility for, *what was* and *what is.*

Not only are sustained thought and the flow of affect inhibited by anal fixation, but (it follows) so are the beginnings of commitment to people and to ideas, ideals, and even to things. The capacity to feel meaningfulness and to hold values is compromised. The healthy development of the ability to love (an achievement that follows the anal period and depends on the flexibility of affect) is adversely influenced. Subsequent transformational refinements and adjustments of ego and superego functioning will be unfavorably inhibited by fixation. With regression, there will be a re-assumption of constrictive anal narcissism.

The devaluation and the de-individualization inherent in "too much" anal defensiveness can lead, ultimately, to the reduction of *everything* to shit—shit here connoting the grey, the undifferentiated, the meaningless. This meaninglessness is a defense against, a cover for, the underlying murderous "bad" shit. Another defense against this emanation of murderous anality would be its transformation into the opposite (the other side of the same "anal" coin, arrived at by the mechanism of idealization [see Chasseguet-Smirgel, 1978, 1984]): "good" magical shit, the golden stuff of the alchemist and of Rumplestiltskin, which promises eternal bliss. Both extremes (with their clamorous moral and aesthetic auras) are disguised by the defensive shift, the sphincteric reduction, to the indifferent and the undifferentiated. These latter appear in as-if defensive involvement and inauthentic value systems; in the façade of boredom and of not caring, of "who gives a shit?" The underlying defensive motivation for fixation at and regression to the anal level is the need to control and to contain primal affect—characterized by Abraham as "unrestricted cannibalism" (1924, p. 488): to kill and to eat. The emotional sphincter is needed to master murderous orality. (Paradoxically, one can also speak of "anal rage," the anal transformation and expression of this primal affect.)

Chasseguet-Smirgel (1978) has written of the Marquis de Sade as exemplifying those who live in an "anal world," where all is reduced to the same matter, where all differentiation is to be eliminated. She sees this reductive degradation as the essence of anal sadism and explains it primarily as a reaction to envy of the father's penis.[5] The degradation toward nothingness is, I believe, a developmentally derived defensive phenomenon (a particular kind of regression that flowers during the anal period); it is a forerunner of the repression barrier that is to be erected after the oedipal period. All the basic psychological dangers (which include narcissistic injury—envy of the breast as well as of the penis) can bring on the threat of regression toward nothingness: toward nondiscrimination, anonymity, need-fulfillment rather than love; loss of identity and individuality; loss of the ability to care about others; and, finally, dehumanization. If any developmental level gets too charged with archaic affect (cannibalism and murder), an anal sphincteric regressive defense that revives narcissism can be initiated.

Vertical Splitting: A Literary Example

Part of the defensive panoply available during the anal period is the possibility of a vertical splitting of the ego in the service of isolation and denial. This means a massive disowning of, and compartmentalizing of, aspects of one's personality, such that one can alternate between them if need be. Freud described the phenomenon masterfully in relation to the Rat Man: "He is made up of three personalities—one

humorous and normal, another ascetic and religious and a third im-
moral and perverse" (1909, p. 278). As an illustration I offer some self-
observation of the great poet W. H. Auden. The material illustrates a
"splitting" that occurred in conjunction with a regression to the anal
level; this event had followed conflicts involving submission to—and
evoking fear and hatred of—a castrative, invasive, phallic mother. (One
can only speculate as to whether Auden, like some of the patients I cite,
had experienced actual anal overstimulation which enhanced fantasies
of anal submission. In any case, Auden, who characterized his preferen-
tial homosexual *activities* as oral rather anal, was left with a compulsion to enact the *fantasy* of exciting anal submission and with a corresponding anal defensiveness to ward off overstimulation.) I quote from
Humphrey Carpenter's (1981, p. 11) excellent biography of Auden:

> [His mother] was musical, and she encouraged Wystan to learn the piano.
> He proved to be competent at it if not specially talented. He also had
> quite a good treble voice, and sometimes sang duets with her. When he
> was eight she taught him the words and music of the love-potion scene
> from Wagner's *Tristan und Isolde*, and together they sang this intensely
> erotic duet, Wystan taking the part of Isolde. She was, Wystan said as he
> looked back at this, sometimes "very odd indeed."
>
> He loved her deeply, but felt that their close relationship had set up a
> great tension in himself. He once wrote a few lines of verse about this,
> which he did not publish:
>
>> Tommy did as his mother told him
>> Till his soul had split;
>> One half thought of angels
>> And the other half of shit.

The idealization of shit (in the homosexual Auden's anal practices)
would have, transiently, merged the two "halves"—reversing the impulse to degrade the castrative, destructive parent, and distancing fear
and hatred of parents and of self. (Not shitty sex, incest, and murder,
but *Tristan und Isolde* and Love–Death!) Richard Wagner, *not* an
overt homosexual, sometimes successfully transfigured and idealized
his own (split-off) nasty and perverse "half" in his music: his greed
and unscrupulousness about money, his mysogyny, his penchant for
stealing other men's wives, his sadism, his anti-Semitism—all can be
found transformed and idealized in *Das Rheingold*, *Die Walkeure*,
Parsifal, as well as in *Tristan und Isolde*. And, in *Tristan*, both the
love-potion scene and the Liebestod are idealized realizations of fantasies of sex-and-death as eternal fusion with the mother.[6]

Notes to Chapter Two

1. Much of my theory is derived from the first of Robert Fliess's three fine volumes in his "Psychoanalytic Series," an uneven and sometimes erratic but always brilliant compendium of insight comparable in terms of clinical usefulness to the works of Freud and Abraham on which they are based. For example here is a statement about the castration complex. (It is a "non-anal" example but it is particularly applicable to my "goose" patient (see Chapter 4.):"One could show that man's fear of castration is, paradoxically, often the stronger the more completely he has identified himself with the 'castrated' woman; and that the woman's feeling of inferiority is frequently the more pronounced the more she has deluded herself about owning a penis" (1956, p. 195). I regret the neglect of these books by most psychoanalytic scholars.

2. In a similar vein, Glover (1935) is, without naming it, refering to the anal phase of libidinal development when he calls the time "roughly between the ages of eighteen months and three to three and a half years . . . [the] phase of 'obsessional primacy'" (p. 132).

3. What I call sphincter defensiveness is a counterpart, a sort of physiological forerunner of the ego's defensive functioning; see "Introduction," this chapter.

4. The sad diminution of creative promise is illustrated in pathologically exaggerated form in the famous story of Kaspar Hauser, which I discuss in Chapter 5.

5. In a later (1984) work, Chasseguet-Smirgel makes clear that she sees regression to the anal universe as being in the service of eradicating "the differences between the generations: the inevitable period of time separating a child from his mother (for whom he is an inadequate sexual partner) and from his father (whose potent sexual organ he does not possess)" (p. 2). I agree with her completely; my view of the reduction of everything to undifferentiated shit is a complementary one stressing general defense; it includes not only the motives she emphasizes but also the need to compromise between fulfilling aggressive impulses toward degradation and destruction and defending against their murderous intensity. Viewed developmentally, and from the perspective of my clinical material, the *bedrock* of what requires defense seems to me to be the murderous intensity of the aggression-laden archaic affects that go on as development progresses (having, one hopes, undergone some transformation) to infuse the oedipus complex.

6. Auden (1977, p. 42) once expressed his lifelong psychic subjection to his mother:

> A long time ago I told my mother
> I was leaving home to find another;
> I never answered her letter
> But I never found a better.

3

Healthy Anality and Anal Creativity

HEALTHY ANAL PSYCHIC STRUCTURALIZATION

By stressing the modifications and integrations of the anal period, I am not questioning the importance of the crucial ensuing oedipal period for healthy psychic development as well as for subsequent psychopathology. The period that is dominated by conflicts over the oedipus complex is the time when transformations and resolutions necessary for true maturity should take place, including the consolidation of the superego; the culmination of the establishment of a repression barrier; and the beginning of true object love. These phenomena of the oedipal period are inevitably partly shaped by the preceding development. We know too little about any given individual's strengths (innate and acquired talents) to be able to predict specific results, which will depend on how well (as well as *how*) the difficulties present during the anal period are transcended (*cf.* M. Kris, 1957).

The control and achievements of the anal period are, forgive the pun, fundamental for psychic structure formation. They help to establish a necessary, and not necessarily pathological, obsessive–compulsive scaffolding that becomes part of the functioning of the developing ego and superego; and which is needed for stability and for enhancement of identity, and for psychological separation from the parents. These attainments, after the advances and transformations of the oedipal period, go on to make for the ability to suspend "disbelief in the selfhood of someone else" (Trilling, 1955, p. 94) and to love others. These complicated developmental advances are based on the interplay of biological givens (inherent maturational patterns) with environmental, specifically parental, influences; and on the internalization of the parents. These glib phrases cover up so much that is not known.

A. Freud places the anal phase from ages one and a half to three and a half years (1947, p. 221). Transformational achievements that follow depend on the individual's having attained a proper balance between anal defensiveness and the expression of anal and other drive impulses. A "healthy" and balanced anal defensiveness implies a flexibility that becomes a quality of the functioning of the psychic structure during the anal period of structural development. Transformations are required for functional stability, and the outcome should enable control of archaic affect without too much emotional constriction, permitting the discharge of modulated oral, anal, and destructive impulses. The implied existence of this kind of "healthy" anal defensiveness in obsessive–compulsive mechanisms renders the presence or the restoration of those mechanisms (despite their sometimes obvious pathology) a source of reassurance to the therapist when seen in patients who have suffered psychotic breakdowns. And, I repeat, all of us neurotics (notwithstanding my warning against generalizations of this sort) are and need to be, in part, obsessive–compulsives.[1] Healthy anal psychic development is required to be able to hold on to familiar and controllable representations of the external world, and—above all—to representations of the parents, which have become part of one's self-representation. The return to this holding on to what once promised stability and rescue is achieved by regression to anal defensiveness and anal narcissism.

E. Glover (1935) in dealing with pathogenesis points to what he calls "the root-problem of affect" (p. 135). (This would correspond to Fliess's "archaic emotions.") Melanie Klein's theory has clearly influenced what he writes. Glover is describing the early ego (past the first six months of life):

> the child is during this period at the mercy of violent fluctuations in affect, which in turn induce a violent pendulum-swing between introjective and projective processes. Just how violent and urgent these affects are can be conjectured from the painful affects associated with melancholiac and paranoid states respectively. These co-called pathological states have already helped to modify the more catastrophic dangers with which the child feels itself to be threatened in the earliest months of life. They have helped, but at a price. The infant, *hounded by the threat of overwhelming affect*, alternately clings to and lets go its cherished mechanisms of introjection and projection. It is this confused, bewildered and agonized state of psychic affairs *which the obsessional phase sets out to overcome.* . . .

The infant not only produces more rapid alternations but smaller doses of anxiety attached to less important ideational systems. It compounds affects and in that way reduces the necessity for excessive anxiety or guilt feeling. *It compounds them so closely, indeed, that the subject soon gives an appearance of lack of emotional feeling. . . .* This is the supreme virtue of obsessional technique (my italics; p. 139).

Glover's "obsessional phase" would refer to the ego development (adaptation and defensive psychic structure formation) of the anal-sadistic stage of libidinal development where body ego is being rapidly (though never completely) transformed into psychic ego. He is clearly indicating a healthy obsessionalism which expresses healthy anality, and he has indicated the main thrust of anal defensiveness—the reduction of emotion.

HEALTHY ANALITY; ANAL CREATIVITY

There is what I will call a kind of "body creativity." It stems from the child's experience of fecal and urinary products as stuff that he/she can produce. In more than one language, excretion is alluded to as "making." Both "making" and "moving" (another frequent paraphrase for defecation, which also connotes locomotion) involve metaphoric conceptions of excretion that have magical meaning for the child. The feeling of magical power is acquired in early life, but it burgeons during the anal developmental stage as a quality conferred by the primitive ego on body processes—part of the omnipotence and enchantment of narcissism. The magic of shitting, "making," "moving," can be good or bad, white or black, magic. The child can feel that what he "makes" is wonderful and/or terrible. These qualities depend on how the excretory products have been emotionally invested from within; this, in turn, has been greatly influenced by parental affects and attitudes (which are, in the course of development, both identified with and reacted against.)

This anal creativity probably has earlier oral prototypes; but these are vague. More familiar are later relevances. The passage of the excretory products through the highly charged erogenous zones (anus and urethra) will come to be connected psychically (and to be confused regressively) with intercourse and genital sexuality. The anal passage of stool will specifically serve as a prototype in fantasy for the concept of giving birth (another itself major unconscious equivalent for the production of all sorts of physical and mental creations, ranging from the making of material objects, tools, and toys to the thoughts and works of genius.)

Feces were once, in childhood, felt to be vibrant and animate, part of one's body. Even after evacuation they continue to have for the child (and to retain, in frequent regression for the adult) animation and narcissistic magical power. At first the child will feel that his feces can do wonderful and terrible things—Freud believed feces were the prototype of gifts, experienced first by the child as gifts to the parents. (The gifts can be experienced as either powerfully beneficent or terribly poisonous and destructive [see Orgel & Shengold, 1968]; or they may be perceived in more mild and modulated fashion.)

Dr. Edward Knight of New Orleans, when discussing one of my presentations on anality, gave a homely illustration of anal creativity, one that combines a fantasy of birth with creative narrative potential. He told of a three-year-old boy who came into the parental bedroom carrying a chamber pot containing three turds: one large, one middle-sized, and one small (this sounds like Goldilocks and the Three Bears); the boy exclaimed with great joy, "Look, I've made a daddy, a mommy, and a me!"

CREATIVE ANALITY: FLAUBERT

Here is a good example of anal metaphor used in a letter written by Flaubert to his mother during his great adventurous trip to Egypt. Its use illustrates some of the rich and contradictory meanings of anality, evoking not only its defensive and its expressive aspect, but also its healthy dynamism and creative potential.

I must first set the scene. The year was 1850. Six years earlier, at age 23, Flaubert had had his first sudden attack of what were called epileptic seizures, which had relieved him from the conflict that ensued when his father insisted that he choose how he was to earn a living. The attack had marked the beginning of a lifelong intermittent and finally chronic semi-invalidism that was to keep Flaubert at home with his mother, able to devote himself fully to his writing. Flaubert's father had died in 1846, two years after his son's epileptic attack. After this, Gustave lived alone with his mother at Croisset in Normandy (until his sister also died and his niece became part of the household). Madame Flaubert was a zealous guardian of her darling son.

In 1850, at age 29, Gustave had recently broken off with his Parisian mistress, Louise Colet, an older woman whose demanding nature and jealousy of his friends and especially of his mother he had found intolerable. He had completed the first version of *The Temptation of St. Anthony*, on which he had been working for years, and he believed it to be his first book really worthy of publication. However, when he read it aloud to two trusted friends (this took 32 hours), he was devastated by their advice to burn it. His identity as a writer was threatened. Shortly after this, he traveled to Egypt with Maxime DuCamp, one of the friends who had advised him to abandon his book. He had wrung permission from his mother only after his brother, a physician, had helped to convince her that the trip would be good for Gustave's health. Because his friends had made him doubt himself, "he was sick at heart as he made himself ready to travel" (Steegmuller, 1972, p. 101).

As it turned out, Flaubert was exhilarated by Egypt; he was the active, excited observer in the country of that Saint Anthony about whom he had been studying and writing for so long. This helped him with the pain of having passively experienced his friends' rejecting criticism. In his flush of good feeling, Flaubert found himself full of desire for all sorts of sexual adventures, about which he wrote to his friend Bouilhet (the other of his two discouraging critics). The excerpt that follows is from the more circumspect correspondence with his mother:

> When I think of my future . . . when I ask myself: "What shall I do when I return? What path shall I follow?" and the like, I am full of doubts and indecisions. At every stage in my life I have put off facing my situation in just this same way: and I shall die at eighty before having formed any opinion concerning myself or, perhaps, without writing anything that would have shown me what I could do. Is *Saint Antoine* good or bad? That is what I often ask myself, for example: who was mistaken—I or the others? However, I worry very little about any of this. I live like a plant, suffusing myself with sun and light, with colors and fresh air. I keep eating, so to speak; afterwards the digesting will have to be done, then the shitting: and the shit had better be good! That's the important thing. (Steegmuller, 1972, p. 109).

Flaubert is manifestly using shit and shitting to refer to his future books and his vocation as a creative writer. There is here a definite self-degrading tone that represents an active turning on himself defensively in an attempt to master the terrible narcissistic injury received passively when his friends rejected *Saint Antoine*. The letter shows typical obsessive–compulsive doubting, symptomatic of many periods of writing inhibition for Flaubert in which he defensively just managed to hold his own. But this is a predominantly optimistic letter, which he ends with a kind of Rabelaisian resolve to heal himself. The healthy physical exuberance of his trip is apparent in his comparison of himself to a flourishing plant, and in his peasant-like allusions to animal processes such as eating and shitting. This capacity for exuberance is, I would speculate, in no small part due to Flaubert's physical distance from his mother. And, supplementing this physical distancing is the psychic distancing provided by anal defensiveness, which is being used not only to dilute a severe narcissistic blow, but also to ward off preoedipal and oedipal impulses toward his mother. In a letter to Bouilhet, he says that one of the sexual adventures he and DuCamp are seeking is to perform sodomy on a boy; and 10 days after the just-quoted letter to his mother, Flaubert tells Bouilhet of going to a bath-house to seek an available bath-boy fancied by him and DuCamp. (Flaubert had many sexual experiences in Egypt—with both sexes, but chiefly with female prostitutes. These encounters were idealized in romantic descriptions to Bouilhet; Flaubert also caught syphilis in the Orient.) Flaubert's letters from Egypt are full of anal references and metaphors; they express his fascination with the "arses" of women and boys; there are frequent references to defecation and to beating. All this gives the correspondence an exotic anal redolence. Perversion and degradation are mixed with health and creative potential. These are vivid and marvelous letters (as are most of Flaubert's, full of wisdom, wit and gossip about art, politics, and life).[2]

The creative "shitting" Flaubert returned home to do turned out to be, at least on the surface, far-removed from his exotic idyll in the Orient. He was to begin the years of preparation for and execution of his great realistic masterpiece, *Madame Bovary*.

In letters written later in his life, Flaubert alternates between phallic and passive anal metaphors of his literary creativity. When, in 1857, he was doing research and struggling to write his second published novel, *Salammbo* (one more directly related to his experiences in the Orient), he wrote to a friend on a day when he had done some work, "Finally I'm beginning to have an erection. That's the important thing. But how hard it's been to get it up! Will it stay?" (1857–1880, p. 5). In a letter written several months later, he was still complaining about lack of progress:

I'm not going ahead, which is better than continuing to make mistakes. I stopped because I felt I was on the wrong track. I'm baffled by the psychology of my characters. . . . I'll be in Paris Tuesday or Wednesday of next week . . . Once there, I swear I'm going to go in for some monstrous debauches, to restore my morale . . . *Perhaps by sticking something up my ass I can give my brain a good fucking.* I hesitate between the column in the Place Vendome and the obelisk. . . . It's true I've gone through similar periods before and come out of them all livelier. But this one is lasting too long, too long! (my italics; p. 6)

(Note that one of the "phalli" Flaubert considers using in this fantasy of fucking himself anally is Egyptian: the obelisk. This fantasy not only echoes the bisexual and anal fucking of his Egyptian journey, but also evokes the fascinating and frightening power of that bisexual creature of Egyptian origin so full of oedipal and preoedipal significance—the Sphinx.)

Flaubert did get over this writing inhibition; we know neither whether he needed the aid of "monstrous debauches" nor, if he did, what these consisted of. He did finish *Salammbo.*

Sublimation of anality (the ability to turn from direct discharge of the anal–sadistic drives to adaptive and creative "making") implies "healthy" anality. And the kind of sublimation of which a creative genius like Flaubert is capable implies mysterious and magnificent health—mysterious because psychoanalysts know too little about gifts, genius, and creativity. What little we have done in this direction (studying the ego, object relations, traumata, as well as drive endowment) is but a scratching of the surface, and we need a new genius of the order of Freud to be able to say, "Look!" and show us the way (if indeed there *is* a way) to the psychoanalysis of gifts and of artistic creativity.

Notes to Chapter Three

1. Compare Glover, who foreshadows my ideas of anal defensiveness: "For the task of the obsessional neurosis is an important and difficult one. It is to permit a regressive flight from the anxieties induced by advancing development, *and at the same time to stem that regression*" (my italics; Glover, 1935, p. 131).

2. Flaubert's letter writing is consistently vibrant and vivid, partly because of his wit and intelligence, and partly through an emotional openness

conveyed by his fondness for body and animal metaphors (see Barnes, 1984). He frequently uses oral, anal, and phallic imagery so that his language almost throbs with body-ego resonance. For example, in writing to Louise Colet of the pallidness of the writing of a mutual friend, the poet Leconte de Lisle, he says:

> . . . he lacks heart. By this I do not mean personal or even humanitarian feelings, no—but *heart*, almost in the medical sense of the word. His ink is pale; his muse suffers from lack of fresh air. Thoroughbred horses and thoroughbred styles have plenty of blood in their veins and it can be seen pulsing everywhere in them, under the skin and the words. Life! Life! To have erections! That is everything, the only thing that counts. . . . All the power of a work of art lies in this mystery, and it is this primordial quality, this *motus animi continuus* (vibration, continual movement of the *mind* [my italics; I would translate this word as *soul* rather than *mind*]—Cicero's definition of eloquence). . . . you can judge the excellence of a book by the strength of the punches it has given you and the time it takes you to recover from them. And then, how dauntless are the great masters! They pursue an idea to its furthermost limits. In Moliere's *Monsieur de Pourceaugnac* there is a question of giving a man an enema. Not just *one* enema is brought in: a whole troupe of actors carrying syringes pour down the aisles of the theatre! Michelangelo's figures have cables rather than muscles; in Rubens's bacchanalian scenes men piss on the ground; and think of everything in Shakespeare, etc., etc., . . . I think the greatest characteristic of genius is, above all, *power* [Flaubert here has been demonstrating and discussing some of the sources of his own creative power]. (1830-1857, p. 193)

4

Defensive and Healthy Anality Contrasted

THE RAT AND THE GOOSE

A several-times divorced, currently unmarried man (a Don Juan in fantasies that he had done his best to act out for most of his adult life) came into analysis to undo the disturbing exigent quality of his sexual impulses and to reduce his need to perform feats of sexual skill and endurance. The pressures of libidinal daydreams and impulses often led to lapses of memory and to interruptions of thought. These minor thinking defects, he believed, interfered with his ability to achieve, frustrating his intense ambition to succeed. He tried to deny his wish for eminence and had partially replaced it by becoming a collector. His character and habits were marked by what Abraham calls "the libidinal overemphasis of possession" (1921, p. 385). He had done well as a collector; and he was a most accomplished seducer. But he had not prospered in his profession, where he usually ended up, like Mozart's Don Giovanni, submitting to the Commendatore he had tried to get rid of. The despised boss or rival would become for him a terrifying punitive father-figure, whom he would first provoke—only eventually to yield (as the Don had succumbed to the Stone Guest who dragged him down to hell). He did experience intermittent respite from the need for punishment, and, after a long time in analysis, was beginning to do well more consistently at his work.

The analytic material presented here occurred in two sessions following the last day of the month, when the patient had been given his bill. (He was usually compulsively prompt and could be expected to hand in a check the next session.) I was about to leave for the traditional end-of-summer vacation, and this anticipated event had absorbed much of the patient's recent attention, characteristically evidenced by his disowning and negating interest. This display of not caring about being abandoned had been interspersed with typical defensive preoccupations and activity. He was trying to launch an affair with a recently met, attractive married woman. This was not the first time that he had initiated a sexual liaison during the summer exile from the analysis.

In the first of the two relevant sessions the patient did not pay and did not mention his bill. Toward the end of a rather resistant hour in which he appeared to be waiting for some disapproving response to a recital of elaborate seduction schemes, he complained that the session had been empty and that I had been silent. "I've been *sitting* here for forty-five minutes and nothing has happened," he said—referring to his supine position on the couch in a "slip" that had reversed our roles. He noted his mistake and, uncharacteristically, started to associate to it. He had a vivid memory of sitting on the toilet for long periods of time when he was five or six years old: "I used to wait for my mother to come in and wipe my anus. I can really feel what it was like. I was too old for her to be doing that kind of thing. She would come and ask: 'Schon?' [Ready?] [German was spoken in the family's intimate life]; I would answer 'Schon,' and then she'd wipe me." This material (to underline the content by way of metaphor) emerged at the "tail end," the last five minutes, of the session.

At the start of the next hour (his bill still ignored), the patient reported that in the elevator coming up to my office he had had the fantasy that his anus was being wiped with paper money. (In a later session, he recalled a longer version of the mirrored dialogue that had usually preceded getting his anus wiped: "Schon? Papier?" [Ready? Paper?], and the rejoinder, "Schon. Papier.") "It wasn't clear who was wiping me," he went on about his fantasy in the elevator. "Maybe it was somebody else, maybe I was doing it myself." There was a pause— this patient often talked in peristaltic rhythm (rushes and pauses)— followed by a rather assertive: "I have *no* feelings about that fantasy." I responded that it was not clear whether he was disclaiming emotions or anal feelings or both. He then started to sound angry: "I don't know what the hell you mean by 'anal feelings'; that 'anal feelings' is your phrase and it has absolutely no significance for me. I don't suppose you are about to explain it to me either. I think you just do not want me to talk about my plans to have sex with G [the new woman]."

Again a pause followed. "Now I remember what I said yesterday about wanting my mother to wipe me. I see myself leaning forward on the toilet—opening my buttocks, leaning over, and staring downward as if I'm reading a book lying open on the floor. (Later on, this memory was connected with autohypnosis: "just staring straight ahead" when reading while eating or on other occasions that evoked forbidden contact and overwhelming affect [see Shengold, 1967].) It's a good feeling, a gentle massage of my anal sphincter; and my head is lying in her lap." Here the tone changed suddenly from nostalgia to sarcastic anger: "Well, if it felt so nice, why didn't I learn to do it for myself? I was five or six—mother was about forty, the same age as G! Why did she do it?"

It was obvious that despite having so far described only good "anal feelings," the patient in his anger was accusing his mother of having done something wrong. His mother had in fact consistently overstimulated him (some of her exhibitionism had already been remembered)—or, more accurately and more damaging, had alternated between overstimulation and desertion, leaving him often in the care of older siblings.

The patient then continued his associations with a disquisition on the anal feelings he had earlier disowned and the knowledge of which he had projected on to me. "The light, massaging anal feelings are good feelings. I love being lightly touched there. But there are other kinds of anal feelings, at least two others, maybe more. There is one that is almost painful. If I get even a pinprick anywhere, my anus closes up tight and there is a sudden deeper feeling—way up my ass. It's even worse when I have to get a hypodermic needle. [He showed no awareness that he was alluding to the analyst and his genitals here with the "pinprick" and implied injection of the "hypodermic needle."] That sudden tight closing of my anal sphincter is like a deep pain. And yet it is also exciting."

The Goose and Goosing

I responded that he was not talking just about touch, but about penetration. "Yes! Penetration means submission and humiliation and anger. I always hated being goosed. I hate being goosed. It's like a terrible, a really terrible invasion of privacy. When I was little, there were two friends who used to goose me: Lenny Schmidt and Lenny

Shane—two Lenny S's. [The last names I have approximated; the first names are as the patient reported.] Lenny Schmidt was a good guy, but Lenny Shane wasn't. He was good-looking, and bigger than I was; but he was a wise-ass and a thief. The name 'Shane' reminds me of what I told you about what was said when I was on the toilet: 'Schon?' 'Schon.'"

At this point I remarked, "There is another Lenny S here now: Lenny Shengold."

"That's fantastic! This is too ingenious to be true. There *is* another Lenny S sitting here with me big as life!" The patient was clearly excited and seemed to be enjoying the flow of his associations. "Shengold . . . Schöngold, the good-looking one [*schön* = handsome in German] . . . Shengold . . . why you are the Golden Goose, the goose that lays the golden eggs!" The patient was at this point in excellent humor.

This man had somehow retained a healthy capacity for humor in spite of, or at least alongside of, his severely obsessional yet impulse-ridden character. He often used humor defensively to distance himself from and to avoid responsibility for what frightened him or made him feel troubled. Yet his humor was also a saving grace, something good from his childhood that had been preserved and had been preservative. That he was capable of humor suggested to me that this man's predominant emotional shallowness might be defensive. I stress his transient and fragile healthy ability to see his body and himself as a joke (which existed alongside masochistic trends and a need to be punished) to contrast it with material derived from literature which follows.

The Goose Imago

The associations to the goose and goosing had brought excitement, confusion, and ambiguity to the patient's associations. I felt that the Golden Goose was for him an incarnation of the large and powerful invasive presence, "big as life," who could stimulate and penetrate him anally. (I judged his predominant connotations of the Golden Goose to refer to it as a parent-figure, as opposed, for example, to the Golden Goose as *child* depicted in the fairy tale by the Grimm brothers.[1] In my patient's fantasy of the Golden Goose as invading parent, the goose appears to be masculine, or at least it is endowed with phallic power. Yet the goose itself is literally a feminine creature, the male being called the gander. It is supposed to be a stupid bird, and for centuries a foolish person has been called a goose. It is regarded as a dirty creature, with anal connotations, perhaps because like all poultry it can be domesticated but never toilet trained; the goose is connected with incontinence—anality, as it were, without a sphincter. "Goose" was a term in 17th and 18th century England for a venereal disease ("Winchester goose"—see Partridge, 1937, p. 343) and also for a "dirty" woman, a prostitute (*e.g.*, W. H. Auden's "Mother Goose" in Stravinsky's opera *The Rake's Progress*). The goose is vulnerable— "Feather by feather the goose is plucked," runs an Italian proverb— both due to its stupidity and because it has no anal sphincter, which facilitates "goosing" (see definition to follow). The goose lays eggs as the child drops feces (golden eggs). The "Goose that Laid the Golden Eggs" was killed and eaten by her foolish (goose of) an owner in Aesop's fable.[2] Geese are eaten by the animal and human predators of the world. Yet the goose can be a fierce and attacking creature, frightening to children: "There are . . . few more aggressive birds than geese" (Lorenz, 1963, p. 186); "the fighting urge of the Egyptian goose . . . seems insane to the observer" (Lorenz, 1963, p. 153). The goose's bill is a curved cutting tool with toothlike serrations around its edge and is used for both defense and attack. The goose can close its bill to cut and bite off, as a child can cut off a fecal column with his anal sphincter. The goose appears in ancient records from Egypt and China and is mentioned in the Bible. It is thought to be the first bird to have been domesticated by man. Despite the implications of foolishness and filth, the goose was worshipped as a god in ancient Egypt. Contradictions abound, as with most anal symbols and attributes.

The verb "to goose" that my patient had used is 20th-century American lingo defined by a standard dictionary of slang as "to poke or threaten to poke a finger into someone's anus to produce shock or annoyance" (Wentworth & Flexner, 1960, p. 224). Other definitions (from an English dictionary of the underworld): "to tickle on the buttock . . . to commit sodomy" (Partridge, 1937, pp. 229–230).

These ambiguous connotations show that the goose can be viewed as an imago evoking anal erogeneity and cannibalistic, anal, and phallic libido. The goose, like the anus in fantasy, can bite and be bitten. In both the fable by Aesop and the folk tale by the Grimms, the golden goose is an attribute of its owner, a detachable (i.e., castratable) gift that endows its master with special power. As such, the goose imago can be used to depict the preoedipal parent (*e.g.*, the goose as an Egyptian god), the best-known symbol of which is the Sphinx in the Oedipus legend (a creature of Egyptian origin that has the wings of a bird). The primal parental figure, endowed with cannibalistic destructive phallic power, is encountered in everyone's psychic development. Its mental representation persists with pathogenic intensity when strong sadomasochistic tendencies are present, for example, in children who are traumatically beaten and seduced (overstimulated) by their parents (see Shengold, 1967, 1979).

The Goose and the Rat

Shortly after the session in which he talked about being goosed, the patient in his associations shifted from the goose metaphor to the rat metaphor. Both animals have stirred man's imagination. Ethologists have noted ways in which both creatures resemble man—for example, here is Lorenz's description of greylag geese:

> All the truisms in our proverbs seem to apply equally to geese . . . in the greylag goose and in man, highly complex forms of behavior, such as falling in love, strife for ranking order, jealousy, grieving etc., are not only similar but down to the most absurd detail the same . . ." (1963, p. 187)

Comparisons to the rat, in contrast, usually refer to man's inhumanity: Men and rats are often portrayed as the two creatures in danger of exterminating their own kind by virtue of their intense intraspecific murderous competitiveness. The rat's formidable teeth and ravenous omnivorousness; its associations with filth, plague, and the Black Death; and its destructiveness and inexterminability, make it a much more frightening symbol than the goose. Certainly when my patient brought in his rat associations he was dealing with what was for him the most terrible item in his list of anal feelings.[3] He had once read Freud's Rat Man case and brought up a distorted, detailed, personal version of the "rat torture" fantasy that obsessed Freud's famous patient.

About a week after the analytic hours described above, he came to his session in great agitation, angry with me and frightened by the depth of his anger: "God, I feel beside myself. Here I said that I didn't know what anal feelings are—and now all I do is think about money and feel things in my ass and at the same time I feel like screaming. I feel as if there is a rat up my ass. I remember reading about that somewhere. For me the idea of a rat up my ass is like the worst thing in the world [cf. Winston Smith in 1984]. That feeling could make me kill. This is almost too diabolical." (These last words were an echo in a threatening minor key of "This is too ingenious to be true.") In later sessions the patient talked of having "a devil up my ass" (cf. the anal devils and rat-like creatures in the hells of H. Bosch and J. Callot).

In this hour he was expressing the full cannibalistic intensity of the feeling of being penetrated. The feeling of being goosed threatened to become the feeling of being overwhelmed and destroyed by anal invasion and overstimulation by the biting rat. The patient was on the way to remembering traumatic enema experiences (cf. Heimann, 1962, p. 402, on enemas "registered as attacks"). For him, the primal parent was predominantly a phallic mother who evoked anal erogeneity and oral-sadistic libido. (Cf. Mother Goose, to whom the male can be subject: "Old Mother Goose when she wanted to wander/Would ride on the back of a very fine gander" [old English nursery rhyme].) In relation to such a figure, the patient's mental representation of his anus could shift regressively, in Abraham's (1924) terms, from the place that contains and expels to the place of destroying and being destroyed. In other words, it could shift from the place of the comparatively benevolent, although paradoxically incontinent, and occasionally frightening goose to the place of the demonic,[4] cannibalistic rat. Both the rat and the goose can symbolize the anus and the invader of the anus (the biting rat can be bitten, the goose can be goosed)—this makes for a possibility of using these images as metaphors for the confluence of subject and object, which appropriately alludes to narcissistic aspects of sexual involvement; see the discussion of fascination in Chapter 6.

Rabelais' Goose

I am going to present some contrasting variations on these "anal" themes from François Rabelais (1494–1553). Rabelais was a man of the Renaissance, and expressed himself passionately for naturalness and tolerance, and against the restraints of traditional scholars and theologians. His views can be epitomized by a proverb of William Blake's: "Damn braces: Bless relaxes" (1793/1958, p. 98). At first a monk,

Rabelais left the restrictive and censorial Benedictine order for the more liberal Franciscan, and then abandoned his church calling to pursue, most successfully, his profession as a physician. He was born in a farmhouse; perhaps that furnished a vantage point, heightened by his medical work, for his healthy view of the sexual and excremental functions. His writings show his belief that child rearing and education should be based on common sense (see Frame, 1977). Like Shakespeare (who was born just after the French writer's death), Rabelais believed in the natural order of the universe; both authors celebrate the healthy expression of the body's appetites. There is a good deal of ambiguity and some contradiction in Rabelais' ideas, which are expressed by way of, and probably passed censorship because of, his humor. His great joke was—*the* great joke is—the human body, the ultimate source of unconscious conflict.

Little is really known about Rabelais' personal life, and almost nothing about his life as a child (see Frame, 1977). The heroes of his books, Gargantua (= great gullet) and his son Pantagruel (= great gullet) are giants. Although these two are grossly overindulged as children, they do not suffer from overstimulation. Indeed, indulgence makes the young Gargantua thrive and prepares him for his eventual rather rigorous (although quite sensible) education. It may be that Rabelais had a (not necessarily conscious) need to deny the possibility of damaging overstimulation occurring as a result of the wildly permissive child-rearing he described; he therefore granted his heroes miraculous size and inherent ego precocity, so that they are too large and too mature to be pushed beyond the stimulus barrier. (Freud remarked that Rabelais was substituting grandiosity for infantile helplessness [1900; see Appendix 2].) Rabelais' conscious intention was probably to disguise through humorous exaggeration his politically dangerous plea for a more natural and less restrictive way of bringing up children. To return to my patient, what had been destructive for him is healthful and developmentally sound (*i.e.*, basic to the establishment of psychic structure) for Gargantua.

Gargantua, the giant child of giant parents, was conceived, born, and raised with much surfeiting of appetite—his parents', his nurses', and his own. Nothing was hurried. He was in the womb for 11 months and was born able to talk (he cried for "Drink!"). He would devour enormous draughts of his mother's milk, because she "could draw from her breasts two thousand one hundred and three hogsheads and eighteen pints at one time" (1534b, p. 24); he also drank enormously of wine and beer. At 22 months:

> He cried very little but he beshitted himself at all times. For he was wondrously phlegmatic of bum. . . . (p. 25) From three to five years of age, Gargantua was, by his father's orders, brought up and instructed in all proper discipline. [This is a joke, but it is also seriously meant. Rabelais believed in "natural," reasonable discipline, as he makes clear in his ideas on education.] He spent his time like other small children: namely, in drinking, eating and sleeping; in eating, sleeping and drinking; in sleeping, drinking and eating. He was forever wallowing in dirt, covering his nose with filth and begriming his face. He wore his shoes down to a frazzle, lay with his mouth gaping to catch heaven knows what . . . he used to piddle on his shoes, brown up his shirt-tails, wipe his nose on his sleeve, clear his nostrils into his soup, and dive headlong into the foulest muck at hand. (p. 36)
>
> [Gargantua's governesses made great sport with his "codpiece," his penis]: Every morning his governesses prinked and dizened it with lovely nosegays and fine silken tassels. Their favorite pastime was to feel and finger his organ, to knead and mould it lovingly, as pharmacists handle ointment and salve to make a large, solidified cylindrical suppository. Then they would burst out laughing for joy at the sport as, under their skilled hands, it would prick up its ears. (p. 38)

When the boy was five, his father Grangousier (= great gullet) visited him after an absence; it is the same age as my patient in his memory of waiting to be wiped. The father wanted to test the boy's intelligence, and also to check up on his nurses, and so he examined them "as to whether they had kept [the boy] sweet and clean. Gargantua at once spoke up. He himself, he said, had taken such pains that there could not be a cleanlier lad in the length and breadth of the land" (p. 41). The boy goes on to prove to his father that he has gained control both of his intelligence and of his anal sphincter, illustrating both with the same series of anecdotes; one such instance:

> "There is no need to swab the arse," Gargantua proceeded, "unless it is beshitten. Now it cannot be beshitten unless you have first shat. Therefore you must shit ere you wipe your rump." (p. 44, modified translation)
>
> "O my splendid little boy, how intelligent you are! I shall very shortly present you as candidate for the degree of Doctor of Philosophy; you are wise beyond your years!" (p. 44)

To return to Grangousier's curiosity about how Gargantua learned to stay clean: "How is that," asked Grangousier.

"Through profound and diligent research," Gargantua explained, "I have invented a means of wiping my bum—it is the most lordly, excellent and expedient technique every seen."

"What does it consist in," Grangousier asked him. . . . "Once I mopped my scut with the velvet scarf of a damozel. It was pleasurable; the soft material proved voluptuous and gratifying to my hindsight. Once, too, I used a hood from the same source and with the same results. The next time it was her neckerchief; again her crimson satin earpieces, but they were bespangled and begilt with beshitten jewelery that scraped my tailpiece from end to end. . . .

(Note that Rabelais has Gargantua begin his experiments with ass-wiping by using articles of a woman's attire; this symbolizes contact with a detachable attribute [extruded fecal column, castrated penis] of the phallic mother. Whatever damage is done can be undone by re-attachment of the detached, and Gargantua reassures himself by proceeding on to a phallic symbol that belongs to a boy, which resembles a similar phallic symbol belonging to an adult male: "I recovered from this thanks to a page's cap with a plume to it like those the Swiss guards sport" (p. 42).

Gargantua makes lists, (like Don Giovanni, like my patient), and he is starting a great list of his wiping efforts. As he describes these efforts, he can experience, as had my patient, a variety of "anal feelings." In the course of making the list, although there are allusions to danger, the boy shows little fear of the destructive power of the phallic mother. This is already evident in his description of being "scraped" by the damozel's earrings, but the symbolism and danger become more explicit with:

Next, [shitting] behind a bush, I came upon a March cat . . . and I put it to excellent advantage though its claws mildly lacerated my perinaeum. But I was fit again on the morrow for I employed the gloves of my charming mother. (p. 42)

Compare this with what my patient added to his own list a week or so after the two sessions referred to earlier: "I have a terrible feeling in my anus that comes with the thought of being hurt or cut. I picture myself at the bathroom door, terrified and trying to get in to be with my mother, because I *scraped* my knee. Why does the idea of my knee being scraped cause such terror? [Freud, I did not tell him, connects the knee (Latin *genu*) with the genitals.] I needed to get to my mother and have her comfort me . . [pause] . . to wipe me gently." The preoedipal phallic mother can be both castrative and comforting.

Gargantua's list goes on for pages; here is its end and climax:

> But to conclude: I affirm and maintain that the paragon arse-cloth is the
> neck of a plump downy goose, provided you hold her head between your
> legs [there is a warning of castrative danger here]. Take my word of honor
> on this score and try it for yourself. You will experience a most marvel-
> lously pleasant sensation in the region of your scutnozzle, as much
> because of the fluffy under plumage as because the bird's warmth, tem-
> pering the bumgut and the rest of the intestines, actually reaches your
> heart and brain . . . in the Elysian Fields . . . they are happy, to my mind,
> because they swab their rumps with a goose." (pp. 44–45)

In this predominantly sunny, healthy, "farmyard-view" of the anal
functions and anal contents (contrast it with the bitter, sadistic tone of
Jonathan Swift's obsessive preoccupation with anality—see "Anal Influence on Genital Sexuality: Swift and Kundera," this chapter), there
is a demonstration that the *happy* control of the anal sphincter paves
the way for the *happy* use of intellectual power, and for a satisfying
sense of identity. The healthy establishment of the ego, the "I," is—to
change slightly what I have quoted Freud as saying—in the first place
the *happy* establishment of the body ego. Rabelais here confirms that a
gigantic step forward in the differentiation between self and other,
between being controlled and controlling, between passive registration
and active thinking, is the mastery of the anal sphincter. The *happy*
attainment of mastery implies the ability (as Fliess says) to contain and
neutralize aggression and rage; and this mastery is a prerequisite for
successful confrontation with the intrapsychic danger (for both sexes)
of castration.

Castration

I am returning after this long digression to the analytic session in
which my patient began the catalog of *his* anal feelings. He continued
by talking about his relationship with one of the Lenny S's, the good-
looking one who was a "wise-ass and thief," who goosed him, and
who would often steal his toys, "like my favorite softball, and other of
my precious things. And then he would deny it and I wouldn't be sure
when I saw them later in his house that the ball and the other toys were
really mine. And I'm still not sure of anything [*cf.* Gargantua's unself-
conscious certainty]." Another pause followed. "My precious things—
that's a rather precious expression. I think of my penis and balls."

I responded: "I think you are saying that wanting your anus rubbed affects your feeling about, and in, your penis and balls." My intervention was followed by an intense (although transient) reaction of disavowal and denial that, paradoxically, confirmed my comment and illustrated the effect the patient was denying: "Nonsense! What difference would that make at five or six? The penis isn't important then . . (pause) . . what an astonishing thing to say! How could I say that? I guess what I feel is how weak and inadequate my penis *is*. I certainly used to feel that when I was a teenager. [Then followed a very long, disconnecting silence.] I'm thinking of the new woman I would like to fuck. She should be very easy to get. She's very frustrated in her marriage."

I then said: "You are thinking about intercourse to reassure yourself that your 'weak and inadequate' penis will work."

"Yes, my precious and long thing; well, even if it's not as long as I'd like it to be, I can keep it up for a long time."[5]

In the course of this session the patient's attention had shifted from the back to the front of his body. This was a defensive displacement; but it also recapitulated a maturational (and a partially environmentally determined) erogenous spread and linkage, analagous to the connection and flow of erogeneity from anus to penis represented in Gargantua's use of a goose. My patient stressed the feeling of penile inferiority engendered by the frightening intensity of anal cravings. The threat of castration is also adumbrated by Rabelais: the bliss-providing goose must have its head carefully held when it is "between your legs." (Here is a reflection of Fliess's speculation that castration is "in the last analysis conceived of as effected through biting" [1956, p. 96].)[6]

The spread and the simultaneousness of anal and genital erogeneity has both an enhancing and an inhibitory developmental potential. It is an economic question—the predominant direction determined by tolerances and intensities. For Gargantua, the spread of anal stimulation leads primarily to genital excitability and erection; Rabelais describes the giant as a healthy proto-Don Juan at five:

> May the drunkard's pip rot your guts if the little lecher wasn't forever groping his nurses upside-down, arsey turvey . . . and if he wasn't beginning to bring his codpiece into play and turn it to account. (pp. 37–38)

Rabelais entitled the chapter that follows this quotation—the one that celebrates the five-year-old's codpiece and his nurses' delight in it—

"Of Gargantua's Adolescence." The title is ironic, perhaps, but it also alludes to the knowledge that what is overstimulating and tormenting at five can become not only bearable but intensely, compellingly pleasurable with the potentiality of genital discharge in adolescence. This is made explicit in Gargantua's subsequent poetry wherein we see the generation of poetic as well as of genital powers that results from Gargantua's ebullient control of his anus, and from his openness to phallic sensations. Implicit is the absence of castration anxiety. Grangousier says:

> "Ha! my little rapscallion! You've been wetting your whistle to pipe poetry like that!"
> "Ay, surely, my lord and king," the lad answered. . . .
> "Listen":

> > In shitting yesterday I did know
> > The tribute to my arse I owe;
> > Such was the smell that from it slunk
> > That I was with it all bestunk.
> > Oh had but then some brave Signor
> > Brought her to me I waited for
> > > Whilst I was shitting.

> > I would have plugged her water-gap
> > And joined it close to my flip-flap
> > Whilst she had with her fingers guarded
> > My jolly arsehole all bemerded
> > > Whilst I was shitting."
> > > (composite translation; *cf.* 1534c, p. 68)

In Gargantua's poetic daydream, the benevolent woman holds his anus closed while he puts his penis in her "cloaca." The anal touching grants a "control" that enhances his phallic power.

In contrast, my patient was dealing with the overstimulation of the *pre*adolescent in reaction to his mother's anal touch: a cloacal opening response on *his* part that was predominantly anal. This anal, feminizing passivity was augmented by, as I subsequently found out, the castration anxiety evoked by his mother's exhibition of her genitals "in the bathroom," again when he was around five years old. The anal touch endangered his potency. The overstimulation had come into his associations with the goose; this linkage was later to evolve into the "worst thing in the world," the rat in his rectum); and in the session I am presenting the goose material had led him to intimations of castra-

tion and to references to his compulsive and joyless "Don Juanism."
The anal stimulation and passive craving stirred up before and during
the session threatened the good narcissistic cathexis of his genitals.
The passive intensities were accompanied by "anal rage" (see Shengold, 1967) and intense castration anxiety. With this, the patient was
repeating his childhood. To reduce the dangerous anal overstimulation (which threatened defensive anal sphincter control) and to shore
up the feeling of phallic power against the castration threat, he resorted to fantasies of sexual conquest—thoughts of the seduction of
women and to feats of genital prowess. In these fantasies, he was active
and not passive, and was pushing in a progressive libidinal direction,
trying to make genital rather than anal erogeneity the focus of body
affect. It was the same path as that taken by young Gargantua in the
last-quoted poem, but my patient followed it compulsively—out of
defensive necessity. Moreover, my patient's fantasies and sexual actions contained the return of the repressed: the penis-to-cloaca direction involved in the opportunity to identify with the seduced and
submitting woman. At the end of the hour he specifically brought out
the fantasy of surrendering to the primal parent, the phallic woman as
preoedipal mother (see Blos, 1965): "I never have been able to tell
you," he ended the session, "and I don't want to tell you now . . .
[pause] . . . B [his favorite mistress of long-standing] likes to play
around with my ass. It's part of the excitement of being with her. I like
it. Yet having my anus played with decreases my erection. But I make
up for it by going on to prove that my penis is OK in fucking."

Primal Affect, Aggression, Oral Sadism

My patient's terrible anal feelings and his castration fears both had as
their deepest layer the ultimate traumatic danger of psychic annihilation that stems from the earliest period of structural and libidinal
development—the time of unfused aggression, of incipient ego formation, and of the threat of the breakdown of the stimulus barrier. This
time of danger is in the first year of life during the oral–cannibalistic
phase of instinctual development, when the child desperately needs the
care of a loving mother to master what Fliess calls "archaic affect":

Among the "uncontrollable stimuli" swamping the ego and producing
anxiety in the case of the loss (or the nonexistence) of [a normal affection-

ate] mother, oral–sadistic ones should, I believe, be assigned a most prominent place. (Fliess, 1956, p. 79)

The cannibalistic wishes—to eat and to be eaten—and their attendant dangers continue as part of the instinctual mix of all subsequent development: "The mouth [of the second oral stage] is transferable onto all subsequently dominant erogenic zones" (p. 86). This biting mouth is the essence of the terrifying rat image, creeping through all libidinal and erogenic phases (again, recall in 15th- and 16th-century paintings of hell by Bosch and the Colmar School those ubiquitous devil-creatures, some of them rat-devils, who have faces on their behinds and whose anuses are mouths with teeth). Fliess's concept of the transferable mouth is also illustrated in a castration jingle quoted by my patient: "Roy, Roy, the cabin boy /The dev'lish little nipper, /He stuffed his ass /With broken glass /And circumcised the skipper."

The spectacularly toothed and "dirty" rat is connected mainly with anal erogeneity—a portentous and threatening connection because of the importance of anal sphincter control for the taming of overwhelmingly intense affect. To repeat Fliess's central contribution to the concept of defensive anality:

> It is often as though the anal sphincter were charged with the mastery of regressive and archaic affect, intrinsic to whatever phase of development, because it is the strongest [sphincter]; and as though the ego chose anal-erotic elaboration upon instinctual strivings of whatever nature as the most reliable means of preserving its organization. (1956, p. 124)

In the oriental torture that obsessed the Rat Man, the rat's teeth destroyed the anal sphincter. To tame the cannibalistic affects symbolized by those teeth, healthy control of the anal musculature must be achieved. Gargantua accomplished this spontaneously and easily; he had that most important requisite for sound maturation: a good relationship with his parents and their substitutes. For those like my patient, whose egos are threatened by the access of primal affect caused by anal overstimulation, there is (as the quotation from Fliess suggests) a paradoxical outcome: the reinforcement of the very anal erogeneity that has set off the psychic danger. My patient had to *over*cathect the anal sphincter to attempt to control his emotions and body feeling. He said, "I am a rat burrowing up my own asshole," thereby expressing not only his regression to anal narcissism and his need for defensive anality, but also the continuing aggressive tension turned against himself. When the rat imago is predominant, and especially when the rat (as it were) bites itself, "archaic affect" is not being effectively warded off. Indeed, my patient's anal–defensive attempts were only partially successful, and the spillover of cannibalistic urgency was making for a qualitative confluent modification of castration fantasies. Thus, the developmentally advanced danger situation of castration was given a more regressive cast, involving feelings, especially anxiety, appropriate to the fantasy of castration by biting.

People like my patient, who are traumatically overstimulated, have a greater than usual need for good parenting to overcome the psychic trauma; but, so often, the parenting (unlike Gargantua's) is faulty, and the parent may even be the source of the overstimulation. The compulsive overcathexis of the anal and urethral sphincters makes for an anal fixation. After these sessions, my patient in his complaints repeatedly used the metaphor of "having a hook up my ass." Gargantua had held and used the hook-shaped head and neck of the goose for his own purpose and pleasure, but for my patient, the "goose" was an ever-present and barely controlled danger—a hook that anchored him to his anally invasive mother and threatened to break loose and tear him apart like the penetrating murderous rat of the Chinese torture that haunted Freud's Rat Man.

Integration of Transference and Memory

"It's too ingenious to be true," the patient had said in an obvious attempt to disown and to distance his feelings in and about the session. Yet this proved to be a most important analytic hour, a turning point toward restoring meaningful and lasting emotional and body-feeling connections to the patient's thought—linkages basic to the flow of insight (see Shengold, 1981). Not only did the intensity of his feeling have to be borne and "owned" by the patient, but he had to connect his impulses and associated emotions and erogeneities with his parents— the much-needed and yet overstimulating "objects" of his drives. It was by way of his transference onto me of the emotionally loaded mental pictures of his parents (linking past and present) that conviction about his body feelings, memories, affects, and drives could be achieved. This conviction was needed to consolidate his identity as a man with the power to integrate what he had called "the pieces of myself" (such as the goose and the rat). Subsequent to these analytic hours, he was able to see that his not paying his bill until after much delay was a provocation to the analyst to "come in"—an acting out of a fantasy in which he wanted his anus not only wiped, but penetrated. This led to memories of enemas and of beatings (especially of being spanked) that he connected with conflict-ridden wishes for (phallic) mother and father to force him to open his sphincter. He was terrified of the intense rage involved with his anal wishes, and of the threat of loss of the sphincter control needed to contain his feelings. The terrible anxiety he had felt as the object of his mother's exhibitions of her genitals, combined with the fear of feminine passivity associated with his wishes to be penetrated, made (at a developmentally crucial age) for a multiply motivated intense expectation of castration. At the same time, his oedipal conflicts (which I have not stressed here) were expressed primarily in regressive anal fantasies. His mother's absences in later childhood (currently relived in relation to my vacation) mobilized his contradictory sexual desires and their dreadful consequences in his analysis: "At five they sent me to camp . . . there were pretty girl counselors. Did *they* wipe my anus when I was there?" he wondered. "I don't remember. As usual, I don't remember. What I do remember is that I was terrified that they would *see* my penis" (*cf.* Gargantua and his governesses).

Thinking and Anality

My patient's conflicts about his anal wishes, and his fears and compulsions concerning his penis were worked through over a long period of time, and along the way, his ability to remember and to think was favorably affected. Fliess points out that "the interpolation of 'delay through thought' does not exist in orality, but is at first performed in the subsequent anal stage" (1956, p. 110). The analysis allowed for a concentration on, and a release of feeling involving, the anal sphincter, which in the lived-out transference repetition fostered a delayed development: an enhancing, anticastrative flow of libido and of sexual power to the genitals that resulted in a safer and less exigent feeling of erogeneity there. This went along with a restoration of mental power (recall that a similar combination was present for Gargantua). Abraham (1921) wrote, "The preponderance of anal over genital erotism makes the neurotic inactive and unproductive" (p. 382). The relative "deinstinctualization" of his anal sphincter made it easier for my patient to remember, to think clearly, and to become more productive and successful. The diminution in rage and in his need for punishment and revenge reduced his compulsion to be a Don Juan and made possible the experience of joy in sex, and even brought the intimations of being able to love.

The Goose and Rat Metaphors

In his analysis the patient was able to experience something of Abraham's (1924) two hypothetical levels of anal libido development: the retentive, holding level he (paradoxically) associated with the (incontinent) goose—anal erogeneity here is compatible with, even sometimes contributing to, erection and genital functioning. This level led him to the more terrifying anal-sadistic level of libido with the destructive fantasies (full of teeth) he associated with the anal imago of the rat. The intensity of feeling involved with the rat usually operates (as in my patient's case) to decrease genital excitement and potency, or— dependent on the compromises achieved in basic motivational unconscious fantasies—can form a narrowly channelled compulsive flow of urgency that is found in perversion (or an approach to perversion).

As subjects, objects, part-subjects, and part-objects, goose and rat, anus and penis, rectum and vagina, father and mother, analyst and patient had appeared and disappeared, and were coupled and then disconnected in my patient's associations. Thus, he paid tribute to the ingenuity of the unconscious, to the elaborate, time-transcending interweaving of metaphor accomplished by our inherently "poetry-making" (Trilling, 1947, p. 52) minds. The metaphors—blended and contrasted, transformed, worked over and dissected in the analysis—had evoked emotions and body-feeling, had effected heightenings and diminutions of this man's sense of identity. For it turned out that what he suffered from most was not the sexual compulsions and memory defects of which he had initially complained, but the consequences of the regression to and the fixation on defensive anality. For him, defensive anality meant a sense of emptiness and falseness, a dehumanization of which he had to become fully, painfully aware. He once said, "My God, I am not a human being. I live in pieces" (*cf.* the quotation from Chekhov's *The Three Sisters* quoted in Appendix 1). And, indeed, his life, with his constant disowning and doubting and isolation, amounted to a kind of "as-it-were" existence that I have described in other patients (whom I have called victims of "soul murder" [1979]). Winnicott has dealt with "as-if" personalities extensively; but never better than the English poet Matthew Prior (1664–1721), whose Jack and Joan carry out existence:

> Without Love, Hatred, Joy or Fear,
> They led a kind of as-it-were;
> Nor Wish'd, nor Car'd, nor Laugh'd, nor Cry'd:
> And so they liv'd; and so they dy'd.
> (Prior, 1718)

My patient's sense of identity (the ability to suspend the "as-it-were") came with the eventual realization of how much and how well he was able to use his mind to put ideas and feelings together: to condense, to separate, to recombine flexibly, and, especially, to integrate.

Although we may isolate connecting strands from the complicated, chaotically dimensioned warp and woof of our psychic fabric for our analytic work and understanding (and of course some linkages are, as with my patient, isolated by pathological overuse), there are no separate lines of development in nature for such complex synthesized structures as "the self," nor are any major aspects of our mental organizations, such as defenses, object relations, or narcissism, discrete by nature. This becomes obvious in the study of metaphoric imagos, such as the goose or the rat, which stand not only for the self and the object, but for so many of their parts, attributes, and functions.

For my patient, it was above all the rat imago—the rat-devil in his rectum—that required an exorcism which was achieved, in part, through his analysis. The analysis reduced the power of the cannibalistic mouth "transferable onto all subsequently dominant erogenic zones" (Fliess, 1956, p. 86). But before the goose and the rat could be dealt with, they had to be recognized and acknowledged as his. "I am an angry, scared little boy with a rat up my ass," the patient came to be able to say with feeling and with conviction. That was for him the breaking of the cul-de-sac, the beginning of the road back toward fuller humanity, toward a Rabelaisian renaissance. Rabelais himself connects the lowest and the highest in man; the bottom and the top; the body and the soul; the anal (by way of the goose) and the most valued functions of a human being. Gargantua reports that the warmth of the neck of the goose "tempering the bumgut and the rest of the intestines, *actually reaches your heart and brain*" (my italics,

p. 45). The full life of the emotions and the intellect is traced to the happy mastery of the anal sphincter. (But the great French writer also expresses the reversible nature of things anal: The fear and destructiveness associated with loss of control are alluded to with greatest intensity in Book 3, Chapter 22, where Panurge finds that "the most terrifying place in Hell is not Satan's jaws but under Proserpine's shitting stool" [Bakhtin, 1942/1968, p. 378]. Rabelais was probably parodying Dante, and Bakhtin's comments bring together the jaws and the anus, supplying the components that constitute the terrifying attributes of the imago of the rat.)

Valenstein (1973) states that the "the nature of the object tie during the earliest period of life is critical for the qualitative structuralization of affect out of primal and primitive affects" (p. 372). This case provides an illustration of the continuity of this state of affairs beyond the earliest period and focuses on a specific element: "the nature of an object tie" as it develops in relation to, and as it influences, anal erogeneity and anal defensiveness. Anal sphincter control (as Fliess says) is crucial for the taming of "primal and primitive affects" that is requisite for the attainment of a separate and full identity and for the health-giving capacity to care about other people.[7]

ANAL INFLUENCE ON GENITAL SEXUALITY: SWIFT AND KUNDERA

The anally preoccupied great satirist Jonathan Swift (1667–1745), whose moral universe is far darker than that of the sunny Rabelais, depicts in more than one work the potentially inhibiting or enhancing influence of cloacal activity on genital excitement and potency (see Brown, 1959). Sometimes he portrays both effects in the same work. Sphincter *control* is central. In a poetic jibe at a resented relative and patron, Swift wrote: "The Problem, That my Lord Berkeley stinks when he is in Love":

> Love's fire, it seems, like inward heat,
> Works on my lord by stool and sweat.
> Which brings a stink from every pore,
> And from behind and from before . . .
> So, when a weasel you torment,
> You find his passion by his scent,

We read of kings, who, in a fright,
Though on a throne, would fall to sh____ [shite]
Beside all this, deep scholars know,
That the main string of Cupid's bow.
Once on a time was an a____ gut, [arse]
Now to a nobler office put,
By favour or desert preferr'd
From giving passage to a t____; [turd]
But still, though fix'd among the stars,
Does sympathize with human a____ [arse]
Thus, when you feel a hard-bound breech,
Conclude love's bow string at full stretch,
Till the kind looseness comes, and then,
Conclude the bow relaxed again.

(1702?, pp. 61–62)

Some optimal level of relaxation of the anal sphincter is necessary to ensure erection, and Swift shows, symbolically, that constriction brings "love's bow string at full stretch." There is a similar ambiguity in *Strephon and Chloe* (written almost 30 years later, 1731). Chloe is so faultless, so like a goddess that Strephon is afraid to approach her on their wedding night, so:

... awfully his distance kept ...
How could a nymph as chaste as Chloe
With constitution cold and snowy,
Permit a brutish man to touch her. . . . [But]:
Twelve cups of tea (with grief I speak)
Had now constrain'd the nymph to leak.
This point must needs be settled first:
The bride must either void or burst.
Then see the dire effects of pease;
Think what can give the colic ease.
The nymph oppress'd, before, behind,
As ships are toss'd by waves and wind,
Steals out her hand by nature led,
And brings a vessel into bed;
Fair utensil, as smooth and white
As Chloe's skin, almost as bright.
Strephon, who heard the fuming rill
As from a mossy cliff distil,
Cried out, Ye Gods! what sound is this?
Can Chloe, heavenly Chloe ____? [piss]
How great a change! How quickly made!
They learn to call a spade a spade.

They soon from all constraint are freed;
Can see each other do their need.
On box of cedar sits the wife,
And makes it warm for dearest life;
And, by the beastly way of thinking,
Find great society in stinking.

(pp. 7-11)

In another part of this poem Swift contrarily cautions mothers to tell their daughters to hide their excretions if they want their husbands to make love to them:

Keep them to wholesome food confined,
Nor let them taste what causes wind.
'Tis thus the sage of Samos means,
Forbidding his disciples beans . . .
Carminative and diuretic
Will damp all passion sympathetic.

(p. 8)

These contradictions between inhibition and enhancement of desire in the anally preoccupied (and often oedipally regressed) are commonly seen in men who need to split their sexual lives in two, performing easily (like Strephon after Chloe pisses) with degraded women while inhibited with those who are connected with the idealized, nonsexual mother. A modern author, Milan Kundera, whose novels feature a variety of compulsively unfaithful men who nonetheless long for fidelity, describes Franz in *The Unbearable Lightness of Being* as having to divide his love life between wife and mistress. He can make love to his mistress only in a city other than the one in which he lives with his wife. Kundera (1984) links the inhibition to Franz's tie with his mother ("For twenty years he had seen his mother—a poor, weak creature who needed his protection—in his wife" [p. 117]), and, in the following passage, makes Swift-like reference to the inhibition caused by smells:

The ban on making love with his painter-mistress in Geneva [his home city] was actually a self-inflicted punishment for having married another woman. He felt it as a kind of guilt or defect. Even though his conjugal sex life was hardly worth mentioning, he and his wife still slept in the same bed, awoke in the middle of the night to each other's heavy breathing, and inhaled the smells of each other's body. True, he would rather have slept by himself, but the marriage bed is still the symbol of the marriage bond, and symbols, as we know are inviolable . . . he wished to separate the bed he slept in with his wife as far as possible in space from the bed he made love in with his mistress. (1984, pp.84–85)

(Kundera portrays similar regressive oedipal anal inhibitions and facilitations in the women in this novel—for example, in the theme of Sabina and the sexual excitement she derives from the black bowler hat associated both with defecation and with her father.)

ANAL PERSPECTIVE

Human beings have to come to terms with the contradictions inherent to anality and anal narcissism. Contact with the excremental can (and should in the course of proper development) be transformed into a perspective that provides insight—insight that can reduce narcissism to realistic proportions: the sense of values that finds in feces and in anality a reminder of the transitoriness of everything, of our animal origins, and of mortality. Freud's mother rubbed her hands together to show her indulged and beloved "Goldener Sigi" the dirt from which we are all fashioned; and Montaigne reminds us that "Perched on the loftiest throne in the world, we are still sitting on our own behind" (quoted in Auden & Kronenberger, 1962, p. 59). And, as Crazy Jane says to the Bishop:

> A woman can be proud and stiff
> When on love intent;
> But Love has pitched his palace in
> The place of excrement;
> And nothing can be sole or whole
> That has not been rent.
> (Yeats, 1933, p. 255)

Anality must be experienced, and if then it can be transcended, it can give perspective, wisdom, and, as Swift and Kundera remind us, sexual power and joy. If anality is denied and it prevails unconsciously, we either exist in isolated abstract defensive sterility or remain mired in compulsive *thing-ness,* living in our own cloaca even though we may pretend it is a palace.

For a poetic didactic lecture on healthy anality and anal perspective, here is a contribution from W. H. Auden, whose anality I have written about in Chapter 2. He knew his Freud, and he shows us (as Freud said) how much we have to learn from poets—including here the danger of being "weak-sphinctered." (I am indebted to Dr. Brian Robertson for directing me to Auden's wise and wonderful poem.)

The Geography of the House
(for Christopher Isherwood)

Seated after breakfast
In this white-tiled cabin
Arabs call *the House where*
Everybody goes,
Even melancholics
Raise a cheer to Mrs.
Nature for the primal
Pleasures She bestows.

Sex is but a dream to
Seventy-and-over,
But a joy proposed un-
    til we start to shave:
Mouth-delight depends on
Virtue in the cook but
This She guarantees from
Cradle unto grave.

Lifted off the potty,
Infants from their mothers
Hear their first impartial
Words of worldly praise:
Hence to start the morning
With a satisfactory
Dump is a good omen
All our adult days.

Revelation came to
Luther in a privy
(Crosswords have been solved there)
Rodin was no fool
When he cast his Thinker
Cogitating deeply,
Crouched in the position
Of a man at stool.

All the Arts derive from
This ur-act of making,
Private to the artist:
Makers' lives are spent
Striving in their chosen
Medium to produce a

De-narcissus-ized en-
    during excrement.

Freud did not invent the
Constipated miser:
Banks have letter boxes
Built in their facade,
Marked *For Night Deposits*,
Stocks are firm or liquid,
Currencies of nations
Either soft or hard.

Global Mother, keep our
Bowels of compassion
Open through our lifetime,
Purge our minds as well:
Grant us a kind ending,
Not a second childhood,
Petulant, weak-sphinctered,
In a cheap hotel.

Keep us in our station:
When we get pound-notish,
When we seem about to
Take up Higher Thought,
Send us some deflating
Image like the pained ex-
    pression on a Major
Prophet taken Short.

(Orthodoxy ought to
Bless our modern plumbing:
Swift and St. Augustine
Lived in centuries,
When a stench of sewage
Ever in the nostrils
Made a strong debating
Point for Manichees.)

Mind and Body run on
Different timetables:
Not until our morning
Visit here can we
Leave the dead concerns of
Yesterday behind us,
Face with all our courage
What is now to be.

                    (pp. 16–19)

ANAL NARCISSISM REVISITED

Our psychic world develops from the inchoate to the narcissistic to one full of others. Abraham (1924) describes the anal stages as "[lying] somewhere between narcissism and object love" (p. 486). As the self and the object representations become more expansive and variegated, danger situations change, but none ever disappears. A regression toward any kind of "body-ego narcissism" brings with it a reactivation of old dangers, but also of old ways of mastery. Return to domination by the "anal–sadistic organization" provides a kind of haven, which I am calling anal narcissism; this haven promises the predictable and the orderly, but it contains its own perils of anal destructiveness. This danger of destroying and therefore of losing much-needed others (like the parents) diminishes as narcissism is regressively increased and, at least delusionally, no other is needed. But this regressive, narcissistically enhanced anal defensiveness provides an unhealthy imbalance with scales tipped toward the elimination of affect and of object-related emotional achievements consolidated subsequent to the anal stage. Anal narcissism involves a regressive reduction of ego to body ego, dominated by the "sadistic–anal organization"; the whole psychic apparatus (impulses, defenses, symptoms, and character) once again acquires an anal cast. Relationships become self-centered and hollow; people are reduced to things; values to "stuff." Alongside this degradation is a concomitant disguising and ameliorating idealization inherent to narcissism. (See Hanly, 1982, for a formulation similar to mine.)

In his 1920 paper, *The Narcissistic Evaluation of Excretory Processes in Dreams and Neurosis*, Abraham exemplified in several dreams the narcissistic nature of the connection of anal and urethral sensations and impulses with love and with hate; he pointed out the "enormous power that the dreamer ascribes to her excretions" (p. 319). Abraham felt that this grandiosity was part of narcissistic omnipotence, and he hypothesized that the feeling of the omnipotence of bowel and bladder functions is a pre-stage of the child's assumption of the omnipotence of thought. One of my patients remembered defecating into the ocean edge at about age three, and having had the conviction that the forbidden act would bring terrible punishment because her feces would "poison the world." The patient was cosmically inflating (in her narcissistic cosmos) the kind of destructive impulse shown by "a small Hungarian boy" quoted by Abraham (1924) "whose family lived in Buda-Pesth. [He] once threatened his nurse with these words:

"If you make me angry, I'll ka-ka you across to Ofen [a district on the other side of the Danube]" (p. 427).

To use a term I will elaborate on later, the child is *fascinated* with parts of the body ego and of the increasingly differentiated *other*: first with the mouth (and the breast = part-of-me); then with the cloaca/anus (and the fecal stick = me/not me); then with the genitals (and that which stimulates them: one's own hand, and the hands and sexual parts of the other). There is a developmental continuation and an admixture of these *libidinal/narcissistic on the way to becoming libidinal/object-related* positions, with easy regression and the possibility of fixation and arrested development. The fascination (a tremendous heightening of awareness of parts of one's own body and of related parts of the surround; see below in Chapter 6) means a pervasive consciousness of body parts. This is created and augmented by the pressure of the instinctual drives: combinations of oral, anal, and genital libido with derivatives of aggressive drive (*e.g.*, in sadism and masochism); and of the so-called "partial instincts" (especially voyeurism and exhibitionism). We live intermittently in narcissistic erogenic worlds alive with projected intense sensations whose center is a part of one's own body: an oral world, an anal world, a genital world. "When I come into your office now, my vulva and anus start to throb and the walls seem to shimmer," said a female adult patient, smitten by an overwhelming sexual transference. In children, even at ordinary times of seemingly nonsexual lesser sensory awareness, there is still the fervid intensity of what Wordsworth called "splendour in the grass . . . glory in the flower." For better and for worse, for feelings that are both "good" and "bad," this physiologically determined body-ego intensity from the paradise and the hell of our earliest existence pervades anality, and can bring later anal phenomena to tumultuous life.

Notes to Chapter Four

1. In Grimms' "The Golden Goose," Dümmling—his name attests to his being himself a "goose"—is given a goose with golden feathers. Whoever tries to pluck them out has his hands adhere to the goose. A symbolic explication suggests discovery and punishment for masturbation, perhaps especially for anal masturbation.

2. The fable can be interpreted as a symbolic object lesson for mothers,

warning against the consequences of satisfying their cannibalistic and symbi-otic urges, while children are enjoined to abandon their narcissistic interest in uncontrolled defecation and train their anal sphincter to follow mother's demands—or else!

3. He reminded me at this juncture of Freud's Rat Man, and indeed he turned out to be one of the "rat people" I have described in two previous papers (1967, 1971).

4. The rat becomes the devil, since, to quote Freud on anal erotism (1908), "the devil is most certainly nothing more than a personification of the unconscious instinctual forces" (1908, p. 10).

5. I was very active during this session; there was probably some counter-transference involved, stemming from shared excitement over the patient's unusual, active, and seemingly responsible participation in the analytic work. There was a certain amount of repetition-in-action within this session. I will leave it to the reader to judge how much this was a hindrance and how much an enhancement to analytic progress.

6. There is also an injunction in one of Gargantua's effusions in verse that illustrates the spread of feeling toward the genitals: (His arse-wiping monologue inspires him to poetry):

> He who his arse with paper wipes
> Shall on his balls leave shitty stripes.
> (my translation of *Tousjours laisse aux couillons esmorche/Qui son hord cul de papier torche* [1534/1973, p. 93])

This warning that you had better watch out for your balls when paper is being used is especially relevant to my patient. For him, paper alluded to the stimulating detachable link between his mother and his anus, and to its symbolic representation in money (when he paid his bill he called the check he gave to me "Shen-paper").

7. See Appendix 2 for related material on Freud and Rabelais.

5

A Literary/Historical Example of Anal-Narcissistic Defensiveness: The Soul Murder of Kaspar Hauser

INTRODUCTION

The story of Kaspar Hauser provides an instance of the effects of deprivation in psychic development—effects which were reacted against by anal defensiveness and narcissistic regression.

In the 1830s the fate and character of the foundling Kaspar Hauser aroused curiousity, indignation, and political controversy. His name was as well-known to European newspaper readers as that of Dreyfus at the end of the century. Kaspar was one of the most famous people in Europe. During the few years between the discovery of the unfortunate boy tottering down a street in Nuremberg and his eventual murder, a visit to Kaspar Hauser was considered part of the Grand Tour for distinguished visitors to the kingdom of Bavaria. Despite the many books and thousands of publications about Kaspar Hauser, his story has not, as far as I know, been the subject of psychoanalytic investigation. The case of Kaspar Hauser can teach us much about child development under conditions of deprivation, and it has special relevance to anal-narcissistic defensiveness. Above all, Kaspar's story illustrates that crime for which Ibsen (1896) declared there is no forgiveness: soul murder. Soul murder refers to killing the joy in life and interfering with the sense of identity of another human being. It is primarily a crime committed against children (see Shengold, 1975a, 1975b, 1979).

The actual term "soul-murder" was probably coined by the compassionate jurist Anselm von Feuerbach, who wrote a widely read (and widely translated) pamphlet on Kaspar Hauser in 1832. Von Feuerbach was a distinguished judge who had drawn up a reformed penal code for the kingdom of Bavaria, which was used as a model by many of the other German states. It is likely that his book on Kaspar was read by the judge Daniel Paul Schreber, whose use of the phrase "soul murder" in his *Memoirs* (1903) caused it to become well-known in psychiatric circles. (Freud's famous study of paranoia based on Schreber's book appeared in 1911.) The term "soul murder" should be understood to indicate the actuality of external traumata—traumata that contribute to psychic pathology by influencing the basic motivating fantasies of the individual victim.[1]

Part of the explanation for the neglect of Kaspar Hauser by psychoanalysts may be that the facts of the case have never been definitively established. Those critics who have declared that Kaspar Hauser was an impostor and a simulator are in the minority, but they have not been, and perhaps never can be, completely refuted. Psychoanalysis requires that the patient has, or at least will ultimately acquire, the motivation to tell the truth. And if Kaspar were a wilful liar, then psychoanalytic understanding of his story is compromised. I am aware of this risk, and of the weak position of the psychohistorian and the psychobiographer who are obliged to derive their data not from a patient in analysis, but from the unprivileged distance of secondary written sources. With Kaspar Hauser I have proceeded under the assumption—which can be questioned—that his original story was, by and large, the truth as best he could tell it. This is my own impression, derived from reading the source material (see also the introduction to the English edition of Wasserman [1908/1928]); it is supported by the fact that all the original witnesses of Kaspar in Nuremberg who had the opportunity to study him, believed in him (see Singh & Zingg, 1939, pp. 276, 295). Handwriting experts and professional and amateur students of crime have defended Kaspar's veracity, but there is also a considerable literature of disbelief. I fall back on the secondary assumption that if Kaspar Hauser was an impostor, he was an impostor of genius, and that his story nonetheless has relevance to students of soul murder and anality (as does the relevant fiction of Dostoyevski, Strindberg, Ibsen, Proust, and other great psychologically minded literary geniuses).

The English translation of von Feuerbach's (1832) pamphlet has a long title that summarizes its story: *Kaspar Hauser. An Account of an Individual Kept in a Dungeon, Separated From all Communication With the World, From Early Childhood to About the Age of Seventeen.* Kaspar "came into the world" (p. 40), as he put it, on May 26, 1828, when he was discovered stumbling down a Nuremberg street, carrying a letter addressed to the Captain of Cavalry stationed in the town. Kaspar could neither stand nor walk properly. He appeared to be about 16 years old. He did not seem to understand the questions put to him, and kept repeating a few barely intelligible phrases or words of jargon. (It was later discovered that he usually attached no particular meaning to his few sentences, expecting them to convey whatever he had to express.) The boy's words were interspersed with groans, tears, and unintelligible sounds. Here is von Feuerbach's description:

> He appeared neither to know nor to suspect where he was. He betrayed neither fear, nor astonishment, nor confusion; he rather showed an almost brutish dullness . . . his tears and whimpering, while he was always pointing to his tottering feet, and his awkward and, at the same time, childish demeanour, soon excited the compassion of all present . . . his whole conduct . . . seemed to be that of a child *scarcely two or three years old*, with the body of a young man. (my italics; pp. 3–4)

The boy showed aversion to all food but bread and water. He astonished the observers, when pen and paper were brought to him, by being able to letter out the name *Kaspar Hauser*. It seemed to be the only thing he could write. This ability made several of the policemen think the boy might be trying to deceive. The official and casual observers had the definite impression that the boy was not insane, but a kind of "human savage" (p. 5)—a "natural man" (Rousseau was still fashionable, and so were tales of children brought up by animals). Von Feuerbach, who saw the boy shortly after the first observers in 1828, described him as seeming "to hear without understanding, to see without perceiving, and to move his feet without knowing how to use them for the purpose of walking" (p. 4).

Kaspar seemed "mild, obedient and good-natured" (p. 71). He passively complied with the teasing and pestering of the hordes of visitors who came to stare at him as if he were a zoo animal when he was first lodged in the tower of the Vestner Castle that was used as a municipal jail. Kaspar kept his good humor even when subject to the "not very humane experiments" (p. 71) of citizens who set out to be amateur psychologists. Indeed, Kaspar seemed incapable of anger.

He appeared to be unable to differentiate between animate and inanimate objects; he had no sense of distance or perspective. He did not recognize himself in the mirror and kept looking for a person concealed behind it. He was bothered by light and habitually looked away from it, usually at his feet. His sleep had the quality of deepest hypnosis—it was almost impossible to waken him. All this aroused the curiosity and sympathy of the citizens of Nuremberg, who flocked to see the boy.

When found, he had been dressed in old and ill-fitting clothes. He wore a white kerchief marked in red with the initials K.H. The letter he had been carrying was badly spelled; the writer called himself "a poor day labourer (with) ten children . . . the mother of the child only put him in my house for the sake of having him brought up. But I have never been able to discover who his mother is." The writer claimed that the boy had been with him for 16 years, since he was six months old, and that he had never been allowed out of the house. "I have taught him to read and write" (p. 12). He had taken the boy to Nuremberg "to become a cavalry soldier as his father was"—when he was first found, Kaspar had kept repeating a phrase like this. The letter concluded: "If you do not keep him, you may kill him, or hang him up the chimney" (p. 13). There was another note, written in Latin but by the same hand, supposedly from the boy's mother, asking the laborer to bring up and educate the child and then send him to Nuremberg when he became 17 years old, to the Sixth Regiment of Light Horse, to which his father had belonged. This note ended: "I am a poor girl and cannot support him. His father is dead" (p. 13). Handwriting experts have concluded that these two notes were not written by Kaspar himself.

The Family Romance

The discovery of Kaspar became notorious and a political issue because of the legend that grew from an investigation into his origins—a widely believed legend that still has not been definitively disproved. Kaspar was alleged from the first to have been the victim of an evil plot—perhaps the illegitimate son of a high-born lady or a priest. But what most took hold of the popular imagination was the story that Kaspar was the legitimate Crown Prince of Baden, son of Stephanie Beauharnais. This niece of Josephine Bonaparte had been given by Napoleon as wife to the reigning Grand Duke Charles of Baden. It was said that the child's kidnapping had been arranged by Charles' morganatic wife, the Countess of Hochberg, in order to get the throne for her own offspring. This seemingly wild romantic tale (hinted at by the sober von Feuerbach) was taken up by antimonarchists, and Kaspar's assassination in 1833 was widely believed to have been politically motivated. It was cited as an example of the iniquity of the nobility of Europe. Prince Metternich, an inveterate persecutor of anyone connected with Napoleon, was said to be one of the instigators of the plot. (The morganatic line of Hochberg did ascend to the throne of Baden shortly before Kasper Hauser's release from confinement [see Singh & Zingg, 1939, p. 276].)

The Baden story was supposedly disproved in 1875 by the publication of the records of baptism and of post-mortem examination, dated 1812, of the infant Crown Prince who was said to have been kidnapped. But supporters of the legend maintained (based on "documents" that can no longer be verified—see Evans, 1892) that a dead baby of a peasant girl was substituted for the true heir of the Grand Duke Charles, and that the stolen baby (the Kaspar Hauser-to-be) was then put in the care of a wet-nurse who was told he was the illegitimate son of an aristocratic lady. She kept him until he was three or four years old, after which he was brought up in the cellar that he remembered and described in 1828. (I discuss later the psychological basis for believing that there were three or four years of relatively adequate mothering for Kaspar.) In proof of the boy's aristocratic descent, supporters cited Kaspar's fine, fair skin, his delicate and beautifully formed hands and feet—the latter showing no signs of calluses ("as soft as the palms of his hands" [von Feuerbach, 1832, p. 14]) nor, beneath the bleeding welts caused by the recently acquired boots, of having worn shoes, and a vaccination scar (an aristocratic designation in the early 19th century). A series of publications in the 1880s and 1890s (chiefly in England and Germany) revived the story of the stolen Baden heir. The truth seems beyond any establishing and, says the *Encyclopaedia Britannica* (1910, p. 70), "the evidence is in any case in complete confusion."

KASPAR'S HISTORY

With the help of tutors, but especially due to the efforts of prison-keeper Hiltel's 11-year-old son Julius (a constant companion in the prison tower where Kaspar was first kept in Nuremberg), Kaspar soon learned to speak and became able to tell his story. The Mayor (*Burgomeister*) of Nuremberg had Kaspar brought to his home almost every day; he extracted a history from the boy that was later supplemented by Kaspar's own written narration. Binder's account is quoted from and commented on by von Feuerbach:

> He neither knows who he is nor where his home is. It was only at Nuremberg that he *came into the world* [my italics; von Feuerbach, p. 46, calls this an expression Kaspar "often uses to designate his exposure in Nuremberg, and his first awakening to the consciousness of mental life".] Here he first learned that beside himself and "the man with whom he had always been" there existed men and other creatures. As long as he can recollect, he had always lived in a hole . . . which he sometimes calls a cage . . . where he had always sat upon the ground, with bare feet, and clothed only with a shirt and a pair of breeches. (pp. 41–42)

Apparently Kaspar had been unable to stretch out to his full length (this was confirmed by the peculiar configuration of his knees) and had slept sitting up with his feet extended. It was discovered that he had been habitually drugged with opium in his water (Kaspar recognized the taste when given a few drops in his water by his guardian). He never saw the face of the man who brought him his food and water, cleaned him, changed his clothes, and cut his nails while Kaspar was in his stuporous sleep. In the "hole" he had two wooden horses and several ribbons, and playing with these was the main occupation he remembered. The "hole" had been his womb, his universe, a timeless anal–narcissistic world:

> How long he continued to live in this situation he knew not; for he had no knowledge of time. He knew not when or how he came thither. Nor had he any recollection of ever having been in a different situation, or in any other than in that place. (pp. 42–43)

Kaspar, while in the "hole," had not had his narcissism checked by reality. He had considered himself "as it were the only being of his kind" (p. 138). For some time before he was taken to Nuremberg, the man "with whom he had always been" had, *standing behind him*, taught him to spell out his name on paper by repeatedly guiding his hand. After that, Kaspar spent much time lettering out his name. The man had also tried to teach him to walk. Formerly, the man had almost never spoken to him, but he began to make Kaspar repeat the phrase about wanting to become a horseman like his father. Recounting this story evokes the moral indigation of the good von Feuerbach. He calls it an account of:

> the criminal invasion of a human soul. [K]aspar's mental condition, during his dungeon life, must have been that of a human being immersed in his infancy, in a profound sleep, in which he was not conscious even of a dream. . . . He had continued in this *stupor* [my italics] until, affrighted with pain and apprehensions, he suddenly awoke, stunned with the wild and confused noises and unintelligible impressions of a variegated world, without knowing what happened. (p. 47)

Von Feuerbach's "stupor" is more than a metaphor:

> [K]aspar sinks, even yet, whenever he rides in a carriage or waggon, into a kind of death sleep, from which he does not easily awake . . . and, in this state, however roughly soever it may be done, he may be lifted up or laid down, and packed or unpacked, without his having the least perception of it. When sleep once has laid hold of him, no noise, no sound, no report, no thunder is loud enough to wake him. (p. 50)

Kaspar was in what we would now call a hypnotic or hypnoid state, spontaneous and defensive as well as having in the past been induced by opium. These undoubtedly protective alterations of consciousness (one of the mechanisms for "anal–narcissistic defensiveness") must have added to the boy's confusion. Von Feuerbach's accusation continues:

> Not only the brutish den and crippling position to which he was confined, and his coarse diet . . . but (principally) the cruel withholding from him of the most ordinary gifts, in which nature with a liberal hand, extends even to the most indigent;—the depriving him of all the means of mental development and culture—the unnatural detention of a human soul in a state of irrational animality [represents] an attempt . . . to exclude a man from nature and from all intercourse with rational beings, to change the course of his human destiny, and to withdraw from him all of the nourishment which nature has appointed for food to the human mind. (p. 52)

Von Feuerbach, nurtured on Rousseau's *Émile* and using his common sense, clearly sees that deprivation has crushed the boy's emotional as well as mental development; and he sees the irreversibility of the deprivations:

> [K]aspar, having been sunk during the whole of the earlier part of his life in animal sleep, has passed through this extensive and beautiful part of it, without having lived through it. His existence was, during all this time, similar to that of a person really dead: in having slept through his

youthful years, they have passed by him, without his having had them in his possession; because he was rendered unable to become conscious of their existence. This chasm, which crime has torn in his life, cannot any more be filled up [von Feuerbach was writing while [K]aspar was still alive and under his immediate observation]; that time, in which he omitted to live, can never be brought back, that it may be lived through; that juvenility, which fled while his soul was asleep, can never be over-taken. How long soever he may live, he must for ever remain a man without childhood, and boyhood, a monstrous being, who, contrary to the usual course of nature, only began to live in the middle of his life. Inasmuch as all the earlier part of his life was thus taken from him, he may be said to have been the subject of a partial *soul-murder*. (my italics; p. 56)

Soul murder is achieved by a combination of torture, deprivation, and brainwashing. One person who has absolute power over another enforces submission and an identification with the oppressor, who is justified or even idealized by the victim.[2] The most likely victim of soul murder is a child, such as Kaspar. I have stated elsewhere (Shengold, 1975a, 1975b, 1979), following Orwell, that in order for soul murder to be effective—that is, for the break in identity and integrity to be maintained—the power of rational thought must be interfered with, the victim's ability to know what has happened to him must be compromised. Von Feuerbach sees the parallel to brainwashing:

The deed done to [K]aspar differs from the crime that would be commit-ted by one who should plunge a man of sound intellect, at a later period, into a state of stupid idiocy, unconsciousness, or irrationality [this "man" could be Orwell's Winston Smith], only in respect to the different epoch of life at which the blow of soul-murder was struck; in one instance, the life of a human soul was mutilated at its commencement; in the other it would be mutilated at its close. (pp. 55–57)

The terrible anger evoked by torment and overstimulation in soul murder is added to the untamed rage that every young child has to master. Under the totalitarian regimen necessary for soul murder, the child must suppress his anger. Not only would expression of it bring punishment, but the victim must try to keep destructive feelings from the psychic images of good parents or a good Providence in order to maintain some kind of promise without which there is no motivation to continue living. So the unavoidable rage must be smothered. (The danger is similar to that generated by the ordinarily expectable access of rage during the child's anal phase of instinctual development.) The need to master the destructive feelings toward the parental figures makes necessary an attempt to turn the overstimulating and the over-meaningful into the indifferent and the undifferentiated. This trans-formation is accomplished by what I am calling "anal defensiveness," and Kaspar's "stupor" was probably his way of achieving it. The rage that remains conscious is largely turned against the self, with the tormentor becoming (like Big Brother) delusionally "good." All this was true for Kaspar.

Kaspar's passivity and gentleness impressed everyone and even chastened some of the thoughtlessly cruel experimenters who were among his early visitors. Kaspar wrote in his narrative: "They teazed me also with all sorts of things which caused me shocking pain" (Von Feuerbach, 1832, p. 166). Von Feuerbach adds:

> Before Hauser was brought to the Burghermaster Binder . . . the most frightful suffering was caused him by the ignorance and wantonness of others. They forced upon *him*, to whom even the smell of such things was the cause of terror, tobacco, and snuffs, and spirituous liquors, and placed him consequently in a condition even to frighten the savages themselves who caused or allowed it. (pp. 166–167)

Kaspar did not get angry. And he could not be angry with "the man with whom he had always been," who, he said "never did him any harm" (p. 43). After he had learned to talk, Kaspar expressed a wish to go back to "the man":

> At home (in his hole) . . . he had never suffered so much from head-ache, and had never been so much teazed as since he was in the world. . . . He had therefore no fault to find with "the man with whom he had always been" except that he had not yet come to take him back again, and that he had never shewn him any thing of so many beautiful things which there are in the world. [When von Feuerbach expressed his] surprise that [Kaspar] should wish to return to that abominably bad man, [Kaspar] replied with mild indignation, "Man not bad, man me no bad done." (p. 71)

Although the only thrashing Kaspar told about was the one ad-ministered just before he was taken to Nuremberg, there were many scars on his limbs, and he did expect to be beaten once when he had made noise (p. 28). Also, his reaction to storms strongly suggested that he had been beaten. One day when it began to thunder (this was in 1829, when Kaspar was writing down his thoughts), Kaspar said:

> Me should not dare go out just then, there is a great man outside who is very angry . . . when it has thundered I always stooped down . . . when it

> thundered it has given me a very painful pressure upon the head, as if
> some one had struck me on the head with the hands . . . Then said I, as
> the storm was gone by, "Mother [Professor Daumer's mother] now you
> say that the man shall not be angry any more . . . then she said, "I tell the
> man he shall no more be angry". (Daumer, 1832, pp. 153–154)

Still, von Feuerbach is quite right to stress that it is not so much the
physical cruelty that is criminal but the terrible deprivation of the
"natural" rights of the child to the benevolent parental care and
contact needed to develop a sense of identity, a sense of reality, and the
capacity for emotion and thought that make up a child's human
qualities—his soul.

In contrast to his blunted awareness of his own anger and pain,
Kaspar was very sensitive to these feelings in others: "He expressed his
indignation against a boy who struck the stem of a tree with a small
stick, for giving the tree so much pain" (von Feuerbach, 1832, p. 91).
Von Feuerbach tells how Kaspar once, a year after his release, expressed anger toward his former captor:

> It was in the month of August, 1829, when on a fine summer evening, his
> instructor shewed him, for the first time, the starry heavens. His astonish-
> ment and transport surpassed all description. He could not be satiated . . .
> "That," he exclaimed, "is indeed, the most beautiful sight that I have ever
> yet seen in the world. But who has placed all those numerous beautiful
> candles there? Who lights them? Who puts them out?" . . . At length,
> standing motionless, with his head bowed down, his eyes staring, he fell
> into a train of deep and serious meditation. . . . He sank trembling upon
> a chair, and asked, why that wicked man had kept him always locked up,
> and had never shewn him any of those beautiful things. He ([K]aspar)
> had never done any harm. He then broke out into a fit of crying . . . and
> said that "the man with whom he had always been" might now also be
> locked up for a few days, that he might learn to know how hard it is to be
> treated so. Before seeing this beautiful celestial display, [K]aspar had
> never shewn anything like indignation against that man; and much less
> had he ever been willing to hear that he ought to be punished. (pp. 95–
> 96).

The first attempt on Kaspar's life took place in October 1829,
when he had lived for over a year with Professor Daumer, who had
taught him to read and write. A false newspaper report had recently
appeared that Kaspar was engaged in writing his memoirs. While
Professor Daumer was away, someone had hit Kaspar over the head
with a sharp cutting instrument and Kaspar was found dazed and
bleeding in the professor's cellar. He had seen the entirely black head

of a man (his face apparently covered with a black veil) and thought it was the chimney-sweep: "the black man stood suddenly before me and gave me a blow on the head" (p. 128); then the man had run away. Kaspar had lost consciousness and, when he had come to, had gone to the cellar to hide. His first, quasi-delirious words when he was found show that he identified the black man with "the man with whom I have always been":

"Man! Man! Mother [the Professor's mother] tell Professor—man beat—black man—like sweep . . . The man kill me! Away! Don't kill! I all men love; do no one anything. . . . Man, I love you too; don't kill! Why the man kill? I have done you nothing. Don't kill me! I will yet beg you may not be locked up! Never have let me out of prison, you would even kill me! You should first have killed me, before I understand what is to live. You must say why you locked me up" and etc. (p. 124–125)

The confrontation may not have been an actual recognition—Kaspar did not remember *ever* having seen the "man." The blackness of his attacker's head may have connoted the darkness of the "hole" of his early life. (Kaspar had described the walls of his prison as "very black," p. 161.) Whether or not the would-be killer was the "man," Kaspar's "black" expectation of him is clear, beneath his need to love the murderer.

[Kaspar] declared afterwards that if the unknown who had held him in confinement, and whom he steadfastly maintained to be the very person that had attempted the murder, were discovered, he would beg for him, as, notwithstanding [the attack], the man had brought him up as a child, and had not killed him. (Daumer, 1832, p. 181)

The incident confirms the statement of Robert Fliess (personal communication) that, to the unconscious, the black man is the father (here the father-figure) in the dark.[3]

The years of soul murder had made it impossible for Kaspar to feel any sustained anger—von Feuerbach speaks of his "indescribable goodness' (p. 145). The boy was "incapable of hurting a worm or a fly, much less a man" (p. 111). Kaspar's reaction to angry and hostile displays by others sometimes revived the cannibalistic intensity that he almost always suppressed in himself. For a long time he refused to eat meat; he at first had considered animals to be human beings. (He kept telling the Daumer's grey cat to go wash himself.) Professor Daumer reported:

With an expression of infinite sorrow [Kaspar] once said to me, "Mr. ＿＿ has killed today in his sporting, a hare and two birds, which I still saw bleeding. How is it possible (continued he) that men can have no pity for these animals, which have done no hurt to anyone?" When he was told men kill these animals in order to feed on their flesh, he replied, "A man might eat something else, bread for instance as I did." (p. 179)

Kaspar's defensive overreaction to his aggressive impulses was extreme.

And Kaspar's sexuality had also been suppressed. The jailer, Hiltel, in whose family Kaspar lived after his first days in Nuremberg, watched the boy closely, often observing him without Kaspar's knowledge, and saw no signs of sexual interest. He told of the boy's "innocence and ignorance" (von Feuerbach, 1832, p. 93). The boy had no feeling of shame about his nakedness when given a bath by the jailer's wife. (This afterwards changed to an exaggerated modesty.) Kaspar distinguished men from women only by their dress. He "expressed his desire to become a girl" (p. 30)—this was taken to mean that women's clothes pleased him more because they were more colorful. Although in 1832 Kaspar would tell von Feuerbach of his plans to study hard, make a lot of money, and settle down with a wife, it was von Feuerbach's impression that Kaspar regarded a wife simply as: "an indispensable part of domestic furniture. He never thinks of a wife in any other manner than as a housekeeper or as an upper servant, whom a man may keep as long as she suits him, and may turn away again" (p. 136). Von Feuerbach says: "In his conduct in all the various relations of life, he showed that his soul was spotless and pure as the reflex of the eternal in the soul of an angel" (p. 30).

From the very first Kaspar seemed incapable of humor; the boy showed no capacity for, or at least no interest in, abstract thought. His imaginative power had been stifled, his recourse to fantasy blocked. He said that he began to dream only after he slept on a bed for the first time when he was living with Professor Daumer. (At first he took the dreams for real occurrences.)

Kaspar's passivity was so intense that von Feuerbach calls his obedience to all those who acquired paternal authority over him "unconditional and boundless" (p. 73). When asked by the judge why he always felt obliged to "'yield to such punctual obedience,' he replied, 'the man with whom I always was taught me that I must do as I am bidden'" (p. 73). Yet despite this presence of the imago of "the man" in his primitive conscience, Kaspar was not without rebellion and resistance; brainwashing and the protective deadening provided by "anal defensiveness" had not been completely successful: The compliance that extended to his behavior did not always result in his acceptance of the ideas or the information given to him by the "fathers." (He had a special resistance to indoctrination by ministers—men in *black*.) Kaspar needed to be convinced by the power of his own senses, and these developed rapidly under the benign tutelage of Professor Daumer. Not authority, but his own experiments—his own use and new "ownership" of his body[4] gave conviction. His soul was not dead. Von Feuerbach describes a characteristic vacant and mindless facial expression, adding: "but, if any thing pleasant affected his mind, a lovely, smiling, heart-winning sweetness diffused over all his features the irresistible charm that lies concealed in the *joy* of an innocent child" (my italics; p. 15). Killing the capacity for joy is one of Ibsen's definitions of soul murder.

KASPAR'S EMOTIONAL AND MENTAL DEVELOPMENT

Speculations about what happened to Kaspar during the first years of his life can be valuable only if they are based on the boy's behavior and reactions after he "came into the world" and was observed by others. Von Feuerbach says of his belief in Kaspar's story:

> And thus we see an instance in which our estimation of the degree of credit which we are to give to the narrator of an almost incredible occurrence, is made to rest almost altogether upon psychological grounds. But the evidence furnished in this instance upon such grounds, outweighs that of any other proof. Witnesses may lie, documents may be false but no other human being (can produce) the very personification of truth itself. Whoever should doubt [K]aspar's narration, must doubt [K]aspar's person. (pp. 59–60)

It is "Kaspar's person" that gives credence "upon psychological grounds" not to the specifics, but to the substance of the two time elements that involve the boy's infant years in the story and in the legend. The letter purportedly from "the man" said that the child was six months old when he was abandoned. The legend has it that Kaspar was in the care of a wet-nurse until he was three or four years old. There can be little doubt (based on the work of observers of children) that there must have been some approach to adequate mothering in Kaspar's infancy. He was not one of those feral children who have had so little human contact that they can never be taught to achieve even a semblance of human identity. The presence of "the man with whom he had always been" is not enough to explain the degree of differentiation of self and the potential for educability that was in Kaspar from the beginning in Nuremberg. I assume that the infant was separated from the primary mothering figure at six months and given over to a substitute up to age three or four.[5] With the child-rearing in upper-class families of the time performed mainly by servants, such an "abandonment" might have produced little more disturbance than what could have occurred if the wet-nurse had been replaced at six months in the parental home. If the loss of the primary mother-figure took place at the age of six months without any adequate substitute mothering, one would expect, based on the work of René Spitz (1945, 1946; Spitz & Wolf, 1946) with "anaclitically depressed" infants who lost their mothering in the second half of the first year of life, that Kaspar would also have, as described by Mahler[6]:

> succumbed to inanition and literally died as a result of the symbiotic object loss. Yet in those cases in which the mother was restored to the anaclitically depressed baby, and when this occurred within a reasonable period of time (after separation), before the infant's vulnerable ego had suffered irreversible damage, the infants did recover. (1986, p. 3)

Body Ego Differentiation and Identity

The substitute mothering of the first few years must have been good enough to allow Kaspar to develop an adequate body ego and some sense of separate identity. He was not (in Mahler's terms) autistic. It turned out (16 years later) that he could learn to separate the concept of his self from that of others, and that he was able to make use of a parental figure as a "beacon of orientation in the world of reality" (Mahler *et al.*, 1975, p. 3; *cf.* Dahl, 1965, on the basis of Annie Sullivan's ability to educate Helen Keller being the child's good early mothering before the sensory deprivation at 19 months).

That Kaspar never remembered anything of his earliest childhood and of the hypothecated substitute mother whom he lost, one can attribute to the repression resulting from the many long years of trauma and deprivation in the "cage" (the excremental place that stood not only for trauma and deprivation, but also for protective deadening). Much of this time was spent in timeless drugged hypnosis.

(I have seen massive reactive amnesia for early years, also frequently involving hypnotic defense [*cf*. Fliess, 1953; Dickes, 1965; Shengold, 1971], in patients who had been severely and chronically traumatized in early childhood.)

Kaspar demonstrated an exaggerated version of a defense or repressive barrier that, in usual development, begins to operate (and to affect memory) during the anal period (before the time of the consolidation of the massive repression barrier that we recognize as occuring in the oedipal phase). The need for this anal–narcissistic defensiveness was expressed by Kaspar in his previously quoted regressive wish (after having been overstimulated and "teazed" by flocks of curious visitors during the first months at Nuremberg) to be taken back again by "the man" to "the hole." The "hole" was an externalization of the anal space surrounded by the anal sphincter, the place for sphincter defensiveness and narcissistic withdrawal: where life was orderly and predictable in its way; controlled by "the man" from the outside and by the compliant child from within. The tyrannical brutishness and deprivation brought on stupefaction that helped to blot out pain and overstimulation; yet the regimen also provided minimal but crucial environmental attention that kept Kaspar at the center of his caged world (a center shared by the fearsome godlike "man").

The undifferentiating, deadening effect of sphincteric defense contributed to the fact that Kaspar had no distant memory at all. Only the recent contrasting heterogenous events in relation to the journey to Nuremberg had interfered with the sense that things were as they "had always been."

I propose to take von Feuerbach's (1832) estimate literally. He believed that the boy showed the mental advancement of a "child scarcely two or three years old" (p. 5). Although his original development may have gone beyond this in some ways, a mental level more or less appropriate to this age was what he preserved under the comparative mindlessness of the years in captivity. If, guided by Anna Freud (1965), we try, despite the dearth of data, to look at Kaspar's "developmental lines" (p. 62), it would seem that his ego development suffered less from the trauma and the regressive deep-freeze of the years in the "hole" than did his instinctual development. As (I postulate) a separated body ego and some sense of identity had been established before the caging, Kaspar turned out to be able, comparatively quickly— when released into "the world"—to learn to walk, to talk, and to read. He was able to learn to distinguish the animate from the inanimate, and to complete the process of separating the image of himself from others and of differentiating those others. These achievements helped him to function, to do work. Although he made a most promising beginning, he was not able to learn to hate or to love (*cf.* Freedman & Brown, 1986).

Libidinal Development—Kaspar's Anality

We know nothing about Kaspar's "oral" line of development—from "sucking to rational eating" (A. Freud, 1965, p. 69); when "found," he would only ingest bread and water and showed fear and disgust toward anything else. Of the developmental instinctual line—"from wetting and soiling to bladder and bowel control" (A. Freud, 1965, p. 72), we can only speculate. Presumably these developments took place early. We do not know what regimen the "man" imposed on Kaspar, or what was done about defecation and urination in the "hole." Kaspar said that he was "cleaned" by "the man" (who apparently characteristically stood behind him), but he gives no specific details about elimination of body wastes. There is no mention of Kaspar's toilet habits after he "came into the world." Is this mid-19th-century reticence—or does it mean that there were no problems and that Kaspar required no toilet training? Some guidance must have been required for Kaspar to learn to make use of the water-closet—Kaspar mentions being in the water-closet when he was attacked in 1829. An inference that he had been sphincter-trained long before emerging in Nuremberg can be derived from Kaspar's characteristic obsessive cleanliness and tidiness. The following description is of Kaspar after several months in "the world":

> A most surprising and inexplicable property of this young man, was his love of order and cleanliness, which he carried to the extreme of pedantry. Of the many hundreds of trifles of which his little household consisted, each had its appropriate place, was properly packed, carefully folded, symmetrically arranged etc. Uncleanliness, or whatever he considered as such, whether in *his own person* or in others, was an abomination to him. (my italics; von Feuerbach, 1832, p. 75)

The obsessive–compulsive character that Kaspar went on to develop, and his obedience and suppression of anger show an anal and a predominantly masochistic tie to the "man" who cleaned him and who always kept behind him. This character pathology implies an internalization of the "man's" *control* by way of the excretory sphincters, which would result in a severe pre-stage of the super-ego, marked by sphincter morality and sphincter defensiveness. The anal stage was probably as far as Kaspar's libidinal development proceeded in the "cage." The anal manifestations when he was observed appear mainly in attenuation, sublimated, and in typical defended fashion—that is, reversed in reaction formation. Von Feuerbach says: "He observed almost every grain of dust upon our clothes; and when he once saw a few grains of snuff on my frill, he shewed them to me, briskly indicating that he wished me to wipe those nasty things away" (p. 75). The sadistic part of the anal impulses showed only through the reversal into masochism. The automatic obedient orderliness (the reaction against angry soiling impulses) represents the effect of the counterpart use of the anal sphincter as an emotional sphincter.

Higher Libidinal Levels and Anxiety

There is no evidence of Kaspar's progress to the phallic oedipal level. His desire to be a girl was understood in terms of wanting feminine attire. This may be valid—it suggests the boy's expunged sexual (alongside the eradicated hostile) feelings. I suspect that Kaspar's "femininity" was primarily related to his fear of aggressiveness, which was not necessarily accompanied by sexual stirrings arising from negative oedipal impulses. Whatever the pregenital instinctual mix beneath the inhibited defensive surface, Kaspar *appeared to be* asexual. Although he was minutely observed without his knowledge in the first weeks he spent in the Nuremberg Vestner Castle tower prison, there is no hint of masturbation; his observer stated that Kaspar's "whole demeanour . . . was a mirror of childlike innocence" (p. 33).

Kaspar's wish for women's clothes might have involved worries about his body. Kaspar was initially without exhibitionistic shame, but went on to develop exaggerated modesty. There are not enough details available to determine whether he was dealing with, or if he went on to develop, castration anxiety. It seems relatively absent. When first found, Kaspar was thought to be absolutely unafraid—his only concern seemed to be his painful feet. When he began to recognize the external world, and anxiety did show (usually in reaction to seeing what he interpreted as anger or to excessive or strange stimuli), it was expressed mainly through somatic reactions: muscular spasms, cold

sweats, vomiting, headaches. Were these pregenital conversion symptoms? Sometimes they appeared unaccompanied by conscious anxiety
(see von Feuerbach, 1832, p. 110). On other occasions (see pp. 105,
153–154) Kaspar felt terror (of strange foods and smells, of storms and
thunder, of black creatures) and would seem to have suffered from
what Schur (1953) describes as "somatic discharge phenomena of uncontrolled anxiety" (p. 80). Mitscherlich (1963/1973) speaks of Kaspar's "pre-genital, almost pre-verbal anxiety" (p. 162). This primitive
anxiety was eventually tamed. From the start "in the world," Kaspar's
anal–narcissistic defenses were formidable; he showed massive isolation, denial, and a powerful autohypnosis—all operating toward regressive narcissistic withdrawal. He returned to these defenses when
they were needed in later years. We know too little to work out from
Kaspar's anxiety and his symptoms the specifics of the devastating
damage done to his instinctual endowment. With all of the shifting of
parental figures that Kaspar had to endure, we do not hear of any
indications of anxiety in relation to separation. Instead, there was a
reaction of brutish dull apathy. (This is very well brought out in
Wasserman's [1908] novel *Caspar Hauser*.) The apathy was the negative emotional surface of the reduction to nothingness, to "shit,"
which is at the core of anal defensiveness. Apathy and mindlessness
were an adaptive reaction—with too much pain and loss it is better to
be a soul-less *thing*.

Development of Nondefensive Ego Aspects

Anna Freud (1965), alluding to maturation of ego potentialities, sets
forth the lines of development "from egocentricity to companionship,
from body to toy . . . from play to work" (p. 79). I have postulated that
there had been some advancement past body ego establishment and
some psychic ego consolidation, from which Kaspar regressed in "the
hole." There, he had only "the man" and some toys (two wooden
horses and some ribbons) for companions. Toys function for all children as magically alive "transitional objects," facilitating by repetition the shift of psychic interest from the child's body and the body of
the primary parent onto others. This "transition" was only partially
achieved by Kaspar; it could have been completed only when there
were organic, alive *others* to identify with and learn from—in Nuremberg. In the "cage," Kaspar must also have used his toys to develop

some sense of mastery over his environment. Anna Freud (1965, p. 80) describes how the opportunity to move toys around tends not only to displace interest from the body openings and their functions, but also provides pleasure in motility and some sense of mastery of it. Moving and adorning his wooden horses must have been so meaningful to Kaspar, who desperately needed some maturational outlet to compensate for his cramped limbs and lack of locomotion. It is therefore no surprise that Kaspar was passionately fond of horses—first toy ones, then real ones. The word for horse was one of the few he had from the first: "to every animal he met with, whether quadruped *or biped* . . . he gave the name of 'Ross' (horse)" (my italics; von Feuerbach, 1832, p. 23); and he begged so piteously for a "Ross" that he was immediately given wooden horses by the people in Nuremberg:

> For hours together . . . has [K]aspar sat playing with his horses without attending in the least to anything that passed around him or by his side (p. 23). . . . [K]aspar often dragged his horses backwards and forwards by his side, without changing his place or altering his position. (p. 28).

During the first few weeks it was obvious that the boy considered his new toy horses to be alive—he tried to give them food and water, and was distressed when one, made of papier-mâché, started to deteriorate. Much later on he learned to ride real horses, and did it well. It was one of the few talents he was able to maintain. The passion for real horses can be understood (literally and symbolically) in relation to fulfilling Kaspar's wish to be "a rider like my father was"—to have and to become a good father. But his riding was also a continuation of the "transitional" attachment to the "companions" of his imprisonment.

Separation and Individuation

In Mahler's (1972b) terms, Kaspar, when "found," had already "hatched out . . . beyond the symbiotic orbit" and had entered and partially traversed the subsequent separation individuation phases "on the way to object constancy" (p. 488)—all in relation to a primary mothering person (for Kaspar, probably a substitute mother acquired at six months). In the "cage," where he undoubtedly regressed, he could continue his development towards individuality only in relation to the "man with whom I have always been." There, Kaspar was deprived of what Mahler calls "the greatest step in human individuation. [The toddler] walks freely with upright posture" (1972b, p. 491). (I, too, believe this is the greatest *active* step in the child's *individuation*; individuation comes *after*—as Mahler indicates—the *separation* involved with the acquisition of body and psychic ego.)

The power to move away from the mother—the advance through "crawling, paddling, pivoting, climbing and righting himself . . . [to] . . . free upright locomotion" (1972b, p. 490) usually takes place from seven to 18 months, just prior to the anal period of development so important for coordination and mastery. For optimal mental development and individuation to proceed during this time, the infant must have adequate mothering—a mother to return to for "emotional refueling" (p. 491). I think it can be assumed that Kaspar had gone through this development (Mahler's "practising subphase") and that he had learned to walk in his second and third year of life. It was then, during the latter part of the anal developmental period, that he was deprived not only of proper mothering, but of the powers of locomotion—both so vitally needed for the development of psychic structure. My assumptions would help to explain how "the man" was able to teach Kaspar to walk so relatively quickly—it was a relearning. Kaspar did not walk well when he was first discovered, but it was a wonder he could do it at all. It took him many months to learn to walk properly. Kaspar could not at first climb or descend stairs—he saw everything in a flat perspective and had no concept of *up* and *down*. The riding of horses provided the acme of his mastery and of his joy in locomotion.

Mahler's (1972b) description of the child during the months after he has achieved the power to walk away is appropriate to the 16-year-old Kaspar after he had reacquired that power and had a need, similar to the young child of 10 to 18 months, to learn about the outside world:

> With the spurt in autonomous functions, such as cognition but especially upright locomotion, the "love affair with the world" (Greenacre, 1957) begins . . . the world is his oyster. Libidinal cathexis shifts substantially into the service of the rapidly growing autonomous ego and its functions, and the child seems to be intoxicated with his own faculties and with the greatness of the world . . . the elation of this sub-phase has to do not only with the exercise of the ego apparatuses, but also with the infant's delighted escape from re-engulfment by the still-existing symbiotic pull from the mother. (p 491)

Kaspar's "elation" and "intoxication" (as with the more disturbed rather than the normal child) was accompanied by a strong sense of the loss of the symbiosis and a longing to return to the timeless bondage with, and the (anal) control by, the "man." The intensity of wanting to be re-engulfed and to merge is part of the reaction to the chronic overstimulation involved in soul murder. It is a defensive narcissistic regression.

Yet Kaspar's elation was very real. There was a marvelous flowering of his mental powers in the year or so after his release. Acquiring language and the ability to walk seemed to free his soul. From the first weeks in the prison tower, there was a hunger for contact with people. The many visitors, says von Feuerbach (1832), tended to "awaken [Kaspar's] mind more and more to attention, to reflection and to active thought, according as his self-consciousness became more clear" (p. 36). What was revealed with the quick acquisition of speech sufficient "at least in some degree to express his thoughts [was] so active a mind, so fervent a zeal to lay hold on every thing that was new to him, so vivid, so youthfully powerful, and so faithfully retentive a memory" (p. 37) as to astound the observers. Here was a rebirth, a psychological birth. ("The biological birth of the human infant and the psychological birth of the individual are not coincident in time" [Mahler *et al.*, 1975, p. 3]). Kaspar's rebirth was a wonder—the citizens of Nuremberg were enthralled; but it did have something of the exaggerated quality of caricature. It could not be completely what occurs with the natural development of a child, so beautifully recalled by Wordsworth:

> There was a time when meadow, grove and stream
> The earth, and every common sight
>   To me did seem
>   Apparelled in celestial light,
> The glory and the freshness of a dream.
> (1803, p. 403)

Von Feuerbach also uses the metaphor of light, describing Kaspar's fervent apprehension of the universe in terms of luminescence and incandescence.

Although Kaspar's "love affair with the world" was less than full, he was helped toward the feeling of glory by the world's love affair with him. People flocked to see him, and he evoked parental feeling—compassion and attention: "From being the adopted child of the city of Nuremberg . . . he became the child of Europe," says von Feuerbach (1832) of Kaspar in 1829 (see also Lang, 1904, p. 118). Kaspar lived with a series of parent-substitutes, who at first took an intense and benevolent interest in him. Prison-keeper Hiltel took him into his home; the *Burgomeister* of Nuremberg and Judge von Feuerbach were immediately and intensely involved (he stayed at their houses); Professor Daumer (Kaspar's tutor) took the boy to live with him, and with his mother and sister promised to become a second family; Lord Stanhope, the Earl of Chesterfield, declared his intention to adopt Kaspar. These people began to provide what Kaspar had been so cruelly deprived of—the narcissistic promise of a continuing parental acceptance (the never-outgrown need derived from the craving of the infant for the fond and accepting gleam in the eye of the nursing mother).

The Developmental Phase of Practising—Active Mastery

The striving to know, connect, and remember had an intensity that Kaspar expressed in an active, motor fashion. This, too, has its parallel in normal development. The child of one to one and a half years is described by Mahler (1972a) as being in the "practising subphase," during which the child uses its intellect and its muscles to get away from the mother and absorb the environment. Kaspar, perhaps in part to compensate for the years of cramped confinement and motor inhibition, used his muscles (especially his eye and facial muscles) to help comprehend and integrate—as though they were grasping extensions of his mind:

> Whenever any person was . . . introduced, Caspar went up very close to him, regarded him with a sharp staring look, noticed every particular part of his face, as his forehead, eyes, nose, mouth, chin, etc., successively . . . and, as I could distinctly perceive, at the very least, he collected all the different parts of the countenance, which at first he had gathered separately and piece by piece, into one whole . . . And now he knew the person; and, as experience afterwards proved, he knew him forever. (Von Feuerbach, 1832, p. 64)

This muscular/psychological "grasping," a coordination of muscular action and thinking, is part of the anal body ego mastery of the renaissance of Kaspar's psychic development. We see a creative comprehending holding on, which is a counterpart to sphincteric action— a holding that involved the peripheral musculature. When he was trying to absorb a new fact or idea or word, or "whenever he endeavoured to connect any thing that was unknown to him with something that he knew" (pp. 65–66), Kaspar would (during those first weeks) first go into spasms of his facial muscles, and then those muscles would become impassive and rigid. Kaspar insisted on active "practising"—he would accept something as true only if he could verify it with his own senses. He was convinced that the balls of a ninepin alley ran of their own volition until Professor Daumer had him roll a ball of crumbs for himself; he had to plant beans and watch them grow to accept that plants come from seeds.

This interconnectedness of muscular action, locomotion, and the acquisition of the power of thought is usually mastered during the anal phase of libidinal development, as we saw in the achievement of the fictional Gargantua.

Memory and Perceptions

Kaspar's memory ("as quick as it is tenacious," p. 72) and his progress with words was astonishing. Von Feuerbach writes of his first meeting with Kaspar:

> About an hour after we had seen him, we met him again in the street [Kaspar was being conducted from the jail to the Burgomeister's] . . . he mentioned, without the least hesitation, the full name of every one of the company, together with all our titles, which must, nevertheless, have appeared to him as unintelligible nonsense. (p. 73)

Kaspar evidenced an incompleteness in his individuation, consistent with the development of the two-to-three-year-old, by first speaking of himself in the third person: "Kaspar very well." (p. 66), and then he gradually developed the use of "I" and "me." (This attainment, I have already mentioned, is attributed by Fliess to the mastery of the excretory sphincters.)

Kaspar showed some of the natural facility for poetry of the developing child of three. (This was, as with children, "imagist" poetry of personal creative metaphor; Kasper never showed any ability for abstract thought.)

> He called a corpulent gentleman . . . "the man with the great mountain." A lady, the end of whose shawl he once saw dragging on the floor, he called "the lady with the beautiful tail" (p. 67). [In] winter, when the snow first fell, he expressed great joy, that the streets, the roofs, and the trees, had now been so well painted; and he went quickly down into the yard to fetch some . . . but he soon ran to his preceptor with all his fingers stretched out, crying . . . and bawling out, "that the white paint had bit his hand." (p. 74)

Kaspar's favorite activity in the first few weeks of his new life was playing with and bedecking the toy horses he had been given; but this "delight" (p. 32) was then given up for what the prison-keeper called the "more serious and more useful occupations" (p. 32) of learning about people and his physical environment; playing in his mind could more and more furnish *delight*—this was the elation of Mahler's "practising subphase."

Kaspar's sense of perspective was at first remarkably deficient. Everything seemed almost one-dimensional to him. With the acquisition of free locomotion he began to develop rapidly the complicated muscular and mental "measuring apparatus" to estimate distance, dimension and shape:

> In the beginning [Kaspar later said] he could not distinguish between what was really round or triangular, and what was only painted as round or triangular. The men and horses represented on sheets of pictures, appeared to him precisely as the men and horses that were carved in wood; the first as round as the latter, or those as flat as those. But he said that, in the packing and unpacking of his things, he had soon felt a difference; and that afterwards, it had seldom happened to him to mistake the one for the other. (p. 78)

The wise von Feuerbach was aware of the importance of being able to walk, and to coordinate walking with seeing, in order to judge realistically the distance and size of objects; and he attributes Kaspar's (relative) slowness in learning these things to his habit of looking down at his feet on his short and infrequent walks of the first weeks

> in consequence of the irritability of his eyes and his fear of falling, . . . and [thus avoiding] looking out into the vast ocean of light around him, [so that] he had, for a length of time, no opportunity of gaining experience concerning the perspective and distances of visible objects. (p. 82)

This is an example of the need to acquire psychic certainty (here specifically about the physical environment) by way of the body ego. Mastery of and by the body musculature—including and featuring the sphincters—helps construct and expand the powers of the psychic ego.

Overstimulation

Under ordinary circumstances, the child starts with and develops a shield against overstimulation—a development determined both by natural maturation and by optimal maternal care (which is ultimately internalized into the child's own psychic structure). But of course Kaspar's maturation and care had been grossly deficient.

Von Feuerbach was alarmed that the rushing in of new impressions might be providing overstimulation for the eager and precocious boy who was so little acquainted with the mastery of any kind of excitement:

> The unaccustomed impressions of the light and of the free air . . . the almost constant and uninterrupted intercourse with the numerous individuals who thronged to him at all hours of the day . . . the strange and often painful minglings of diverse excitatives which continually flowed in upon his senses; the effort to which his mind was constantly stimulated by his thirst for knowledge, labouring, as it were to go beyond itself, to fasten upon . . . to devour . . . whatsoever was new to him—and all was new to him—all this was more than his feeble body and delicate yet constantly excited, and *even over-excited*, nerves could bear. (my italics; pp. 83–84)

Kaspar did become sick, whereupon he was taken by Professor Daumer to live with him, his mother, and sister. In the Daumer family home he could be educated at a slower pace, and in a private and more peaceful setting. The Daumers tried to become Kaspar's new family. The boy's good feelings and enthusiasm revived; his increasing powers of moving about freely, and of talking and writing brought about a slower, more stable progress. There was less incandescence; changes implying psychic structure began to occur—the boy continued to show strong obsessive–compulsive tendencies that now seemed to be compatible with an emotional openness and enrichment. His innate mental and emotional endowment again began to flower. Kaspar learned finally to distinguish the animate from the inanimate. (He was at first indignant with a much bespattered statue in the Daumer garden for not washing itself.) He started to write down his thoughts. At the Daumers' Kaspar slept in a real bed (rather than a straw one) for the first time, and began dreaming for the first time that he remembered. The soft bed perhaps symbolized the much-longed-for matrix provided by the Daumer family: "[Kaspar] would often say, that this bed was the only pleasant thing that he had met with in the world" (p. 99).

Kaspar's Giftedness

Like many other deprived children who need to make the most of their powers in order to survive, Kaspar had developed certain extraordinary gifts in the course of adapting to his years of imprisonment; these contributed to the initial impression of his remarkable endowment. His sensory perceptions seemed supernormal:

> It has been proved by experiments carefully made, that in a perfectly dark night, he could distinguish different dark colours, such as blue and green from each other . . . when at the commencement of twilight, a common eye could not distinguish more than three or four stars in the sky, he could already discern the different groups of stars and he could distinguish the different single stars of which they were composed from each other, according to their magnitudes and the peculiarities of their coloured light . . . scarcely less sharp and penetrating than his sight was his hearing. (pp. 101–102)

He could recognize at a very great distance (when others present could not even hear) various persons by the sound of their footsteps. His sense of smell was also extraordinarily acute: "He could distinguish apple, pear, and plum trees from each other at a considerable distance, by the smell of their leaves" (p. 106). Kaspar had "less aversion [to] what we call unpleasant smells" (p. 105) than he did to the scent of flowers or perfumes. (This seems to be a reference to the odors of excretion, and could be explained by what Kaspar had become accustomed to in the "cage.")

The Turning Point

Kaspar's diligence in learning and his "steady progress in ciphering and writing" (p. 118) under Professor Daumer's tutelage continued up to the murderous attack made on him in the Daumer home in the summer of 1829. That attack must have had a terribly disillusioning effect. Kaspar had been trying to re-establish his capacity to feel and to love in relation to the parental substitutes. It was toward the Daumers, the Burgomeister, and von Feuerbach that Kaspar had turned the hunger of the deprived child "to extract every drop of human nutrient, every bit of stimulation available" (Mahler, 1968, p. 49). They had so much more to offer than the "man," and must have been idealized into gods by the boy. But with all their riches, and goods, and power, they had been unable to protect him. The "man" had returned and had almost killed him. It had been difficult enough to try to make Kaspar believe in a kindly God (Kaspar was much beset by well-meaning theologians)—the attack reinforced Kaspar's concept of a malevolent murderous Providence.[7] Von Feuerbach (1832):

> Once when the conversation was concerning the omnipotence of God, [Kaspar] proposed the question: "Can Almighty God also make time recede?", a question which contained a bitter sarcastic allusion to the fate

of his earlier life, and . . . concealed the inquiry, whether God could restore his childhood and youth, which had been lost to him in a living grave. (p. 115)

Kaspar stayed on with the Daumers for two years after the attack, but much was changed. As Kaspar looked about him, he began to appreciate the enormity of his deprivation—what it meant not to have and never to have had a real family. At Professor Daumer's, says von Feuerbach, Kaspar:

> began more and more to reflect upon his unhappy fate, and to become painfully sensible of what had been withheld and taken from him. It was only there, that the ideas of family, or relationship, of friendship, of those human ties that bind parents and children and brothers and sisters to each other, were brought home to his feelings; it was only there that the names mother, sister and brother were rendered intelligible to him, when he saw how mother, sister, and brother were reciprocally united to each other by mutual affection and by mutual endeavours to make each other happy. He would often ask for an explanation of what is meant by mother, by brother, and by sister; and endeavours were made to satisfy him by appropriate answers. Soon after, he was found sitting in his chair, apparently immersed in deep meditations. When he was asked, what was now again the matter with him? he replied with tears, "he had been thinking about what was the reason why *he* had not a mother, a brother, and a sister? For it was so very pretty a thing to have them." (pp. 96–97)

Failure of "Rapprochement"

It is during the second 18 months of life that the developing child is vulnerable to the loss of the feeling of elation that accompanies his new locomotive and mental powers. The relative imperturbability begins to fade, and a new jeopardy develops. Mahler (1968) calls this the developmental subphase of "rapprochement": "It is the time when the child's self-esteem may suffer abrupt deflation" (pp. 22–23). The world is so huge, and the child must learn to cope with it. Parentally enhanced control (developmentally, this is anal control) of a limited inner world must now be supplemented by the acquisition of realistic mastery of the outer world. The child must shed much of his narcissism and come to terms with the existence and the claims of "others."

The child is really able to be more independent, but increased mastery of reality brings sadness as the child realizes narcissistic loss—separation from the parents and the fading of omnipotence and magic. After the elation, the child shows "an increased need and wish for his mother to share with him every new acquisition on his part of skill and experience" (Mahler 1972a). It was at a corresponding developmental stage—when increasing knowledge of the world had brought a new fragility and an increased need for parental care—that Kaspar began to appreciate his terrible and irrevocable loss. He had tried with all his will to learn what the world was like, and what he learned turned out to be devastating. Kind as the Daumers and some others were, they were not his parents. They could never make up for the past deprivation of the "mother's spontaneous pleasure in the child's achievement" (A. Freud, 1965, p. 86). The parental substitutes were not strong enough to keep the murderous "black man" away, nor loving enough to dilute Kaspar's own murderous black rage. He had tried to feel as much as possible (to relax his "emotional sphincter"), but his basic affective structure was deficient, and the intensity of his bad feelings was too much for him; there was not enough love to transcend or to neutralize the hatred, and there was too much need for control to let go emotionally. Kaspar was forced toward obsessiveness and depression.

The Good Parent's Loss of Power

Because the Daumers had not been able to protect Kaspar, the municipal authorities took more of a supervisory interest. It may be (as Wassermann [1908] portrays in his novel *Caspar Hauser*) that Professor Daumer became frightened and wanted to decrease his responsibility. At any rate, a decision was made that showed lack of empathy and increased Kaspar's sense that his foster family could not fulfill his needs. Kaspar was sent out of the Daumer home (where he had been tutored by the Professor) to spend a good part of the day attending *Gymnasium* (high school); there he was put into an advanced class with students of his own age. He was expected to act as an independent 18-year-old when his emotional development was that of the three-year-old, who, according to Mahler (1972a), "becomes more aware of his separateness and employs all kinds of mechanisms to resist separation from the mother" (p. 337).

The separation and the exile to school evoked the disapproval and indignation of von Feuerbach (1832): "This poor neglected youth . . . who was still deficient in so much knowledge which other children acquire *at their mother's breast or in the laps of their nurses*, was at once obliged to torment his head with Latin grammar and Latin exercises" (my italics; p. 139). Von Feuerbach saw clearly the need for emotional sustenance that was scanted by taking Kaspar out of the "bosom" of the home-tutoring situation, and substituting "the dry trash of a grammar school" (p. 140). At the school, Kaspar was tormented by comparing himself with his schoolmates and realizing, as von Feuerbach said, that he "should never be able to regain his lost youth, to equal those who were the same age with him" (p. 140). In assenting to this change, Professor Daumer, generally so kindly disposed toward Kaspar (he continued to write about his former pupil up to his old age), played the role of the weak and unempathic parent so often seen in instances of soul murder—the parent who allows the child to be damaged not out of evil intent but out of passivity and inadequacy.[8]

During his last years at the Daumers', Kaspar's intellecual development continued at a much slower rate, and there was a regression of his already stunted emotional growth. The feelings of irrevocable loss, of unfulfillable longings were too much to bear, and the more he learned about the world, the more aware he was of what he would never have. Kaspar became depressed and dull; his incipient anxiety and the all-too-dangerous anger needed to be quelled. He must once again have called upon his old anal–narcissistic and hypnotic defenses.

Another mistake was made in 1831, when Kaspar was taken entirely away from the Daumers, and sent out of the familiar and accepting environment of Nuremberg. The responsibility for Kaspar's expenses had been undertaken by the Earl of Chesterfield, Lord Stanhope (who did not take Kaspar to England to live with him as he had promised); Kaspar was sent to an unsympathetic guardian, Herr Meyer, in Ansbach (see Singh & Zingg, 1939, p. 352). There Kaspar worked as a clerk in the office of von Feuerbach (who lived in Ansbach). When von Feuerbach died in 1833 (a death that many believed was a murder committed by Kaspar's aristocratic enemies—see Wasserman, 1908, p. xii.), Kaspar had lost all the good-parent substitutes. All these relationships had been cut off when they were not yet of sufficient duration or intensity to provide the needed establishment by identification of mental representations of parent figures, and the continuing inadequacy of Kaspar's sense of identity and completeness deprived him of any possibility for enrichment of his meagre emotional life. The high intelligence, the poetry, the beginnings of humor, the passionate intellectual curiosity, the marvelous memory—all faded with the anal-narcissistic defensive restriction of the boy's feelings. In 1832, von Feuerbach noted how much promise Kaspar had lost, how much his soul had shrunk:

> In his mind there appears nothing of genius; not even any remarkable talent; what he learns he owes to an obstinately persevering application. Also the wild flame of that fiery zeal, with which in the beginning he seemed anxious to burst open all the gates of science, has long since been extinguished. In all things that he undertakes, he remains stationary, either at the commencement, or when arrived at mediocrity. Without a spark of fancy, incapable of uttering a single pleasantry or even of understanding a figurative expression, he possesses dry, but thoroughly sound common sense . . . within the narrow sphere of his knowledge and experience, he shews an accuracy and an acuteness of judgement, which might shame and confound a learned pedant. (p. 135)

Kaspar had become an "anal character," a caricature.

> He regulates his conduct with a scrupulous exactness, which, without affectation, approaches even to pedantry. (p. 138) . . . The extraordinary, almost preternatural elevation of his senses, has also been diminished and has almost sunk to the common level. He is indeed still able to see in the dark . . . but he is no longer able to read in the dark. Of the gigantic powers of his memory and of other astonishing qualities, not a trace remains. He no longer retains anything that is extraordinary, but his extraordinary fate, his indescribable goodness, and the exceeding amiability of his disposition. (p. 145)

After von Feuerbach died, even the goodness and the amiability began to recede into irritation and indifference.

Superego and Obsessional Character

Before he arrived in Nuremberg, Kaspar had advanced to and become fixated in the anal phase of libidinal development, with emphasis on its defensive aspects. In the "cage," compliance was enforced ("I must do as I am bidden," p. 73). There were manifestations of some soul-saving bits of resistance in Kaspar's clinging to his conviction in the evidence of his own senses. Kaspar's primitive superego functioned partly inside and partly outside his mind (cf. Freud, 1940, p. 185, on the precursor of the superego, quoted page 36, this volume). For Kaspar, the god-like coercive "man" was always incipiently present, always about to return and take the boy back to the "cage." There was also an internalized imago of the "man," easily transferred to others: "[Kaspar's] obedience to all those persons who had acquired *parental authority* over him, particularly to the Burgomeister, Professor Daumer, and the prison-keeper Hiltel, was *unconditional* and *boundless*" (my italics; von Feuerbach, 1832, p. 73). Following the exposure to these kindly parental substitutes in Nuremberg, some modification, relaxation, and maturation occurred in Kaspar's superego. But the murderous presence continued, inside and outside his mind. The physical attack in 1829 was disastrously disillusioning; there was a reinforcement of the pervasion (in the world and in his conscience) of the murderous "black man." This made for a regression to anal narcissism, sphincter defensiveness, and sphincter morality. The "regressive and archaic affect" (Fliess, 1956, p. 121) of normal development is enhanced in those who have been the victims of soul murder by that terrible rage (so frequently "anal rage"; see Shengold, 1967, pp. 411–412) that the victim feels as both subject and object, as coming from inside and outside. For Kaspar, the increased pressure of rage brought on the intensification of anal defensiveness, as evidenced by the massive hardening of his obsessive characterologic armor. As the stress increased, there was a push toward melancholic withdrawal.

Kaspar's development of obsessive–compulsive character was also determined by the circumstance that the boy's intellectual progress far outstripped the maturation of his emotional and instinctual life.[9] Kaspar's obsessiveness, observed from the beginning in Nuremberg, became more entrenched as his life took on the rigid predictability of travesty. This regression accompanied the series of losses of parental substitutes. It was indeed as if there were a sphincter operating to close off Kaspar's entire emotional life. To protect himself from pain and overwhelming feeling, Kaspar had to reconstitute the anal–narcissistic defensive situation of the "hole"—a sphincter projected onto the environment.

Characterologic Regression

Von Feuerbach describes Kaspar (in 1832 when the boy was living at his home) as being very aware of "the dependence of his person upon the favour or disfavour of men" (p. 138). This awareness was a new version of the registration of his former dependence on the "man."

That original dependence had the form of unconscious assumption—it was the order of the universe. Now that Kaspar had become painfully conscious of his relative helplessness, he developed certain defensive traits; wariness, making minute observations—traits that might have gone on to become talents,[10] or character defects.

> Hence his expertness in observing men which was almost forced upon him in self-defence; hence the circumspect acuteness which, by ill-disposed persons, has been called slyness and cunning—with which he quickly seizes their peculiarities and foibles, and knows how to accommodate to those who are able to do him good or harm, to avoid offence to oblige them, adroitly to make known to them his wishes, and to render the good-will of his favourites and friends serviceable to him. (von Feuerbach, 1832, p. 138)

What might have developed into creative observation and useful adaptiveness became (as part of Kaspar's general withdrawal and retrogression) slyness and obsequiousness. Toward the end there are hints of the appearance of other unpleasant character traits. According to the (admittedly negatively biased) account of Herr Meyer, Kaspar became increasingly crabbed and demanding, complaining and bitter. This distrustful Meyer (who openly said that he believed Kaspar to be a liar) became Kaspar's guardian and repeated the role of the "man" in the reconstituted restrictive emotional "hole" of Kaspar's Anspach existence. This must have brought out Kaspar's suspicion and secretiveness ("Every Man for Himself and God against All"). These qualities, evoked by a hostile or indifferent environment, were intermixed with the angelic goodness that had predominated earlier.

Kaspar's disillusion with the world he had tried so hard to know and to embrace was much more acute than that of the normal child who sadly gives up his feelings of omnipotence and his belief in his parents' magical powers. When this renunciation is done well, it is done largely out of love. But Kaspar lacked this emotional resource. What did he have to make up for the loss of the intimations of immortality?

> Whither is fled the visionary gleam?
> Where is it now, the glory and the dream?
> (Wordsworth, 1803, p. 403)

Wordsworth can take comfort, and justify the loss (after the earliest years) "of splendour in the grass, of glory in the flower" (p. 404), because as a man he had attained what Kaspar never could:

A faith that looks through death . . .
   the philosophic mind . . .
Thanks to the human heart by which we live,
Thanks to its tenderness, its joys, and fears. . . .
                              (p. 406)

It was the deficiency of the heart, in himself but above all in those around him, that resulted in a second, piecemeal soul murder. This is depicted in Wassermann's book, *Caspar Hauser*, which is subtitled *Die Trägheit des Herzens*, literally "the slothfulness of the heart," translated as "The Unheeding World" (see Introduction to the English edition, p. 7). Kaspar's ultimate reduction to a near automaton is imaginatively and chillingly portrayed in Werner Herzog's film by a sequence in which he is trying to play a piece by Chopin on the piano—all the notes are there, but their relation to each other is missing; there is no unifying line of reference that only a sense of emotional relevance could supply.

The Child of Europe, whose fate and aspirations had moved so many, whose soaring intellect had encouraged fantasies of his being restored to noble rank and perhaps even to a throne, had become a prematurely aged, pedantic petty clerk. Twice deprived of maternal love and empathy, his soul withered to a crabbed, anal aridity; and his world had shrunk to an enlarged anal-narcissistic replica of his original "cage."

The soul murder of Kaspar Hauser culminated in actual murder. In 1833, after the death of von Feuerbach, Kaspar was still working as a law clerk in Ansbach and living with Herr Meyer. He was accosted in a park by a stranger who gave him a lady's handbag and, as the youth opened it, stabbed him in the chest with a dagger. Kaspar lived on for three days and was able to tell what had happened. A confused note was found in the handbag. Handwriting experts have established that the writing was not Kaspar's. The assailant was never identified. Kaspar's eager taking of the purse proffered him in this last fatal encounter perhaps shows a kind of greediness to make up for his emotional losses by the acquisition of things.[11] By then he had himself become a *thing*—less than fully human. When he was murdered, his soul was already half-dead.

Notes to Chapter Five

1. I deal with this fully in a separate forthcoming book, *Soul Murder*: *Child Abuse and Deprivation*.

2. A modern instance of soul murder is to be found in Orwell's *1984* where the tortured and broken hero ends by "loving" the "Big Brother" responsible for his ruin. Orwell (1949) projected his own childhood experiences into the future.

3. When first "found," and long afterwards, Kaspar was afraid of black creatures. He ran away from a black hen; he shuddered when he saw a flea, calling it "that black thing," but was also very upset when a man killed it. His aversion to clergymen was partly based on their dressing in black: "When he saw a minister he was seized with horror and dismay" (Von Feuerbach, 1832, p. 116).

4. There was a re-establishment as well as a new establishment of body ego for Kaspar; *cf.* Sacks (1985): "This unquestionability of the body, its certainty, is, for Wittgenstein, the start and basis for all knowledge and certainty" (p. 43).

5. Compare Freedman (1975), who concludes that the incapacity to differentiate self from object and the crippling of the ability to experience affect in children who have suffered prolonged environmental/emotional deprivation is *irreversible* if the deprivation is continued past age four.

6. Margaret Mahler, a Freudian analyst, contributed to psychoanalytic theory as an observer of disturbed and of normal children. Her observations and theoretical conclusions stressed the child's disengaging and "hatching out" from the mother—*separation*; and the evolution of the child's own self image and identity—*individuation*, or the psychological birth of an individual. She viewed this development of the mental representation of the self and of the beginnings of the capacity for the recognition of, and the ability to accept and care for, others—i.e. the capacity for object relationships—as occurring in phases and subphases. This evolution of identity (the separation-individuation processes) takes place alongside and interrelated with the unfolding of the libidinal and aggressive drives and the development of the ego. Mahler postulated a normal autistic phase (psychic chaos and undifferentiation) followed by a normal symbiotic phase (psychic union with the mother); these occur in the first year of life—accompanying the oral period of libidinal development. Separation follows. Mahler conceived of this as a process divided into the subphases of (1) differentiation and the development of the body image (last part of the first year); (2) practising—the start of getting away from the mother with the development of locomotion and the beginnings of thought, the time of the child's "love affair with the world" (10-12 months to 16-18 months) (see also "Separation and Individuation," this chapter); (3) rapprochement—adjusting to the separation from the mother with awareness of the need to return to her periodically (15 to 24 months); (4) consolidating individuation and the beginnings of object constancy—the ability to be able to hold the image of the mother and then others firmly in the

mind in their absence (2 to 3 years). The last three subphases would occur during the anal phase of drive development. The timings are of course approximate and vary with the individual (see Mahler *et al*, 1975).

7. Werner Herzog's 1974 film about Kaspar is titled "Every Man for Himself, and God against All"; it is partly a religious parable, with Kaspar as Christ, killed by His Father.

8. Often the soul-murder victim has experienced various combined effects of both destructiveness and inadequacy in the parents. For example, a sadistic, self-righteous paranoid man picks a masochistic wife, who needs to deny what her husband is and does in order to continue the relationship (and to keep out of consciousness connections with her own past). Both husband and wife repeat their childhood in relation to their own child (this usually means repeating *instead of* remembering)—he actively repudiating his identification with the victim-child by taking the role of tormentor; she as the onlooker (the unconscious abettor) too weak and unempathic to interfere. I would speculate that this may have been the situation with Schreber's parents, and that Frau Schreber might not have dared to interfere with her (probably idealized) husband's crazy, tyrannical and cruel child-rearing practices.

9. Freud (1913, p. 321): "I suggest the possibility that a chronological outstripping of libido development by ego development should be included in the disposition to obsessional neurosis." Anna Freud (1965, pp. 162–163) has emphasized the role of premature ego and superego development, and has also underlined the anal fixation pointed out by Freud.

10. Kipling, another victim of partial soul murder (see Shengold, 1975b), attributed a certain creative potential to the distrust and the need to watch out for his guardians—qualities forced upon him by the persecutions he had suffered as a child:

> Nor was my life an unsuitable preparation for my future, in that it demanded constant wariness, the habit of observation, and attendance on moods and tempers; the noting of discrepancies between speech and action; a certain reserve of demeanour; and automatic suspicion of sudden favours. (Kipling, 1937, p. 365)

11. I speculate that there was a regression to the first days in the prison at Nuremberg, when, "like a little child, he endeavoured to lay hold of every glittering object that he saw; and when he could not reach it, or when he was forbidden to touch it, he cried" (Feuerbach, 1832, p. 22).

6

The Place of Anality in Defense Theory

CLINICAL MATERIAL SHOWING
REGRESSION FROM OEDIPAL CONFLICT TO
ANAL-NARCISSISTIC DEFENSIVENESS

I was several minutes late in opening the door for my patient. The
young man began the session by doubting whether I could possibly
have been late. In the waiting room he had checked his accurate watch
and therefore "knew" the *door* should have been opened; he had felt a
little anger and some fear. He, not the analyst, must have been mistaken. He had wondered if he should just sit there and wait.
"*Certainly*[1], he said in his session, "I would not have burst the door
open."

I responded, "Then you had the thought of bursting the door
open."

"Yes, I always bury my anger."

The patient then started to tell me about the very bad time he had
had the night before the session. A few days previously he had made
what he called a "breakthrough," having had a very pleasurable sexual
experience, during which he had successfully penetrated his girlfriend's vagina, sustained his erection, and ejaculated. But after that
"triumph," difficulties had returned. He felt he ought to be able to
repeat his achievement and this had been increasingly experienced as
an obligation, even as a burden (thus making him feel "a little
anger"). The night before the session he had had considerable trouble
maintaining his erection. He had felt as though the analyst were there
in the bedroom with him and his girlfriend, "looking over my

114

shoulder." His girlfriend had accused him of being angry with her, of reacting toward her as he did toward his formidable mother in his matriarchal family. This "interpretation" (he had an analyst underneath him as well as one looking over his shoulder), delivered as he was trying to make love, further inhibited him and made him angry. Or rather, he said, "at least it started to make me angry. But I wasn't angry with her. What she said was true. And I'm not really angry with you."

I replied: "You say you are *not* angry with me, as you said you would *not* have burst the door open at the start of the session. Both last night and here have to do with *not* being angry when you are concerned about penetrating."

A long pause followed. Then the patient said: "Well, I heard what you were saying to me. But I couldn't listen fully. My mind switched over to doing my accounts and counting money, to putting things in order. It was a way of shutting you out."

I replied: "You needed to shut out being angry and wanting to burst in. You shut out instead of bursting open."

The patient responded: "I guess I have to be able to be angry in order to be able to fuck." I was sure he had "guessed" right, but for him it was only a guess and there was a lot of work ahead before he could make this preliminary insight his own. (I would have worded it: "You have to become less afraid of your anger in order to be able to fuck.")

I want to focus on this patient's defensive shift—his becoming unable to listen to me—shutting me out—while his thoughts became full of anal preoccupations (*i.e.*, money and order). Transiently he was the only one present in his mental world. His experience of successful intercourse had brought fantasies of his impregnating his girlfriend, and he was frightened of the incestuous and destructive phallic force-fulness involved. These forbidden fantasies were again evoked by the desire to "burst open" the analyst's door. The intercourse of the night before the session had involved an awareness of both parents—he had imagined the analyst was over his shoulder, and his girlfriend was not only being penetrated by him, but also had (acting as analyst) "brought in" his dominating mother. The conflicts over both his positive and negative oedipal complexes, and especially over their aggressive components (which could have given rise to rage), had resulted in inhibition of his sexual desire, performance, and pleasure. He had been fleetingly aware of his anger, but characteristically had turned most of it against himself (in a part of the session I have not quoted), condemning himself for his failure and passivity.

When I interpreted his angry penetrating impulses toward his girlfriend and toward me, I had used his own violent and evocative metaphor, "burst the door open"—a metaphor that alluded both to body and emotional sphincters and so tapped into body-ego feeling (see Shengold, 1981). The patient had defended himself with a change in his consciousness, distancing the contact with me, and simultaneously had introduced a seemingly disconnected preoccupation with anal derivatives. The regression to anality added force to his negative oedipal strivings and to his feminine identification. But for the most part, the regression was a defensive shift to anal narcissism. His concern was withdrawn from others and focused on himself. It was withdrawn from people and focused on things, which could then be counted, contained, and controlled. It was withdrawn from sexual destructiveness and focused on order. The dangers associated with overstimulation, rage, and castration (as well as the pleasure that should have accompanied his erogenous arousal) were reduced to obsessive dullness. The patient was transiently the center of a narcissistic world that was anally organized, but where the dangerous anal intensities were ordered and ameliorated. He had automatically subjected his soul, the life of his emotions, to sphincter control. The peopled universe could be reduced to a petty solitary realm where, paradoxically, he could feel grandiose: a large narcissistic toad in a little anal mud puddle. Without responsibility and without awareness, he had lost connection with the incestuous and murderous longings involved in the "bursting open" impulses with which he had started his session.

Another Example of Defensive Anal Narcissism

A business man who tortured himself and all around him with his obsessive–compulsive character traits had achieved in a previous analysis some distancing of his preoccupation with sadomasochistic fantasy, and some ability to have sexual gratification and even to care about others. He had married and fathered children. He returned many years later for more treatment because of hypochondriacal anxiety that recurred when his father was dying. Merely being in analysis calmed him, but he was not working at it. When my summer vacation approached, however, the patient's symptoms and anxiety returned. He was intellectually aware of his anger toward his father and toward me, but he was unable to express it or even to feel it fully. His father's condition had become stable, but his death seemed imminent and might well occur when I was away. The father had recently felt neglected by his son and had threatened to disinherit him. The son was certain that his father would never carry out the threat, but he was, in his intermittently responsible way, full of rage that his father could even have thought of it. What supervened was an anxious preoccupation with his bowels—constipation and recurrent conviction that he was suffering from cancer of the colon:

> I was driving here today and I got stuck in traffic. I became furious. I wanted to ram into the cars around me. I thought of what my father had said about changing his will, and then I began to get scared I would have a heart attack. To calm myself I started to think about being a child again. I used to love to play with toy soldiers. I had my own little world; I would shut my bedroom *door* and have wars with the soldiers. I loved it. It made me feel like a king. Like King Shit. Why did I say that? You know that was a time when I was holding in my feces. I can remember sitting in there with the soldiers and feeling the pain and the pleasure of having a full rectum. I held in my bowel movements all the time. Sometimes it got scary. Once it was so bad I couldn't move my bowels and my father had to take the shit out of me with his hand. That was one of the worst experiences in my life. But I still do hold in my feces. And I'm still only comfortable moving my bowels in my own bathroom.

The patient had needed to calm himself when his helplessness in the traffic "impaction" evoked anxiety and anger. The separation anxiety involved in his impending loss was enhanced by the angry wishes that followed the "anal touch" of his father's threat to disinherit him (and therefore to take away his fecal impaction again). He had reacted by regressing to an anal–narcissistic fantasy of being "King Shit." Once again he was the Lord of the worlds of his body and of the nursery— the sadomasochistic and anal universe he could people with his toy soldiers. He was the Only One, and in full control of his anal sphincter (here again symbolized by a door). Paradoxically (a word tied to "anal reversal" that I have used frequently in this book) and characteristically, the anal regression brought with it the danger of anal overstimulation and an urgent need to discharge his excitement and his "anal rage." This need upset the narcissistic equilibrium (as had the "too-muchness" of his anal retention as a child), and delivered him over again (in his associations) to be, as he subsequently put it, "fucked by my father's fingers." (One can see here a retreat from Abraham's second toward his first anal phase. That is, the successful anal–narcissitic state was taken over by an anal–destructive attempt to hold on to by submitting to his father.) The murderous impulses involved in his concomitant rage reaction were predominantly turned against himself in the form of (anal) hypochondria.

Oral and negative oedipal impulses and dangers can, of course, also be seen in the above material. This patient used to express his awareness of the "archaic affect" involved in oral destructiveness by speaking of his fear of "going berserk," a word etymologically derived from a word for bear, a biting creature. In the course of maturation, the terrifying biting impulses become directed clearly and specifically against the parental figures during the anal phase, when self and object representations are developing. The danger passes from the annihilation of *everyone* (the whole universe merged with the inchoate self) to the murder of the one person without whom one cannot live, the punishment for which is to be murdered in turn. With further development this passes into the oedipus complex. The narcissistic shrinking down of the world can be a regressive defensive response to the preemptory nature of the instinctual drives as expressed in intense emotions and/or body feelings. As the direction toward narcissism proceeds, there are instinctual and ego regressions; the body ego reasserts itself, and the inner world of psychic representations tends toward condensing into one object or even a part-object—toward fusion or even back to chaos. But if the regressions can be (as in health they usually are) partly held up at the anal stage, an attempt to control and stabilize can be made with the operation of anal-narcissistic defensiveness. This defensively adaptive fixation involves a predominantly anal body ego, and a negative and a positive grandiosity with one's own body as the universe. With a failure of the defense, for example, in depression and hypochondria, the negative aspects can predominate; not only the external world, but also the self can be felt as terrifying, devouring emptiness. In contrast, when the body ego is full of idealized and grandiose "good" feeling, and the psychic representations of others are reduced to the level of magical fulfillers of need, there can be a variety of moods, ranging from my patient's feeling like "King Shit" to mania to even more undifferentiated states.

ANALITY IN PERVERSION: MALE HOMOSEXUALITY

"The overt male homosexual" is a descriptive term and not a diagnostic entity. It informs us about sexual object-choice, and implies certain sexual fantasies as well as certain avoidances, being carried out in action. It does not characterize the mind or soul (psyche) of the individual. I am not attempting an explication of the problems involved in the definition and understanding of male homosexuality. I am concentrating only on certain aspects of anality that I have seen in male homosexual patients. We see in such individuals (as we can in anyone looked at from a genetic perspective) mechanisms and developments that stem from every period of instinctual and ego maturation, existing in various complicated dynamic combinations. Male homosexual practices can be connected with oral, anal, phallic, and oedipal (especially negative oedipal) conflicts. There would often seem to be, in homosexuals, quantitative differences in the level of castration anxiety and qualitative differences in how it is reacted to. There is obviously more use of the anus to replace the vagina than in heterosexual men; there is perhaps greater inherent "body-ego narcissism" in being restricted to the body of one's own sex in the choice of an object of sexual desire. Those who engage in anal intercourse are exercising their anal "control" by using their will to relax the anal sphincter, or by inducing or forcing others to relax theirs. The easy reversibility (the term Freud used first for homosexuality, "inversion," literally means "reversibility") of roles in anal intercourse has narcissistic as well as phase-specific ("object-related") anal-reversible implications. Oedipal (including negative oedipal—the father as the son's sexual object) fantasies involve murderous as well as sexual feelings that have to be connected with two much-needed and beloved persons. These currents of feeling that relate to both parents have to be brought together by all of us in relation to a sexual partner.[2] There may be some increased guilty aggressive valence in the male homosexual's need to try to eliminate the *mother* in condensing action upon a *male* partner. At any rate, for both homosexuals and heterosexuals, the aggression and the murder involved in oedipal sexuality (and the need to direct the killing and the sex toward a loved and required parent) often brings on defensive regression back to the period dominated by the "sadistic-anal organization," where there is promise of being able to control murderous incestuous affect. Control, of course, involves willed letting-go as well as willed keeping-shut. The homosexual's practiced (and frequently idealized) control of the anal sphincter is sometimes reflected in heterosexual slang (usually stripped of its idealization): "ass" for female genitals; "piece of ass" for intercourse. Sphincteric control can be the source of narcissistic pride: "What wonders my anus can perform," one patient boasted, evoking for me Glover's "halo in the sky."

Proust

I want to illustrate some mental aspects of anality (in homosexuality and in general) by examining some passages from Marcel Proust's masterpiece, *Remembrance of Things Past*. Here is a description of a homosexual encounter in the section "Cities of the Plain." The narrator and hero, Proust's alter ego, Marcel, is observing the scene (it is a "primal scene") while hidden from view. He sees a meeting in a courtyard between the ex-tailor, Jupien, and the Baron de Charlus—an elderly, snobbish aristocrat who has come to visit a sick, older female relative at what is, for him, an unusual hour. Marcel first notices that the Baron, thinking himself alone, has relaxed his facial expression, which usually presents a mask of haughty masculinity. (The observer-"child" first focuses on part of the riddle of the Sphinx—the mystery of sexual identity):

> Blinking his eyes in the sunlight, he seemed almost to be smiling, and I found in his face seen thus in repose and as it were in its natural state something so affectionate, so defenceless, that . . . what was suggested to me by the sight of this man who was so enamoured of, who so prided himself upon his virility, to whom all other men seemed odiously effeminate, what he suddenly suggested to me, to such an extent had he momentarily assumed the features, the expression, the smile thereof, was a woman. . . . The baron, having suddenly opened wide his half-shut eyes, was gazing with extraordinary attentiveness at the ex-tailor poised on the threshold of his shop, while the latter, rooted suddenly to the spot in front of M. de Charlus, implanted there like a tree, contemplated with a look of wonderment the plump form of the aging Baron. But, more astounding still, M. de Charlus's pose having altered, Jupien's, as though in obedience to the laws of an occult art, at once brought itself into harmony with it. . . . Jupien, shedding at once the humble, kindly expression which I had always associated with him, had—in perfect symmetry with the Baron—thrown back his head, given a becoming tilt to his body, placed his hand with grotesque effrontery on his hip, stuck out his behind, struck poses with the coquetry that the orchid might have

adopted on the providential arrival of the bee. I had not supposed he could appear so repellent. . . . This scene was not, however, positively comic; it was stamped with a strangeness, or if you like a naturalness, the beauty of which steadily increased. Try as M. de Charlus might to assume a detached air, to let his eyelids nonchalantly droop, every now and then he raised them, and at such moments turned on Jupien an attentive gaze . . . each time that M. de Charlus looked at Jupien, he took care that his glance should be accompanied by a word . . . he stared at Jupien with the peculiar fixity of the person who is about to say to you: "Excuse my taking the liberty, but you have a long white thread hanging down your back," or else: "Surely I can't be mistaken, you come from Zurich too; I'm certain I must have seen you there often at the *antique dealer's* (my italics—Scott Moncrieff translates this last phrase "at the curiosity shop"; 1921, pp. 626-627).

The encounter takes place in a courtyard, an "enclosed space" (= rectum; see Chasseguet-Smirgel, 1978). In what is described as a kind of biological rite, Jupien proffers his behind. The narrator emphasizes the voyeuristic stimulus to the anal exhibition (the "extraordinary attentiveness" of the Baron's gaze); the continuing interplay evokes the bewildered child in the antique dealer's "curiosity shop" of the primal scene. What is the "long white thread hanging down your back?"—is it fecal, or phallic? And is it an exotic or a humdrum sight to put beside "Zurich," evocative of the bourgeois Swiss and the middle-class home of the narrator?

Thus, every other minute, the same question seemed to be put to Jupien intently in M. de Charlus's ogling, like those questioning phrases of Beethoven's, indefinitely repeated at regular intervals and intended . . . to introduce a new theme, a change of key, a "re-entry." On the other hand, the beauty of the reciprocal glances of M. de Charlus and Jupien arose precisely from the fact that they did not, for the moment at least, seem to be intended to lead to anything further. It was the first time I had seen the manifestation of this beauty in the Baron and Jupien. In the eyes of both of them, it was the sky not of Zurich but of some Oriental city, the name of which I had not yet divined, that I saw reflected. Whatever the point might be that held M. de Charlus and the ex-tailor thus arrested, their pact seemed concluded . . . one might have thought of them as a pair of birds, the male and the female, the male seeking to make advances, the female—Jupien—no longer giving any sign of response to these over-tures, but regarding her new friend without surprise, . . . At length Jupien's indifference seemed to suffice him no longer; from the certainty of having conquered to getting himself pursued and desired was but a step, and Jupien . . . went out through the carriage gate. It was only, however, after turning his head two or three times that he disappeared into the street, toward which the Baron, trembling lest he should lose the trail . . . hurried briskly to catch up with him.

(Note the metaphor, more extended in the original, of ornithological ritual—individual behavior lost in the "inborn" responses of the "birds.")

At the same instant, just as M. de Charlus disappeared through the gate humming like a great bumble-bee, another, a real one this time, flew into the courtyard. For all I knew this might be the one so long awaited by the orchid, coming to bring it that rare pollen without which it must die a virgin. I was distracted from following the gyrations of the insect, for, engaging my attention afresh, Jupien . . . returned, followed by the Baron . . . "come inside, you shall have everything you wish," said the tailor, on whose features disdain now gave way to joy. The door of the shop closed behind them [= enclosed space] and I could hear no more. I had lost sight of the bee. I did not know whether he was the insect the orchid required, but I had no longer any doubt, in the case of a very rare insect and a captive flower, of the miraculous possibility of their conjunction when I considered that M. de Charlus . . . who for years past had never come to the house except at hours when Jupien was not there, had, by the mere accident of Mme. de Villeparesis's indisposition, encountered the tailor—and with him the good fortune reserved for men of the Baron's kind by one of those fellow creatures . . . the men predestined to exist in order that they may have their share of sensual pleasure on this earth; the man who cares only for elderly gentlemen." (pp. 628–629)

The narrator then steals into an empty shop next to the tailor's in order to continue his observations; hearing replaces seeing:

. . . from what I heard at first in Jupien's quarters, which was only a series of inarticulate sounds, I imagine that few words had been exchanged. It is true that these sounds were so *violent* that, if they had not always been taken up an octave higher by a parallel plaint, I might have thought that one person was *slitting another's throat* [Scott Moncrieff translates this *"strangling another"*] within a few feet of me, and that subsequently the *murderer* and his resuscitated *victim* were *taking a bath* to wash away the traces of the *crime.* I concluded from this later on that there is another thing *as vociferous as pain, namely pleasure,* especially when there is added to it—in the absence of the fear of *an eventual parturition,* which could not be the case here . . . an immediate concern about *cleanliness"* (my italics; p. 631).

The references to cleanliness (and therefore to dirt) and the mention of parturition show that the sexual contact probably included anal intercourse. The entire long passage contains, directly and implicitly, many of Proust's general ideas about sexuality, as well as about homosexuality, which stem from the vantage point of the preoedipal child fantasying a primal scene imbued with anal erogeneity and anal-sadistic libido.[3]

CARICATURE

One sees in the above material the reduction by passionate sexual arousal of individuals to types, to caricature. This applies not only to the Baron and Jupien, but also to the excited third member of the "primal scene," the narrator–observer who is driven to become a sneak and an eavesdropper. The variety of life becomes stylized biological ritual, with stages, seemingly predetermined and implying the abandonment of responsibility and will.

CONTRADICTIONS AND OPPOSITES

Proust presents the polar opposites, the simultaneous contradictions, the "ins-and-outs" that mark anality. What the observer Marcel finds "repellent" he also describes as full of "strange beauty"; the strangeness soon becomes "naturalness"; the commercial materialism connoted by "Zurich" is accompanied by, and could serve to disguise, the "oriental cities" (Sodom and Gomorrah). The "music" (Beethoven) of the reciprocal glances leads to "violent" sounds. The seemingly innocent and banal comparison between the men's sexual approaches and those of birds, bees, and flowers coexists with the pain and killing, the throat-slitting and strangling of Proust's allusions. Murder and love; rage and pleasure; dirt and cleanliness; degradation and idealization—these alternatives are side-by-side in the anal ambit, which features simultaneous sadism and masochism, doing and undoing, passivity and activity, masculinity and femininity.

DENIAL

There is denial inherent in the narrator's analogy to the bee and the orchid, which alludes to the false promise of fertilization in the homosexual congress. Proust makes this manifest by what appears to be unnecessary underlining: "in the absence of an eventual parturition, which could not be the case here" (p. 631). This is the *negation* of an anal birth fantasy, which in the text is both preceded and followed by the idea of dirtiness, expressed again by its opposite—"taking a bath" and "concern about cleanliness." The compulsive attempt to negate the fantasy of anal impregnation and birth simultaneously serves to express the child's denial of the role of the vagina.

DIGRESSION ON DEFENSES: PRIMARY AND SECONDARY IDEALIZATION AND DEVALUATION

According to psychoanalytic beliefs, affects—and reactions or defenses against affects—are derived from very early experiences of pleasure and pain (or "unpleasure," a better translation of Freud's "*Unlust*"). Pleasure and unpleasure are the primary experiential sensory dichotomy. The capacity for affects—pleasure and unpleasure—is related to our instinctual drive inheritance, and the affects develop and change along with the drives. Freud believed that at the beginning of mental life, in infancy, pleasure can be retained in the mind, whereas some structural development is needed before unpleasure can be held and registered. At first the psyche simply blanks out reflexively what does not bring gratification. (This is the sense in which there is no "No" in the Unconscious.) And the capacity to contain in the mind (in order to deal with) life's No's and pains, limits and limitations—is necessary for survival, for testing and getting along in unparadisiacal reality, and, as with Adam and Eve, for the acquisition of human qualities.

Idealization and devaluation are also derived from primal pleasure and unpleasure experiences. Idealization involves a narcissistic, grandiose enhancement of emotional force, granting an urgent, wonderful, vibrant meaningfulness to whatever is invested with it.[4] The luminescent power comes from our earliest childhood:

> There was a time when meadow, grove and stream
> The earth, and every common sight
>   To me did seem
>   Apparelled in celestial light,
> The glory and the freshness of a *dream*.
>   (my italics; Wordsworth, 1803, p. 403)[5]

The dream is a *hallucinatory* experience. In Chapter 7 of *The Interpretation of Dreams* (1900), Freud describes the hypothetical first mental act as being that of a hallucinatory wish fulfillment. The wish starts with unpleasure derived from the inevitable and necessary (to the development of human qualities) frustrations of somatic needs. Because of these exigencies of life, Freud says, the infant requires that the memory-image of an "experience of satisfaction"[6] be reproduced in hallucinatory sensory intensity in an attempt to:

> re-establish the situation of the original satisfaction. An impulse of this kind we call a wish. . . . Nothing prevents us from assuming that there was a primitive state of the psychical apparatus in which . . . wishing ended in hallucinating (p. 566). . . . [A] current of this kind in the [mental] apparatus starting from unpleasure and aiming at pleasure, we have termed a "wish". . . . (p. 598).

There is, then, a hallucinatory intensity posited as inherent in the primal mental activity (i.e., primary process giving rise to a memory-image) involved in the "experience of satisfaction," the pleasure-giving fulfillment of a somatic need. With these "experiences" (they are, of course, hypothetical *proto*-experiences, since we know nothing about when or how they begin to register), all that is bad is banished.

But the bad and unpleasure return with devaluation, the negative side of idealization, which has a corresponding intensity of power, but now directed to the deprivation of meaning, a degrading in the direction of nothingness. The degradation still possesses the potential sensory and emotional force of early idealization—acting like a celestial black hole, devouring the significant surroundings. Idealization and devaluation are primal, perfervid ways of reacting to sensations and emotions; they are directed to parts of the self, of others, and of the external environment. In their primal, beginning-experiential forms they are (and to some considerable extent they remain) attention-commanding mechanisms, clamorous and phosphorescent—providing to the relevant part of the self and/or external world such imperative sensory intensity that everything around that part is dimmed, robbed of significance. Matching the black hole of devaluation would be the metaphor of idealization as the rising sun affecting the lesser sources of light:

> The glow-worm shows the matin to be near
> And 'gins to pale his ineffectual fire.
> (Hamlet 1-V-89)[7]

These qualifying mechanisms, idealization and devaluation (which become part of body ego functioning), develop as the bodily sensory experiences begin to register and to be organized, that is, when the drive-derived sensations, together with proprioceptive and perceptory ones, begin to provide "islands" of body ego. In a sense, the secondary idealizations that continue to exist past the earliest ontogenetic period into later life represent somatically infused psychic shards of Eden. These remnants are manifest in Wordworth's "Intimations of Immortality," and in Proust's experiences of automatic memory, which evoke the oceanic feeling of "Time Regained" (both authors describe feelings that have to do with transcending the laws of time). We retain these (incipiently hallucinatory) presentiments and promises of paradise as remnants of the early timeless and fervent bliss of the "auto-erotic," symbiotic oral stage of union with the mother.

Idealizations have as a kind of central dynamic core the constantly changing mental registrations of experiences of instinctual drive gratification involved in the oral, anal, and phallic (preoedipal) phases, together with the "component instincts" (sadomasochistic, fetishistic, exhibitionistic/voyeuristic) of polymorphous perverse infantile development. It is the interaction in the course of maturation of these forces (derivations of drive) with exteroceptive, interoceptive, and proprioceptive stimuli that results in body ego formation. Primal idealization (the making everything wonderfully good) acquires as its adjunct the primal mechanism of introjection, the taking-in of the good from the outside.

Devaluations become enhanced as part of antithetical and defense activity (related to "the bad" and to aggressive instinctual derivatives). "The bad" arises from experiences of bodily unpleasure (with the use of the mechanism of projection to try to banish it) and from the frustration that follows parental, subsequently internalized, No's. These retarding and reversing functions begin and flourish in the oral period.

Spitz (1965) describes in detail from observation and from theory the child's development of the power of "No." At first, he says "the mother is the child's external ego" (p. 181). Then, especially after the child begins to attain the power of locomotion, the mother begins to say "No," and "the child understands the mother's prohibitions through a process of identification" (p. 181). Spitz connects this power of negation acquired during the oral period (he is dealing with the second half of the child's first 15 months of life) not only with locomotion, but also with the beginnings of thought (as I have similarly connected the developmentally later anal defensiveness):

> The negative headshake and the word "no" . . . represent a concept: the concept of negation, of refusal in the narrow sense of the term . . . it is the minus sign of mathematics . . . (p. 183)

The mother's "No" means that the child experiences unpleasure through frustration; this enhances the (oral) aggressive drive, and:

> a memory trace of the prohibition is laid down in the ego and will be invested with this aggressive cathexis. (p. 186) . . . The mastery of the "No" (gesture and word) is an achievement with far-reaching consequences for the mental and emotional development of the child; it presupposes that he has acquired the first capacity of judgement and negation. (p. 188) . . . With the acquisition of the gesture of negation, action is replaced by message, and distance communication is inaugurated . . . Here begins the humanization of the species. (p. 189; see also Spitz, 1957)

Freud connects the power of defense associated with the registration of unpleasure in physiologically prototypical (and potential body-ego) terms in his paper on negation (1925). He conceives of the origin of the power of judgment as expressed:

> in the language of the oldest—the oral–instinctual impulses . . . : "I should like to eat this," or "I should like to spit it out." (p. 237) . . . The study of judgement affords us, perhaps for the first time, an insight into the origin of an intellectual function from the interplay of the primary instinctual impulses . . . negation—the successor to *expulsion*—belongs to the instinct of destruction. (my italics; p. 238)

Here, negation (as the psychic successor to "expulsion") marks the beginning of qualitative thought, leading the way to the mature power of mind (featuring secondary process) by way of the registration (and potential psychic "control") of the rejectable "outside" and the rejecting "other." The early body-ego concept of expulsion, protoprojection as it were, is the oral equivalent of the quasi-physiological (body-ego) prototype for anal (or sphincter) defensiveness.

Although idealization and devaluation (and their associated mechanisms of introjection and projection) have these earliest oral beginnings, they are greatly augmented during the anal development phase, when psychic reversals become organized and entrenched at the time of a wave of aggressive drive. At this stage of "anal reversibility," either devaluation or idealization (now no longer "primary" and more properly to be identified as distinctive defense *mechanisms*) can be used to disguise the other. With overt perversion, there is some sort of complicated failure of integration of the idealization/devaluation processes and this failure results in a psychic "split," so that the predominant devaluation is surfaced over by a disguising, luminescent layer of idealization: The anus becomes, as Glover says it was for a perverse patient, "a halo . . . in the sky" (1938, p. 294; *cf.* Chasseguet-Smirgel, 1984). The increase in the aggressive drives evokes what I have been calling anal–narcissistic defensiveness. Part of this appears as an egregiously apparent flowering of reversals, with resultant simultaneous contradictions. These contradictions we all retain, and they are enhanced in regressions—but they are most dramatically apparent in the compulsive defensive form in perversions (or as concomitants of perverse impulses). In perversion, the idealizations of sexual aim, object, and impulse (frequently intermixed with the destructive degradations they are meant to negate) can result in striking, bizarre caricatures of what we expect in our ideas of "normal" romantic love. I have exemplified the contradictions and caricature of Proust's descriptions of the first encounter between the Baron and Jupien.

In life, we find a whole range of gradations of these phenomena in every individual. Freud (1937), calling normality "an ideal fiction" says: "Every normal person, in fact, is only normal on the average. His ego approximates to that of the psychotic in some part or other and to a greater or lesser extent . . . (p. 235). I will convert this last sentence to: "His *sexual* life approximates to that of the *pervert* in some part or other and to a greater or lesser extent." In other words, everyone's sexuality is a complicated dynamic mixture of the perverse and the impossible-to-define (but conceptually necessary) "normal."[8] Some idiosyncratic "perverse" sexuality is, then, present in everyone, and not only in regressive sexual foreplay; sexuality that features with varying compulsive effect the idealizations, devaluations, fascinations (see pp. 131 *et seq.*), and avoidances of the pervert, certainly in fantasy, but frequently also in (possibly attenuated) action.[9]

Idealization

Glover (1938), in a paper on idealization, makes several statements relevant to my views. He is discussing "the observation of sexual perversions occurring in certain psychotic types," and notes that some of them "make constant use of the process of idealization" (p. 291). Glover then generalizes about the pervert:

> This [idealization] is a common characteristic of the sexual pervert. However devoid of idealization of adult relations he may be, his *geese* are usually regarded by him as swans [my emphasis—for my "goose" patient

they turned out to be rats as well]. The sexual part-objects treated with this combination of sexual over-estimation and idealization vary with the individual, but my experience seems to indicate that these reactions are more common in the case of objects of anal and urethral sexuality. Next to these come those fetishistic idealizations behind which lies a good deal of sadistic interest. (p. 294)

Glover follows this with an example that also features the typical anal displacement from below to above, and illustrates Fliess's (1973) assertion that *sky* and *blue* are symbols for *arse* and *anal* (p. 89):

In a typical case the anal ring was phantasied as a kind of halo suspended in the sky. It was then contemplated, adored and idealized. The qualities attributed to it were mystical and the whole attitude of the patient was religious in type. (p. 294)

Glover connects these idealizations with anality:

The primitive idealizations have in my opinion a specially close relation to anal-sadism, a relation which renders them subject to part repression. (p. 296)

Idealization continues as a narcissistic phenomenon—a remainder of and/or a return to the self-absorbed overevaluation of early childhood, and to the uniqueness and glory of the limited, sensorily (the halo) and mythically charged contents of one's own garden of Eden. Devaluation (in its primal sense of negative idealization) would have a matching narcissistic intensity and concentration. (Both idealization and devaluation are involved in the related phenomenon of fascination which I am shortly to describe.) When these mechanisms are in full sway, paradoxically, the universe is charged with the most intense, hallucinatory colors—but *emotionally* it is the starkest black *or* white (no *or* yes, good *or* bad); no spectrum exists, no modulation is possible.

It was Freud's belief that only the fulfillment of a wish from childhood, from the concentrated narcissistic, glorious early world (the Eden that denies death and hell), can made one happy. Proust's concept of "unconscious memory," evoked by sensory stimuli, is of an experience that brings happiness by reconstituting part of the past with the hallucinatory intensity of the lost Eden of infancy, a blissful narcissistic *timelessness*. What is basic is reunion with and dissolution into the mother.

When Proust was 32 (shortly after the death of his father), he had what was perhaps his first satisfactory, or at least successful, expe-

rience of intercourse with a woman (the actress Louisa de Mornand—
the mistress of a close friend). He expressed his reaction in a letter to
her: "I feel, meanwhile, happier than a child that has just been given
its first doll" (Painter, 1965, p. 12)—hardly an expression of trium-
phant mature masculine activity; (note also the fetishistic devaluation
of the sexually vibrant woman to an inanimate doll). We cannot know
what Proust really felt; the sexual relationship with Louisa lasted for
some time, but it did not "rescue" him from his predominant homosexuality. The liaison occurred at a time when Proust was sharing the
family home along with his mother, after his father's death, and it
lasted up to the time of hers. He used the affair to some extent to cause
his mother pain—she was greatly distressed that Louisa would come to
the family home to visit Marcel in his bedroom. In Proust's conscious
or unconscious fantasy (reflected in repeated incidents in his fiction),
he was degrading his mother in a primal scene reversal—forcing her to
watch his sexual betrayal of her. But, in a characteristic need to
preserve narcissistic tranquillity, the bad—those parts of Proust's complex feelings that were sadistic, dirty, and offensive (i.e. anal), and
actively, masculinely incestuous (oedipal)—were denied and reversed,
regressively idealized, in the image of the passive and indeterminately
sexed child being given a doll, presumably by its mother.[10]

Primary idealization is conceived of here as furnishing a primal
kind of defensive activity (whose first vicissitude is reversal into primary devaluation). Early idealization and devaluation have introjection and projection as adjunct mechanisms; they are also associated
with Freud's primal repression. These primal defenses in later development (during or past the oral phase) are refracted into various
psychic defense mechanisms: denial, reversal to the opposite, secondary repression, isolation, splitting, (post-primal) projection and identification, secondary devaluation, and secondary idealization.[11]

All these defense mechanisms have a complicated and intertwined
development. Much work has already been done, but we still lack a
satisfactory general hierarchy of a "line of development" for, and
proper definitions of, defense mechanisms; what we now have is full of
lacunae and confusion and perhaps inherently so. (See Weinshel's
[1977] sophisticated discussion and review of the literature, which
shows the interrelation of, and the difficulty in sharply delineating,
the "mechanisms of defense"—especially denial, repression, and negation.)

In this book I am trying to emphasize a major nexus of defensive activity that involves anality and occurs sometime between the early period of primal repression (and primal idealization) and the establishment of the repression barrier that takes place after the oedipal period. This anal defensive cluster would include not only those familiar mechanisms typical of (that is, burgeoning during) the anal developmental period—reversal to the opposite, reaction formation, isolation, devaluation, and idealization—but also the underlying, biologically connected (by way of body ego) concept of anal or sphincter defense.

FASCINATION

Proust, in the courtyard encounter I have quoted at length between the Baron de Charlus and Jupien, portrays the erogenically related phenomenon of *fascination*, a phenomenon accompanied by and allied to both idealization and devaluation. All three involve a regression to or toward that primal perfervid (near hallucinatory) sensory intensity of the early drive-charged body-ego feeling. With fascination, there is an exigent heightening of sensations; the body parts of the self and/or of the other (Fliess's (1956) "partial subject" and "partial object"[12]) function like erogenous zones in early development—providing the equivalent of an erection (to think of the phallic investment) to a part of the body ego. Jupien's fascinating behind functions for the Baron in a way similar to what went on in the Baron's distant past, in the original "transitional" limbo of *part me/part not-me*. Fascination does begin as a transitional phenomenon, stemming from the transition between narcissism and the acquisition of the capacity to care about others. Fascination consists of a concentration on the need-fulfilling bodily parts of the object of sexual desire—on what is needed to fulfill an object-related sexual wish and/or to complete a part of the self. Fascination is accompanied by a heightened consciousness, usually centered on looking that may be simultaneous with showing. The concentration involves a narrowing or shutting off of attention directed toward anything or anyone else (including the ordinary passage of time), while awareness recedes of the world peripheral to the subject fascinated by the object or, more specifically, by a part of the object.

The need-fulfilling part-object, here Jupien's proffered behind, is simultaneously that which promises to satisfy the Baron's urgent body-need, and by way of projected identification, part of the Baron's own body-self. For example, if the Baron were to daydream about Jupien's "ass" bending over for him, the part-object "ass" in fantasy could also be felt as part-subject—as if it were the Baron's own organ. If he were to recall the courtyard scene in masturbatory fantasy, the Baron could be dealing with (and feeling with) his own "ass" while thinking of Jupien's and would be able to play (by way of transient, reversible identification) both roles in a sexual encounter. In the fantasy, the sexual part of the other person would be fascinating—that is, invested with heightened sexualized, idealized narcissistic interest.

Fascination involves a genetically based narcissistic regressive vicissitude inextricably linked to intensified body-affect, evokable at every stage past earliest development. With displacement, fascination becomes intense emotional focusing on the apparently nonsexual parts of the other—for example, on the face. Fascination as I define it might have been called by Kohut a "self-object" phenomenon, the prototype of which would be the infant's not-quite-differentiated concept of existence implied in Freud's "I am the breast/the breast is part of me" (1941, p. 151). At this level of mental functioning, awareness of body feelings comes *"vor allem,"* before everything else, in more ways than one. Past infancy, and especially after the development of the capacity for object relations, experiences of intense erogeneity of whatever kind or admixture usually involve a return to narcissistic or transitional body-ego feeling. A concomitant of this kind of regression (and part of the phenomena involved in idealization, devaluation, and fascination) is some interference with, and the possibility of a transcendence of, the ordinary adult sense of the passage of time.

The transitional concentration on part-objects that is essential to fascination makes for a repetition in later development of a narcissistically saturated step toward the acquisition of the power of "cathecting" (Trilling's "suspending the disbelief in the reality of") another person. Fascination seems to have its *experiential* start as an anal-narcissistic phenomenon (there would be oral forerunners—*e.g.*, the Isakower phenomena) probably because the child develops during the anal phase the responsible awareness that coincides with the beginnings of (and the transition to) true and full relatedness to others. Abraham marked the transition by the passing from the first to the second anal phase. Hanly (1982) points out how Abraham in his late papers achieved an integration of developmental areas in his "careful attention to the interplay of object libidinal and narcissistic factors as well as to the role of the parents" (p. 429). Hanly illustrates the integration by citing Abraham's remarks on anality and on the effects of toilet training. There is persistence into adult life—with old intensities frequently renewed in transient moments (and sometimes in longer periods) of regression—of fascination with anal *parts*, functioning, and products. Most adults continue to feel at least a residue of the child's original passionate attachment to its feces. One woman mentioned looking "lovingly" at the turds in the toilet bowl before "sadly" flushing them away. She had identified with a mother who was obsessed with her daughter's bowel movements. The patient was "sad" at the separation from a part of her self, but also at the loss of a part that represented for her (and connected her with) another person (the fecal stick meaning both *me* and *not-me*).[13]

A regression toward narcissism involving fascination is brought about not only by intense erogeneity, but can also follow severe pain or intense emotional states:

> A person who is tormented by organic pain and discomfort withdraws his libidinal cathexis back upon his own ego . . . . "concentrated is his soul," says Wilhelm Busch of the poet suffering from toothache, "in his molar's narrow hole" [Einzig in der engen Höhle/Des Backenzahnes weilt die Seele]. (Freud, 1914, p. 82)

There is a verbal bridge to anality in this quotation from *On Narcissism* (as well as an illustration of confluent anal and oral sadism). *Backe* means "cheek" and *Backenzahn* is literally "tooth of the cheeks." One might transpose Busch's saying for the anally fixated or aroused: "Concentrated is his soul/ In his backside's narrow hole." The concentration is, at least in consciousness, on a part of the self-representation; the conscious concentration on the parts of another is a normal regressive phenomenon of sexual attraction. Fascination, as I am defining it, blends self-and object-representations. It takes the form of a potential heightening of perception and sensation accompanied by a narrowing of consciousness—a kind of autohypnosis which, if reciprocated, becomes *à deux*; time is suspended and the world shrinks down, as it does for the aroused Jupien and the Baron, to a small place—like a shared anus projected onto the surround, which becomes a sexualized, narcissistic, idealized, intensely sensory, tiny universe mutually cathected with body-ego feeling. And, within this shared narcissistic compass—if all goes well, as it does here with Jupien and the Baron—the lover can say, with Yeats (1914):

> While up from my heart's root
> So great a sweetness flows
> I shake from head to foot.
> (p. 122)

(Or, in regressive terms, again to echo Glover, the perverse lover can be so moved because the anus has become the halo in the sky.)

Fascination and Masturbation: Proust

There is a passage in Proust's early work *Contre St. Beuve* (1908-1909) about his first masturbations, which anticipates (and is more sexually explicit than) one in the published novel *Remembrance of Things Past*. Proust emphasizes the *place* where he masturbated as an adolescent, a little water-closet that was on the top floor of the family home in Combray. (The water-closet was the site of the first attack on Kaspar Hauser.) The room's "anal" connotations are obvious, and these would include anal defensiveness and control. The bathroom or water-closet has a special significance, as a fantasied, if not also literal, appendage to the parental bedroom—the confluence of both rooms representing the venue of the primal scene—where the parents can be seen naked, and where one can also be seen naked. The small, lockable room in the Combray house the boy could associate with both parents; it symbolized a body cavity (cloaca; anus; vagina) and was also part of the symbolic equation *house* equals *body* (and therefore evoked body-ego feeling). For the pubescent Proust, masturbation was accompanied by a heightened focused awareness of all his senses, with a recession of consciousness of the environment peripheral to those few elements that had sexual symbolic resonance.

The *St. Beuve* passage about masturbation is linked by contiguity with material about involuntary memory—one of Proust's basic preoccupations (found in most of his major works): taste or sound or feel or smell automatically bringing about a full-dimensioned psychic recreation of the past. In his books we find the involuntary-memory theme repeated, with minor variations, in relation to incidents in which a rusk, or a madeleine dipped in tea evokes his aunt's or his uncle's *house*; or stumbling against some stepping stones in a courtyard brings back the reality of what it was like to be in Venice; or the tapping of a teaspoon calls forth a long-past railroad journey. (All the memories involve re-creating the ambient environment of the past when in contact with symbolic elements in the current surround that stand for the body, body parts, and for sexual contact.)

Just before the passage about masturbation in *Contre St. Beuve*, Proust recounts a recurring dream that recalls his childhood and expresses castration anxiety. The "castrator" in the dream is a priest (a man in skirts) who in life had tormented young Marcel because his parents had insisted that he wear curls that made him look like a girl.

> I would dream that our old priest was pulling my curls, a thing which had been the terror and tyranny of my childhood. The fall of Chronos [parricide], Prometheus's discovery of fire [defiance of the father], the birth of Christ [compliance and submission to the father], could not have more enlarged the heavens above man's heretofore bowed shoulders than did the shearing of my curls, severing me forever from that frightful dread. I must admit that other pains and other fears replaced it; but the world's axis had been shifted. In sleep, I painlessly re-entered the world of the Old Dispensation, only waking from it when, having tried in vain to elude the poor priest, dead for so many years, I felt my locks sharply tweaked *from behind*. [The castration has anal connotations.] And before falling asleep again, and remembering perfectly well that the priest was dead and my hair short, all the same I was careful to consolidate my *sheltering nest of pillow, blanket, handkerchief and wall*, before returning to that queer world where the priest was alive and I had curls. (my italics; pp. 28–29)

The dream evokes the boy's passage from the stage of development of the body-ego, in which sexual identity-confusion and bisexuality are predominant, to one marked by a clamorous, anxious awareness of the possibility of the loss of the male external genitals. Castration by the father is nearer to consciousness and predominates in the dream. The priest from the narrator's boyhood plays the inhibitory, punitive, and castrative role that "the man with whom I have always been" played for Kaspar Hauser. The consolidated "sheltering nest" of *material* would symbolize a protective maternal *enclosed space*, a womb, in which to hide from the castrating parent. It also can refer to the significant, developmentally subsequent, autonomous *place* of control: the anal sphincter surrounding, as it were, the anal space.

After this passage with its threat of punishment comes the description of the crime:

> And there are other sensations . . . [that] bring with them the poetry of youth . . . La Rochefoucauld said that only our first loves are involuntary. So is it, too, with those pleasures taken in solitude, which later on we only make use of to pass off the absence of a woman, imagining to ourselves that she is with us. But when I was twelve years old, and for the first time, going upstairs to the top floor of our house at Combray, locked myself into the water-closet with its dangling garlands of orris root, it was an unknown pleasure that I went in search of sufficient in itself and not a substitute for anything else. (pp. 29–30)

On "going upstairs to the top floor" (= erection), the boy enters the water-closet (= penetrating or being penetrated). He "locked [himself] into" (an illusion to sphincter control) "the water-closet with its dangling garlands of orris root." Orris is a violet-odored root stalk of some varieties of European irises, sold commonly as "orris root" for use in medicines and perfumes. Its "dangling garlands" would have represented a perfumed phallic symbol, ready to be ingested or inhaled. (The floral elements would also have female connotations.) The passage continues with more odors and the symbols of a witnessed penetration:

> It was an unusually spacious room for a water-closet. The door locked securely, but the window always stood open to accommodate a young lilac which having taken root in the outside wall had pushed its scented head through the aperture. (p. 30)

The primal-scene allusions are obvious here. (The section of *Contre St. Beuve* that precedes what I have quoted [and the section that follows the corresponding (later) passage in *Remembrance of Things Past* (p. 13)] concerns the young Marcel's successful attempt to get his mother to leave his father and to lie down with him in his own bed.) The quotation continues with a description of masturbation that features a narcissistic "widening" of consciousness, a regression "concentrating the soul" (*cf.* p. 133 above), with a special emphasis on the sense of sight focusing on symbolized sexual parts—all elements of fascination as I have defined it:

> So far aloft, in the attics of the house, I was completely alone, but this element of being out of doors added a delicious uneasiness to the sense of security which those sturdy bolts assured to my solitude. Then, in search of a pleasure that I did not know, I began to explore myself, and if I had been engaged in performing a surgical operation on my brain and marrow I could not have been more agitated, more terrified. [The castrating, hair-pulling priest is invoked here.] I believed at every moment that I

should die. But what of that?—*my consciousness, exalted by pleasure, knew itself to be wider and more powerful than the universe which I saw remotely through the window, a universe in whose immensity and duration my everyday thoughts were resigned to claiming no more than a gnat's share* [my italics]. Far as the forest might stretch and the clouds round themselves above it, I *felt* that my spirit extended a little further, was not quite filled by it, had still a little margin to spare. I *felt* [note the merging of perceptions, of feeling and seeing, as subject and part-object contact in fantasy] the lovely swelling hillsides that rose like breasts on either side of the river, supported, like mere insubstantial reflections, on the dominating stare of my pupils. [Seeing does dominate.] *All this world reposed on me, and I was more than it, and could not die.* (my italics; pp. 30-31)

Following this narcissistic engrandizement comes defiance of the father:

I paused to draw breath. Wishing to sit down without being incommoded by the sun which was shining full on the seat [= father confronting the boy's bottom] I quoted to it: "Take yourself off, my boy, to make room for me," [a "catchword, dating from the French Revolution," according to the translator (p. 400)]; and I drew the curtains, though the lilac bough prevented me from shutting the window [= the persistent presence of the father]. At last a shimmering jet arched forth, spurt after spurt, as when the fountain at Saint-Cloud begins to play. [The boy's ejaculation projected out onto the landscape, but magnified and idealized, with grandiose narcissistic implications which reverse his primal scene role.] . . . In that moment I felt a sort of caress surrounding me. It was the scent of lilac-blossom, which in my excitement I had grown unaware of. But a bitter smell, like the smell of sap, was mixed with it, as though I had snapped a branch. (1908-1909 p. 30)

The water-closet as the extension of the parental bed—specifically, although usually unconsciously, evoked in masturbation—is the place of potential castration and physical attack. (*Cf.* Kaspar Hauser; we do not know what Kaspar was doing in the W.C. when he was assaulted—presumably excreting rather than masturbating). Snapping the branch is symbolic of castration—is it the parent or the boy whose branch is snapped? The emphasis on lovely floral *smells* in Proust's narrative serves to disguise and idealize the destructive and dirty (including foul-odored) anal–sadistic connotations of the primal-scene fantasy.

The passage demonstrates symbolic fusion between parental genital part-object and the boy's penis (both symbolized by the lilac bough) by way of a merging of liquids (ejaculate and sap) and smells (lilac and the smell of semen). There is a reversibility in fantasy of subject and object, and therefore also of roles. The previously observed and smelled lilac bough, which had penetrated the window, was the observer of Marcel's masturbation and ejaculation. The body-ego sexual concentration on the overwhelming genital and orgastic pleasure had been accompanied by an expansion of consciousness in which self and the parts of the observable object world that symbolized the body-self had crowded out the rest of the universe: "All this world reposed on me"—"me" here comprises the fused self and object parts—"and I was more than it" (expressing enhancement of self-awareness because of the fusion with self-consciousness filling the shrunken realistic (which is subjectively felt to be an expanded narcissistic) universe—all "exalted by pleasure . . . and [I] could not die [= the timeless bliss of oral merging]."

Marcel is expressing fascination with his own body and his parents', and with parts of the environment symbolizing these—fascination exerted in the course of his genital excitement and masturbation. His concentration in unconscious fantasy is on the symbols of sexual parts of both parent (*e.g.*, lilac branch whole, and lilac branch snapped) interplaying and equated with elements symbolizing his own body parts (*e.g.*, lilac branch, again). Proust closes his description with his continuing involvement with "the gentle lilac scent." This is one of the real but defensively idealized sensory impressions that would evoke a heightened and concentrated awareness in the future (and one that could involve a sublimated fascination), enabling him, in "Proustian" involuntary memory, to recapture the past and, specifically, to relive in consciousness the fascinating, almost hallucinatory moments of his first ecstatic masturbation while evoking its unconscious sensory incestuous matrix.

SCOTOMIZATION

A concept allied to devaluation—a kind of defensive negative of fascination, as it were—has been called "scotomization" by Mahony (personal communication, 1984). Mahony describes an emotional and perceptual concentration on what superficially appears to be a peripheral detail, thereby ignoring what ought to be the central meaningful event. Scotomization, too, involves a regressive return to a sensorily heightened narcissistic world. There is a well-known example in Proust (which also alludes to a fetishistic world)—an illustration of the narcissistic selfishness of the Duke de Guermantes: the incident of the dying Swann and the red shoes. Proust fashioned it from an anecdote told by the main original of the Baron de Charlus, the poet Comte Robert de Montesquiou, about his cousin Aimery:

> Montesquiou's brother Gontran was dying, but Comte Aimery felt unable to give up his plans for the evening. He was overtaken by a tactless informant who cried "Gontran's dead!"; whereupon Comte Aimery merely pushed his wife (who was dressed as a queen-bee) up the steps, declared, in the Duc de Guermantes' very words, "People exaggerate!" and fled majestically into the ball. (Painter, 1959, p. 154)

Proust used this anecdote both rather directly, and then again with some variation in *Remembrance of Things Past*, and in both cases scotomized death by concentrating on an adjunct to, and a symbol for, a body part: the Duchess de Guermantes' shoes.

The impatient Duke (Basin) de Guermantes is hurrying his wife to go get into their costumes for a fancy-dress ball, when:

> He came into collision, outside his front door which they were grimly guarding, with the two ladies with the walking-sticks, who had not been afraid to descend at dead of night from their mountain-top to prevent a scandal. "Basin, we felt we must warn you, in case you were seen at that ball: poor Amanien has just died, an hour ago." The Duke was momentarily dismayed. He saw the famous ball collapsing in ruins for him now that these accursed mountaineers had informed him of the death of M. d'Osmond. But he quickly recovered himself and flung at his cousins a retort . . . : "He's dead! No, no they're exaggerating, they're exaggerating!" And without giving a further thought to his two relatives who, armed with their alpenstocks, prepared to make their nocturnal ascent, he fired off a string of questions at his valet:
> "Are you sure my helmet has come?" . . . "Oh, hell and damnation, everything's gone wrong this evening. Oriane [the Duchess], I forgot to ask Babal whether the *shoes with pointed toes* were for you!" (my italics; 1921, p. 751–752)

The more poignant passage (all the more because of Proust's exquisite comic observations) also involves shoes; it concerns Swann's telling his old friends about his fatal illness. (Because his doctors have warned him he might die at any time, it could be a final farewell.) Again the Duchess and the impatient Duke are going out, this time to a dinner party. When Swann tells them his news, the Duchess insists he is joking:

> "It would be a joke in charming taste," [Swann] replied ironically. "I don't know why I'm telling you this. I've never said a word to you about

my illness before. But since you asked me, and since now I may die at any moment . . . but whatever I do I mustn't make you late; you're dining out, remember," he added, because he knew that for other people their own social obligations took precedence over the death of a friend, and he put himself in their place thanks to his instinctive politeness. But that of the Duchess enabled her also to perceive in a vague way that the dinner-party to which she was going must count for less to Swann than his own death. And so, while continuing on her way towards the carriage, she let her shoulders droop, saying: "Don't worry about our dinner. It's not of any importance!" But this put the Duke in a bad humour and he exclaimed: "Come, Oriane, don't stop there chattering like that and exchanging your jeremiads with Swann; you know very well that Mme de Saint-Euverte insists on sitting down to table at eight o'clock sharp; . . . Forgive me Charles," he went on, turning to Swann, "but it's ten minutes to eight already. Oriane is always late, and it will take us more than five minutes to get to old Saint-Euverte's." [The Duchess says that the doctors must have frightened Swann "quite unnecessarily"] and, lifting her red skirt, she set her foot on the step. She was just getting into the carriage when, seeing this foot exposed, the Duke cried out in a terrifying voice: "Oriane, what have you been thinking of, you wretch? You've kept on your black shoes! With a red dress! Go upstairs quick and put on red shoes . . . "But, my dear," replied the Duchess gently, embarrassed to see that Swann . . . had heard, "seeing that we're late . . ." [The Duke responds:]

"No, no, we have plenty of time. It's only ten to; it won't take us ten minutes to get to the Parc Monceau. And after all, what does it matter? Even if we turn up at half past eight they'll wait for us, but you can't possibly go there in a red dress and black shoes." (1921, pp. 618–19)

There are object-related, perverse, castrative, oedipal, as well as narcissistic meanings for the Duke in the event of the Duchess "lifting her red skirt" and showing her foot; the emphasis on his wife's shoes (a repetitive theme in the novel) suggests a fetishist tendency in the Duke. That the shoes serve as a distraction from death (in both excerpts) can be connected with castration, and the Duke's strong reaction to disharmony of color (perhaps specifically to red and black) could have expressed castration shock as well as aesthetic outrage. For the selfish and unloving Duke, his wife is a need-filling extension of himself—he cares as little for her as a separate person as he does for his footman or for his old friend Swann.[14] His narcissism predominates; his wife's black shoes with a red dress command his furious and threatened attention as part of himself, of his body ego. The Duke's fascination with his wife's shoes (the symbol-product of intense somatosensory *condensation*, which for the Duke is capable of evoking the "experience of satisfaction" that undid the frustration of some primal body-need) serves as a focus of *displacement* for his rage at frustration. The displacement to symbol shuts out (scotomizes) his own bodily and narcissistic involvement, the needs of others, and the fear of death. For the ego in the narcissistic universe, there is no death.

Freud's concept of the early functioning of the mind was of a primary psychic system—"the first psychic agency" (1900, p. 260)—whose workings he called *primary process*. Primary process was described as functioning with free energy, seeking discharge, and "regularly avoiding unpleasure" (p. 600). Descriptively (putting aside psychic "economics"), it aims at "establishing a 'perceptual identity' [with the experience of satisfaction]" (p. 602), doing so at a hallucinatory pitch. Primary process works mainly by way of the mechanisms of *condensation* and *displacement*. (All of this was induced by Freud from his study of dreams.) Primary process, as Freud delineates it, contributes to and is imbued with the defensive modes of idealization and devaluation. Condensation concentrates intensities (as in fascination). Displacement does this, too, but by taking intensity away from somewhere else, leaving "holes" (*scotomization*). Most primary-process characteristics can be seen as relevant to idealization/devaluation (see Freud quote in note 4, Chapter 8).

ANALITY AND PERVERSION

Concentration on anality in perversion allows the individual to deny the difference between the sexes (this is one of the central themes of Chasseguet-Smirgel). The dichotomy of the partners during the anal phase of development, according to Freud, is one of active/passive rather than male/female. With the use of a finger, or the mouth, or a dildo (accompanied by a transformation in fantasy of a body part or a phallic-shaped thing into a phallus), the female can act out the role of the active partner, too—active toward another female (whose receptive organ could be vagina-as-cloaca or anus), or toward a male as passive anal partner (*cf.* Vidal's *Myra Breckenridge*). Fascination with the anus reduces the penis to that-which-can-stimulate-the-anus (*e.g.*, the fantasy of a fecal phallus). Chasseguet-Smirgel (illustrating from De Sade) also points out the devaluation (inherent in anality) that seeks to eliminate the difference between the generations. There is no incest if everything is reduced to shit. Finally, identification with the partner (universal as a transitory phenomenon in the sexual act, but more intense, long-lasting, and perhaps qualitatively different in the perversions), accompanied by the regressive devaluation of person into sexual body part ("ass," "cunt"), can undo the difference between individuals. And—this is my message—the beginnings and height of devaluative de-differentiation (covered over by idealization, the "halo in the sky") occur during the period of anal development, under the domination of anal instinctual drives and organization.

Notes to Chapter Six

1. This is the defensive quasi-certainty which conceals doubt that I mentioned earlier in the book (see "Complexity and Diagnosis," Chapter 1); here it is allied to a negation, unconsciously expressing the opposite of what is asserted as certain.

2. Freud once wrote to Fliess (1887–1902) in reference to their idea of universal bisexuality that he was accustoming himself to thinking of four people in bed when a couple were having intercourse; in relation to what goes on in the unconscious fantasies that involve the partners' parents, the number four is insufficient.

3. After the men emerge, the Baron offends Jupien by asking him about other homosexual partners:

> These questions must have ruffled Jupien, for, drawing himself up with the indignation of a courtesan who has been betrayed, he replied, "I can see you are thoroughly fickle" . . . this reproach must have had its effect on M. de Charlus, who, to counteract the bad impression his curiosity had produced . . . [whispered a proposition to Jupien which must have flattered him] . . . and, [Jupien] deciding to grant M. de Charlus the favour that he had just asked of him, after various remarks lacking in refinement such as *"What a big bum you have!"* said to the Baron with an air at once smiling, impassioned, superior and grateful: "All right, you big baby, come along!" (my italics; p. 632)

4. Vann Spruiell, who has devoted more specific attention to idealization than any other analyst, has devised more precise definitions and descriptive categories for idealization than I am supplying here. There are both resemblances and differences in our respective use of terms: We both connect primary idealization with the very early developmental period and secondary idealization with the time of the emerging ego. Spruiell's work on this topic is currently (1987) being refashioned into a book. For an excellent review of the literature on idealization, see Spruiell 1976, 1979, 1983.

5. I quoted this earlier, in relation to the incandescent sensory awareness, the ardent animation that followed Kaspar Hauser's psychological "birth."

6. Freud himself (1900, p. 565) puts this in quotation marks; he is talking mainly about the baby at the breast.

7. Compare the effect of falling in love from Schumann's *Frauenliebe und Leben*:

> *Seit ich ihn gesehen, glaub ich blind zu sein; wo ich hin nur blikke, seh' ich ihn allein* . . . . (Since I first saw him, I think myself blind; wherever I look, I see only him.) (1840, p. 84)

8. In fantasy, McDougall (1985) says, "we are all omnipotent, bisexual, eternally young, and immortal" (p. 9).

9. Compare Chasseguet-Smirgel (1984):

> I see perversions more broadly, as a dimension of the human psyche in general, a temptation in the mind common to us all. . . . My studies and my clinical experience have led me to believe that there is a "perverse core" latent within each one of us that is capable of being activated under certain circumstances. (p. 1)

10. The devaluation of the woman that I have pointed to in Proust's comparison of Louisa to a child's doll, also reduces her to a part-object (*doll = cunt*). The degradations are disguised by the concurrent idealization, in which the doll has the regressive meaning of the good gift as transitional object. (After Alma Mahler broke with Oskar Kokoschka, he made a doll image of her which he took around with him to concerts, night clubs, etc; he finally destroyed it.)

11. Glover calls the latter "primitive idealization."

12. Fascination is an idealization (with the Baron and Jupien a *mutual* idealization) of a part-object; or, one might say in terms invented by Fliess, *partial object* and *partial subject* are idealized and merge.

Fliess (1956) is referring to two people in sexual activity:

> The ego of both the sexual subject and object regresses to what I suggest calling the "partial subject" and "partial object." *Subject* and *object* in these terms mean what they always mean: each partner is to his own self the subject, to the other an object. *Partial* denotes a reduction of ego . . . ending in a condition in which the ego, topographically, is but an appendage of the genital zone, and, dynamically, the executive of its erogenic function. (p. 204)

The "reduction of ego" to "partial subject" in our daily sexual fantasy and action is a regression to the beginning of ego formation, to the narcissistic period when an "island" of body ego would form in relation to the instinctual drives as "an appendage of an [erogenous] zone" and the "executive of its erogenic function." And our sexual arousal returns us to the exigent, fervently sensual, cosmic centrality of the early body ego and its parts.

13. I have already told Dr. E. Knight's charming story of the three-year-old who joyously dubbed his three anal creations "Daddy, Mommy, and me"—a story that connects fascination with turds to narcissistic/object-related borders. In a personal communication regarding this story, Knight astutely remarked the "anal matters usually seem to include something before and something after," and it follows that both something oral and narcissistic and something oedipal and object-related are simultaneously present in the anecdote.

14. In the reductive, fetishistic way the Duke treats the Duchess, one can see an echo of Proust's own attitude toward women—I am thinking specifically of his having compared his mistress's gift to him of her body to a doll given to a little girl (see p. 130). Like the shoe for the fetishist, the doll can signify a sexual part-object; the thought of the doll shows regression toward a transitional object: a gift from the other which also can mean a part of, or an extension of the self. The doll is completely controllable and can be dressed and undressed at will, allowing for fetishistic fascination with the doll or the clothes (like the helmet or the shoes of the anecdotes just quoted, which were used to reassure the Duke in relation to his fears of castration and death). I am grateful to Shelley Orgel for pointing out this parallel to me.

7

Defense Against Murderous Impulses

MURDEROUS ANAL PRIMAL SCENE: PROUST

The emphasis throughout the Jupien/Baron de Charlus encounter described in Chapter 6 is on seeing and hearing and showing—directly and surreptitiously; it is a primal scene. There is much compulsive curiosity in Proust. Readers of his great novel will be familiar with the theme of the (now grown-up) child's forcing the parents (in a fantasy acted out by using their photographs) to "look" as their offspring engages in perverse sexual acts (*e.g.*, Mademoiselle Vinteuil). Proust, who frequented male brothels and often went just to look, gave to a brothel-keeper the furniture that had belonged to his parents. (Aunt Leonie's sofa is similarly disposed of by Marcel in the novel.) One must conclude that Proust's fantasy of making the parents look was his revenge for his exclusion from what he felt was going on in the parental bedroom of his childhood (where, as shown by the birth of his brother Robert when Marcel was almost two, the "possibility of parturition" *did* exist). The exclusion from the parents' sexual activities was part of the child's torment in the long going-to-bed scene at the beginning of *Swann's Way* (where his victory over his father by getting his mother to sleep in his bed represented, Proust felt, a parental giving in to and a weakening of his will that marked him for life). What went on in the parents' bed was regarded as sadistic and anal; murderous and exciting; dirty as well as fascinating. The dirt and destruction, with typical anal reversal, could be idealized into beauty and myth. But myth is also terrifying; and the noise of "strangling" (in the scene in which Marcel listens to the Baron and Jupien having sex in the next room) evokes the Sphinx (which literally means "strangler"). The Sphinx in the Oedipus myth is a composite creature whose members allude to what the child considers to be the bestial underparts of both parents, and whose riddle, Freud says, is the mystery of where babies come from. In fact, the words "Sphinx" and "sphincter" are both derived from an ancient Greek word meaning "to draw tight" (*O.E.D.*, X, p. 587).[1] The Sphinx, then, is a murderous, castrating sphincter! The "dark woman" who haunted Proust's deathbed dreams and hallucinations symbolized more than death for him. Painter (1965) quotes Proust's dying utterances:

> "She's very big, very ugly . . . very dark! She's all in black . . . she frightens me . . . No one must touch her! She's merciless, she's getting more horrible every moment." [And then later, his last word]: "Mother!" (pp. 361–362).

The last word is equivocal. Is "Mother" the dark, black (*cf.* Kaspar Hauser) woman; and, if so, is she not the bad, "horrible" mother, and (primal scene meaning) the mother in the dark? Or is she the good mother who appears to protect her child from all that is dark and bad (come perhaps to allay his fears by sleeping with him again as when he was a child)? Or both? Probably both.

Surely the dark woman is the Oedipal Sphinx, "merciless" enough to kill and eat her children. In his perverse practices, Proust sometimes expressed simultaneously his identification with this figure, its reversal (with his taking the role as child-victim), and his continuation as the child-observer in the murderous anal–sadistic primal scene. He would hire men to bring him rats (as we have seen, archetypical anal creatures) in a trap (= enclosed space) and watch them beat the rats with sticks or pierce them with a woman's hatpin (Painter, 1965, p. 269).[2] (The hatpin can be equated with the unmentioned sting of the bumble-bee that features so prominently as metaphor in the anal homosexual primal scene quoted on pages 120–122.)

Murder and Anal Defensiveness

There is a repetition of a sadomasochistic anal primal scene involving the Baron, Jupien, and the narrator toward the end of *Remembrance of Things Past*. This time the implication of murder becomes more overt. The greyness of wartime Paris (during World War I) is turning toward black with the approach of night; lights are dimmed behind shutters; shops and bars are closed; there are few taxis and not many people on the streets. "One felt that poverty, dereliction, fear inhabited the whole quarter" (1927, p. 838). The dirty deserted bourgeois district is darkened in reaction to the threat of German bombing—destructive anality reigns in the outside world. The narrator, seeing ahead of him someone he thinks is a close friend, follows him into a hotel and discovers another scene out of an oriental city, from "the old Orient of those *Thousand and One Nights* which I had been so fond of . . . " (1927, p. 837). The hotel turns out to be a male brothel. Hearing talk of beating and chains, Marcel orders a drink and hires a room:

> . . . my curiosity was so great, I . . . turned round and went up . . . to the top of the building [*cf.* the site of his first masturbation]. Suddenly from a room situated by itself at the end of a corridor [*dead end* = *anus*, Fliess, 1973, pp. 86-87], I thought I heard stifled groans. I . . . put my ear to the door. "I beseech you, mercy, have pity, untie me, don't beat me so hard," said a voice. "I kiss your feet, I abase myself, I promise not to offend again. Have pity on me." "No, you filthy brute," replied another voice, "and if you yell and drag yourself about on your knees like that, you'll be tied to the bed, no mercy for you," and I heard the noise of the crack of a whip, which I guessed to be reinforced with nails [= hatpins?], for it was followed by cries of pain. At this moment I noticed that there was a small oval window opening from the room onto the corridor[3] . . . stealthily in the darkness I crept as far as this window and there in the room, chained to a bed like Prometheus to his rock, receiving the blows that Maurice rained upon him with a whip which was in fact studded with nails, I saw, with blood already flowing from him and covered with bruises which proved that the chastisement was not taking place for the first time—I saw before me M. de Charlus. (1927, p. 843)

Jupien, who turns out to be the manager of the brothel, then comes in through another door and the Baron asks him to send Maurice out of the room. The Baron then complains:

> "I did not want to speak in front of that boy, who is very nice and does his best. But I don't find him sufficiently brutal. He has a charming face, but when he calls me a filthy brute he might be just repeating a lesson." "I assure you, nobody has said a word to him," replied Jupien, without perceiving how improbable this statement was. "And besides, he was involved in the *murder* of a concierge in La Villetee." "Ah! that is extremely interesting," said the Baron with a smile. (1927, p. 845) [The narrator continues:] "[Jupien] felt that it was not quite sufficient to introduce M. de Charlus to a young milkman. He would murmur to him with a wink: "He's a milkman but he's also one of the most dangerous

> thugs in Belleveile" (and it was with a superbly salacious note in his voice
> that Jupien uttered the word "thug") . . . "he was in [jail] for assaulting"
> (the same salacious note in his voice) "and practically *murdering* people
> in the street, and he's been in a punishment battalion in Africa. He *killed*
> his sergeant." (my italics; 1927, p. 845.)

Marcel is now the observer of a potentially murderous primal scene.
The narrator notices that Maurice and some other young men who had
been talking in the hotel lobby about the "man in chains" resemble
Morel—the handsome, narcissistic violinist who has been the love of
the Baron's life—who has disappointed and betrayed (and thereby,
along "Proustian" principles, captivated and captured) the Baron.
After Charlus's death, Marcel finds a letter that convinces him the
Baron had really intended to kill Morel. This explains to him Morel's
terror when Marcel urges him to go see the old and sick Charlus. Morel
refuses: "No . . . It is—but never say this to anybody, I am mad to tell
you—it is, it is . . . from fear! He began to tremble in every limb. I
confessed that I did not understand him" (1927, p. 832). The letter
makes Marcel believe that Morel is right to be afraid; the Baron could
have killed. One infers that the Baron might require the anal beating
by "murderers" to keep his own murderous impulses in check.

Murder is being played with in the brothel, dramatically enacted
in the sadomasochistic perverse practices, and portrayed in the fictional stories the men tell one another about criminality. The young
"murderers" who resemble Morel play the parental role and punish
the bad "child" crawling on his hands and knees. Maurice, the milk-
man-"murderer"—a man who gives milk and yet can kill—is a bisexual creature: like the Sphinx, a phallic woman or a man with breasts.
After his orgy, the Baron painfully goes down the stairs to the lobby
and jokes with and is charming to the young men who pretend to be
the thugs and killers. It turns out that *he* owns the hotel/brothel; *he*
has set Jupien up in the business. He is ultimately in control, even
while acting out the complete loss of control. The degrading and
being degraded, the murdering and being murdered, are not experienced directly as impulses: they are essentially denied as they are
compulsively dramatized. It is a triumph of anal compromise and
ambivalence. The humdrum and the stereotyped (the ordinary young
men) can coexist with the bizarre and the dangerous. The precarious is
simultaneous with the controlled, as pain is with pleasure. The servant plays the master; the old man, the naughty child—roles are
instantly reversible, adding to the confusion about what is really

taking place. What can be more banal and benign than the milkman, than the mother giving milk. But they can kill and can be killed. The little anal perverse world, controlled by the Baron, is the dramatic attenuated microcosmic counterpart of the deadly destructive and vulnerable world that threatens to transform the drab banality of wartime Paris. In the curbed theatrical distortion, sex and murder can be safely confluent.

One sees in Proust the attempt to idealize and romanticize the anal control and the anal–sadistic perversions; the Baron and the narrator can view what goes on in the brothel in terms of medieval romance. But Proust presents this view alongside a full and a knowing exposition of the ugliness and dangers of oral and anal aggression. He does this by describing vertical psychological splits (without, of course, using our awkward technical terms):

> And if there is something of aberration or perversion in all our loves, perversions in the narrower sense of the word are like loves in which the germ of disease has spread victoriously to every part. Even in the maddest of them love may still be recognized. If M. de Charlus insisted that his hands and feet should be bound with chains of proven strength [or] other ferocious instruments . . .—at the bottom of all this there persisted in M. de Charlus the dream of virility, to be attested if need be by acts of brutality, and all that inner radiance, invisible to us but projecting in this manner a little reflected light, with which his mediaeval imagination adorned crosses of justice and feudal tortures. . . . In short his desire to be bound in chains and beaten, with all its ugliness betrayed a dream as poetical as, in other men, the longing to go to Venice or to keep ballet-dancers. (1927, pp. 870–871)

And in relation to splits, Proust says about the male prositutes:

> Clearly it was a gross fault in their education . . . combined with a propensity for making money . . . which led these ordinary young men to do, quite innocently one may almost say and for a very moderate reward, things which caused them no pleasure and which must in the beginning have inspired in them a lively disgust. On this evidence one might have supposed them to be fundamentally bad, but not only were they in the war splendid soldiers, men of incomparable courage, in civil life too they had often been kind-hearted and sometimes wholly admirable people. They had long ceased to speculate upon the morality or immorality of the life they led, because it was the life that was led by everybody round them. So it is that, when we study certain periods of ancient history, we are astonished to see men and women individually good participate without scruple in mass assassinations or human sacrifices which probably seemed to them natural things. And our own age no doubt,[4] when history

is read two thousand years hence, will seem to an equal degree to have bathed men of pure and tender conscience in a vital element which will strike the future reader as monstrously pernicious, but to which at the time these men adapted themselves without difficulty. (1927, pp. 867–868)

A PARALLEL CLINICAL ILLUSTRATION

A homosexual man in his middle thirties said, when he was first in analysis and had become aware of insistent sexual wishes toward me as the analyst: "I want you to fuck me, but if you even touched me, I'd kill you." This was so full of feeling that he writhed on the couch as he said it. Paradoxically, he was then often being fucked anally, which he frequently found very pleasurable—fucked usually by anonymous partners, but also occasionally by men who were more meaningful. It was very difficult for him to be the active penetrator in anal intercourse, especially with men he knew, even though some of them wanted it.

I understood that the way he expressed his sexual wish toward me showed that I evoked too much emotion in him—an overstimulated body-feeling was elicited in the transference. The transference was from a parent, and there was a concomitant emotional "too-much-ness." The overwhelming feeling came from preoedipal and oedipal conflicts that endangered the parent as well as himself. He was also risking the debasement and loss of the mental representations of his beloved and idealized parents with the wish and the need to degrade them (and himself) that is part of the destructiveness involved in anal fucking (see Chasseguet-Smirgel, 1984).

I soon learned that the patient was expressing a range of body-feeling, which could be classified (at risk of oversimplication) according to the libidinal anal phases of Abraham. There was a level of anal sadism involving fantasies of anal and penile contact in which being penetrated and penetrating meant being overwhelmed and destroyed or being overwhelming and killing. The patient jokingly referred to anal intercourse as "anal murder." With murderous intensity, this man would bring in associations of the rat (*cf.* Proust—associations that showed that imago's links to oral sadism and anality [see Shengold, 1967, 1971]). The patient was wont to say (at first with a bravado that showed how far he was from feeling it fully and responsibly): "If you can't kill, you can't fuck!" In his everyday life and in his sexual encounters, the patient was rather gentle and, if anything, overconcerned about causing pain (as was the Baron de Charlus). Like the male prostitutes described by Proust, the patient split off and essentially denied his sadistic involvement; occasional fantasies of cruel behavior and sadistic verbal play were as far as he would go.

After a summer vacation, I had installed a newly soundproofed, thickened, metal-rimmed door to my office. After a few sessions, the patient began an hour by commenting on the door:

> My thought is—the door is like that of a padded cell. It makes this room a padded cell [= enclosed space = anus]. Is that hostile? Or dangerous? Am I frightening? Or frightened? I have a strange feeling now—as if I want something in my belly. [The patient was experiencing body-feelings, and seemed confused about subject and object in the "padded cell"— was he in danger, or dangerous?] I have a kind of confession. While you were away, I had sex with a married man, a friend of Y's [his lover]. The man came over to see Y, but he was away, too. The man was very nice, very affectionate. He was willing to do whatever pleased me. He wasn't doing it for money, not like a prostitute, but I knew he expected I would do something for him, give him something. In the sex, he really treated me like a woman: kissed me, fondled my breasts; I sucked him. He put a finger up my ass; he said it was like what he does with his wife. But that first time he couldn't fuck me. He tried, but he couldn't. It left me with a sense of promise. I wanted to see him again. It gave me another strange feeling in my belly. I wanted something anal—to fill him up—I mean to be filled up by him. [Here, too, with the slip, he was confused and substituting active for passive impulse.]

Deserted by his analyst and by his lover, my patient appeared to have enacted a negative oedipal fantasy of being the "wife" to the "married man." What had been revealed in the prior analytic work was the insistent fantasy and finally the memory of having been repeatedly exposed to the sight of his mother's genitals when he was a child. These shocking views supplied, I conjectured, the dangerous open door and padded cell, which attracted, confused, and frightened him.

> I did see the married man again. The second time he fucked me. But it wasn't any good. This seems like a strange thing to say, but there was something "anal" about it. I know that it was literally anal, that's not what I mean. I mean *anal* as wrong, bad, dirty, something hurtful. I don't feel like that when Y does it to me. This guy was married, and a father. You probably are, too. I said this is a padded cell. Maybe you are my father. My father was a nice man. So was this married man. But, you know, he did have a knife strapped to his leg. He said it was to protect himself when he rode on the subway. He did take it off before we had sex.

It makes me think of the metal rim on that door. Padded cell—somebody could go crazy. It is as if the fucking could destroy me, could make me into nothing.

I had pointed out his slip of the tongue when he made it, and here I referred back to it, saying: "Then your having said 'filling him' when you meant to say 'being filled by him' would also make you the potential destroyer." He responded: "Yes, there is danger to both of us in the padded cell." The patient seemed to have been at least aware of the dangers of the anal-sadistic impulses as they focused on the analyst in transference from his father. Here is part of his next session:

That door—it really is like a padded cell in here. I still have this strange[5] desire to be fucked anally. When I am being fucked I am not sure I really like it; I feel anxious to have it over with. And yet I have the fantasy of being fucked forever, as a continual pleasure. It doesn't work out that way. I get impatient for the man to come, to get it over with. There is also the fear of being fucked to death—that can be a wish, but then it's Love-Death, like *Tristan and Isolde* (*cf.* anecdote about W. H. Auden, Chapter 2, in section entitled "Vertical Splitting: A Literary Example")—*ewig*, forever, and then it doesn't feel like fear. Another contradiction, I have the feeling of wanting to be filled up anally; but when my anus is filled it gives me a sense of "voidness," of vacuum, of nothingness. Fucking that is really pleasurable is somehow also connected with this terrible fucking that is not. It's like anal rape, a loss of control, a crushing—like a rat in a trap. [I responded: "That would go along with this room being a padded cell."] Yes, there is danger in my telling you this, in your knowing what I want, what my body wants. Padded cell . . . you'll kill me and I'll kill you. That man's knife could have killed me. I didn't tell you that during those few days that I had the affair with that married man, I had diarrhea several times. There is loss of control in the fucking, like diarrhea. I think of Y going off to school. I was always sad to be going to school in September. I guess I missed my mother. That bitch! That is really ironic. Maybe I feel like a mother to Y, as he is going off to school. I actually cried when he went off. I know that it is good for him to go and the crying really wasn't about him. I felt a longing for my own past. It is really about my mother. Sometimes I even want to get rid of Y. I would be glad for him to go. And yet I miss him. I want the fucking to be loving. But there is something bad, crushing, destructive. My brother still cannot stand to be touched by my mother.

I felt that the patient was threatened by the sadness at the separation from me and from his lover, each of whom could represent his "good" mother. He was frightened by the rage at her expected transformation into the seductive, exhibitionistic, overstimulating "bad" parent with the knife—the phallic destructive mother (the Sphinx of the Oedipus legend) with whom "fucking means murder." This role had also been thrust onto his father, the married man who simultaneously, in his wishes, served as a refuge from mother (his father had notably failed him here) and a reassurance against the castrating and castrated female genitals.

> [A pause followed.] Here's something else that is anal. I always mash my food together, whatever is on the plate—string beans, potatoes, meat, bread—all mushed up and chopped together. It means being undifferentiated and crushed; it means not being defined, losing my identity. Bread crumbles and becomes fluid. [pause] It's like a pile of shit. It's also like a vagina; that's how I see a vagina, a place that will crush me, a mouth that takes everything in. But mushing everything together also makes the vagina mushy. I don't see it defined, with the hair. Defined—as the potato would be if standing alone. [Here "defined" has a phallic meaning: the "defined" potato can "stand."] And if I mix different things into the mush, maybe the woman could have cock and balls, too. *I* could be a woman as well as a man. The married man treated me like a woman. I liked it and I hated it. [pause] I feel so angry.

In this book I am concentrating on some anal aspects of male homosexuality. Here the patient brings in correlated conflicts about phallic women, the oedipus complex, and perhaps, above all, the castration complex—conflicts made more acute by being relived in relation to his analyst. He needs the sphincter defensiveness and the anal organization to help contain his anxiety and his rage, and to control the dangers related to those overwhelming affects—dangers from both the preoedipal and the oedipal periods that make the patient conflate sexual intercourse and murder in fantasies of anal rape.

"BURSTING OPEN" THE DOOR TO THE "PADDED CELL": ANAL RAPE AND SPHINCTER DEFENSIVENESS

I am conflating two metaphors—one used by the male analysand just quoted, who is a practicing homosexual, and one used by the heterosexual male analysand quoted at the beginning of Chapter 6. The resultant phrase, "bursting open the door to the padded cell," seems to me to point to the core of the danger of loss of *anal defensiveness*—the loss of mastery of the anal sphincter, the use of whose psychological counterpart is evoked when the body ego is threatened. *Sphincter defensiveness* is perhaps a better term, because it includes the use of the urethral sphincter [as in "the bread becomes fluid" in the food-mushing ritual just described] and could be understood to complement vis-à-vis the ego the sphincter morality that Ferenczi posits for the superego. I believe that sphincter defensiveness is a major component of what must be a complicated defensive development of the preoedipal period, and that it becomes part of what is transformed into the repression barrier. We think of the latter as formed as an outcome of the oedipus complex. But the barrier does not fall suddenly, like a wet blanket. And its early prototypes, such as sphincter defensiveness, continue to function (as Freud says of the prototype of the superego) "beside and beneath" the later processes. Child analysts and observers have much to discover about the earlier development of the massive repression that initiates the latency period.

Mastery of the anal sphincter makes the frontier between the narcissistic, predominantly destructive first anal stage and the object-related, predominantly retentive second anal stage. (Abraham makes this the genetic transition point between the narcissistic and the transference neuroses.) Sphincter control is correlated with emotional control—control of the "archaic" affects so full of cannibalism and murder. Sphincter control gives the possibility of containment, of closure. (These have their own dangers—the dangers of what can go on in the "padded cell," the dangers of inspissated destructiveness.) Closure is needed for the attainment of boundaries for the body ego and the ego toward subsequent structure-building; containment is needed for the mastery of overstimulation. A "closed" or "closeable" body-ego psychic representation is a basic requirement for a stable self-representation (see Eisnitz, 1980). It follows that to break or to "burst open" this physio-psychic restraint, this closeable "door" (symbolized and evoked by the anal sphincter) threatens to undo the control of primitive destructive affect, to obliterate the feeling of identity, to evoke the primal terror of psychic disintegration. These are the unconscious dangers associated with anal rape, with violation and destruction of the anal sphincter and its controlling powers. The child once felt, and the adult can again become aware of, what I will paraphrase: "With my powerful anal–emotional sphincter I can shut off all feeling and emotions and shut out the rest of the world." With this anal-narcissistic defensive power in mind, one can understand the Rat Man's terror of the rat and the rat torture (Freud, 1909) and the terror of other "Rat people" (which would include several patients cited in this book, also see Shengold 1967, 1971, 1985a): the terror centers on the rat's ability, in order to penetrate, to bite through (and eliminate the shutting power of) the anal sphincter. The fantasy of rape by the rat imago (cannibalistic anal rape) evokes the expectation of destruction of the means to control cannibalistic destruction itself. The psychic reverberations of anal rape include abolition of the power of the sphincter to control, and the regressive transformation of the anus into the cloaca that can no longer contain. The murderous sexual excitement that motivates rape brings out a regressive de-differentiation of the object: to part-object as vagina, vagina to anus, anus to cloaca—with the ultimate aim being ego and body-ego dissolution. In this sense, our most common curses—"Fuck you!" "Up yours!" "Go fuck yourself!"— are expressions of predominant destructive hostility denoting anal fucking and anal rape. (This is stating that psychologically there is a sense in which all rape is anal rape.) As I have tried to show in my clinical material, one must be able to contain and to come to terms with the desire to kill (and to be killed) in order to feel relatively secure with the desire to fuck (and to be fucked). I will illustrate this with two statements by one of the patients described earlier. The first sets out what must be accepted somewhere in the mind: "fucking means murder." The partial acceptance of what was at first a striking intellectual *mot* came late in the analysis, after a "working through" of what anal fucking and rape implied for him: "I have to be able to say 'Fuck you!' in order to be able to fuck! No! I have to be able to feel 'Fuck you' in order to be able to fuck!" (*cf.* the questions Stoller [1979] raises about the inherent involvement of destructive aggression in perverse and in normal sexual functioning). The patient's later statement was made when he could *feel* that "fucking means murder."

For the containment and control of the murderous, cannibalistic affect that marks the beginnings of our instinctual nature, it is necessary that a part of that instinctual nature itself become directed toward the control of instinct—a control that makes for survival and for the attainment of "civilization and its discontents." The price that some have to pay, and that all have to pay in some part, for the defensive burgeoning of, and fixation on anality is the loss or diminishment of openness, of freedom, of spontaneity, of animal spirits, of creativity. But Freud has taught us that to be human is to be able to compromise, and the variety and complexity of our compromises make it possible for most of us to transcend, if only partially, the dangers of emotional deadness and caricature involved in narcissistic anal defensiveness, while retaining elements of the early psychic organization necessary for the structuring of our minds and for the containment of our primal animal nature.

Notes to Chapter Seven

1. I am indebted to Mark Kanzer for pointing this out to me.

2. Painter connects this sadistic rat ritual with Proust's impulses toward his dead parents in a passage from the novel in which the narrator speaks of nightmares:

> with their fantastic albums, in which our parents who are dead have met with a serious accident, that does not preclude a speedy recovery. Meanwhile we keep them in a little rat-cage, where they are smaller than white mice, covered with big red-spots in each of which a feather is stuck [the hatpins?], and address us with Ciceronean speeches. (1965, p. 269)

3. Proust repeatedly uses the device of the narrator (Marcel) spying and eavesdropping on sexual activities; most frequently (as here) he is observing the Baron de Charlus. The "Peeping Tom" contrivances are invariably clumsily presented and unconvincing—the readily available "oval windows" and empty adjoining rooms with thin partitions strike a false note which, I think, gives away the writer's passionate involvement (fascination) with primal-scene fantasies. Proust himself points out an analogous jarring verbal signpost—an awkward or "portentous" (1927, p. 851) phrase that

> unconsciously draws attention to what we wish to hide, that features language so unlike the language we habitually speak, in which emotion deflects what we had intended to say and causes to emerge in its place an entirely different phrase, issued from an unknown lake wherein dwell these expressions alien to our thoughts which by virtue of that very fact reveal them. (p. 851)

The uncharacteristic lack of verisimilitude of the recurrent episodes of peering through windows and transoms and listening through walls and doors suggests to me that Proust was not responsibly aware of the depth of the "unknown lake" in which were submerged his voyeuristic and sadomasochistic impulses of such perverse intensity. Indeed, there are elements in this specific passage—"[climbing up] to the top of the building"; "window opening from the room"—that duplicate the description I have quoted of the narrator's first masturbation (from *Contre St. Beuve*, but repeated in *Remembrance of Things Past*); a description so full of voyeuristic and primal-scene qualities of perfervid fascination. These two scenes, from the first and the last volumes of Proust's many-volumed novel, can be merged to suggest the continuity of the author's preconscious life of sadomasochistic sexual fantasy.

4. More recently, Hannah Arendt would apply the phrase "the banality of evil" to Nazi motivation.

5. Note how often the patient uses the word "strange." Proust in his description of the meeting of Jupien and the Baron repeatedly uses this and similar or related words ("occult," "rare," "grotesque," "oriental," etc.). Both the English "strange" and the French *étrange* are derived from the Latin *extraneus*, meaning external, foreign. The "bad," the "anal," the "queer" is attributed to the other—the foreigner on whom these qualities are projected. Thus, in France, homosexuality is "the English vice"; in England, "the French." Here again, this disowning of impulse is in large part an attempt to distance awareness of wanting to foul, soil, debase, and destroy the idealized image of the parents—that is, to avoid *incestuous* destructiveness.

8

Coda: Final Words on Defense, Integration, Murder, and Soul Murder

The session to follow came late in the analysis. It took place (again!) on the day after I had announced the dates of my long summer vacation. In that next session, the patient, uncharacteristically, had come half an hour late. He apologized. He seemed most upset, almost trembling. Then he spoke of being angry when his wife kept him waiting. The lateness was not his doing, he said. His "stupid" boss had manipulated him into having to stay at work. The boss had acted in a lordly fashion that had made him feel humiliated and full of rage. (Once more, he seemed to be almost shaking, now apparently from anger):

> And I bring all that hate to my session. . . . Why do I feel *so much*? And what does it have to do with money? [Money was a current, hate-provoking topic in the analysis.] And why today? [With a series of questions like this, studded with *whys* and *whats*, I think of the child confronted with the Sphinx and its riddle—where do babies come from?] Lateness and money seem to go together. I feel a kind of stubborn spite about not paying you a bigger fee. I probably can afford to. Here I've just spent money buying myself a new car—a beautiful machine. That machine means so much to me. And I feel you will take it away from me. When I feel this way, life is really terrible.

I replied: "You frequently need to become a machine yourself to turn off too much terrible feeling." Then the patient said, after a pause, "Well, I really could listen to you then." (Frequently, especially if I spoke at any length, he would just turn me off, as if *I* were a machine under his control.)

During this session the patient brought up a childhood fantasy that his fierce and forceful father would run him down with his powerful motor car. He also recalled that just before he was five, there was talk of the parents splitting up. His mother had told him that she was about to leave home and get a divorce and that he would be left with his father. His rejoinder (delivered in a machine-like voice that he reproduced while telling the story) was, "Well then, give me the dessert you put in the freezer for me." (He had to become the freezer himself to stifle the clamorous intensity of the need for his mother's care [= the dessert]; the rage at the frustration of his need; and the terror of the loss of his mother.)

The next day the patient said that he had felt "terrible" during and after the previous session, realizing that he had *really* wanted to keep me waiting. He reacted to this as if it were a criminal impulse:

> I really wanted to waste your time. And the session was a wasted session. That doesn't sound bad enough. I wanted to *waste you*.[1] I had the feeling that I just wanted to take time away from you—precious time that could never be replaced [*cf*. Kaspar Hauser]. You were there just waiting for me. [He had projected onto me the passionate impatience of the child waiting for the godlike parent.] I felt as if I had stolen the time from you, as if it were stealing money, only worse—as if I had committed a great crime. I had the fantasy of your being on your deathbed, with just a few minutes to say good-bye to your wife and children. And that precious time is the time I wanted to steal from you. God, why don't you kill me? And yesterday I really hated you and felt that I could kill you. I really felt it. Why don't you just destroy me?

The patient had "really" and responsibly felt, perhaps for the first time, the murderous intensity of words he had mouthed before, and (most important!) he felt them *aimed at me*. I was another human being for him—he had suspended the disbelief in my separate existence and he was near tears: "I have said before that I wanted to kill you and that I hated you, but yesterday it was really *you*; I felt it as *you*!" I replied: "It sounds as if the session was far from wasted." And he said, "True. I did learn something—but the hatred is so terrible."

I told him that one way to understand what had happened was to see that there had been a reversal. I had announced my taking time away from him when I mentioned my vacation. (This had, of course, reactivated his mother's threat to go away.) He had responded by feeling that he was stealing the control over time from me, and he had put onto me the intense feelings of the small child longing for the parent who was gong away. The frustration of his longing for love had brought on rage—murderous rage. He rejoined:

> Again—I heard you. You are right. But still I feel you must be afraid of my wish to kill you—that's why you bring in longing and love.

> [I replied:] That could be, but I am not aware of it. I think that what you need to get away from, now and since you were a child, is feeling *both* the killing hatred *and* the longing for love from your parents and now from me. If you care, then it is terrible to want to destroy the one you care about.

> [Patient:] Yes! Yes! [pause] And then I freeze my feelings and become a machine. I do feel grateful. Today I can feel both the love and the hate for you. I feel like crying in gratitude—and that makes me feel that it is glorious to be alive; and yet, I could kill you and feel you must want to kill me. I really did want to kill you. I've said that many times, but it's only now that I can also care about you, that I feel I really mean it—that it's *you* that I hate. These feelings, this mixture, is so awful and yet so wonderful—I feel like weeping for myself. I feel like weeping for all mankind.

The patient learned that to be human is to feel love-and-hate. This epiphany-like session was followed by a long period of "working through": repeating, retreating from, and finally consolidating and "owning" the new combination (or recombination) of feelings.

Freud pictured the beginning of mental life as the "yes" of hallucinatory wish-fulfilment brought on by the "no" of environmental frustration of bodily needs (*e.g.*, the unavailable breast). The initial hallucinatory fervidness of psychic functioning leaves its mark in the regressive propensity for fascination that in later life continues to center around bodily and erogenic needs. We postulate (perforce, since memory is of no use in establishing the beginning of the experiential in infancy) that all of the "yes" involved in the hallucinated experience of satisfaction (pleasure) is "good" (this "good" is proto-"inside" and proto-"me"); and that all of the "no" of environmental frustration (and potential unpleasure) is "bad" (this—when registrable later on—would be proto-"outside" and proto-"not-me"). In the course of development, the good and the bad must be integrated as *good-and-bad* in order to deal with the true nature of inner (psychic) and outer reality. With regression toward the time of body-ego dominance and the sway of archaic affect, there follows a defensive partial reestablishment of the narcissistic world, which, although realistically shrunken, can be felt as grandiose and expansive. Dangerous emotional life is transformed and becomes surrounded, as it were, by a "halo in the sky"—a celestially intense sensory and sensual aura that develops from the primal hallucinated image (presumably of the breast) that once promised bliss and actually provided a transient satisfaction of bodily needs:

> But trailing clouds of glory do we come
> From God [the primal parent—forgive me for
> marring the poetry], who is our home:
> Heaven lies about us in our infancy!
>   (Wordsworth, 1803, p. 403)

The glorious heaven can, in reaction to inevitable frustrations and due to our innate destructiveness, quickly be changed into nightmarish hell. This vulnerability of narcissism (the sudden shift from ecstatic gratification to mortification) makes for a defensive need for rapid alternations of idealizations and devaluations, which can then cancel each other out; this threatens to eradicate all affects, meanings, and values.

The primal near-hallucinatory sensory intensities are, of course, peripheral aspects of the prevalent primal or archaic affects of the child's earliest time. Primal affects can be good as well as bad. Both extremes can be glimpsed as they make a transient appearance in later life. "How terrible/glorious it is to be alive," my last-cited patient said in the session in which he felt the bad, the good, and the bad-and-good. But aside from moments of great emotional and sensual intensity, the adult lives in a different world:

> It is not now as it hath been of yore;—
>   Turn wheresoe'er I may,
>   By night or day,
> The things which I have seen I now can see no more.
>   The rainbow comes and goes,
>   And lovely is the rose . . .
>   The sunshine is a glorious birth;
>   But yet I know, where'er I go,
>   That there hath pass'd away a glory from the earth
>   (Wordsworth, 1803, p. 403)[2]

The anal phase comes at a transitional point in development between a narcissistic world and one full of others, of "objects" (as we lamely put it in our jargon). At that time, therefore, the child must master the taming of affects in relation both to the mental representations of his own self (featuring his own body and its parts) and to the mental representations of his parents and the rest of the external world. This taming is made more difficult due to the access of the aggressive drive that we postulate to occur (and observe the signs of) during this time of sphincteric and skeletal muscular activity—an activity that inevitably and properly arouses parental intervention (frustrational as well as enhancing). There results the formation of a system of anal–narcissistic defenses featuring partly new and partly old (regressive) mechanisms. The operation of the entire system is modelled on the prototype of bodily mastery of the sphincters. Sphincter defensiveness develops in conjunction with two other great ego achievements: control over locomotion, and the acquisition of the power of effective thinking (which provides an opportunity to master and control through an active displacement onto mental representations).[3]

I believe that the defensive systems set up in the course of psychic maturation (and especially during the anal phase) can be viewed as individually variegated ways of employing an array of "mechanisms of defense" that effects alternations of idealization and devaluation. (Idealization and devaluation I see as defensive styles that operate in conjunction with introjection and projection.) The defensive systems have a continuing development and they can of course regress, in whole or in part, in the direction of the primal narcissistic world. Alongside their dynamic shifting and blending, idealization and devaluation combinations occur accompanied by splits in the ego, so that psychic "compartments" of idealization can exist alongside "compartments" of devaluation.

The "blending" alternations of idealization and devaluation achieved during the anal phase can cancel each other out, providing a kind of defensive spectrum ranging from the capacity for emotional modulation (establishing a gamut of *good-and-bad*) to two extremes of dehumanization—either in the form of reduction of everything to meaningless, sterile emotional hash (or "shit"), or (with defensive collapse) the breakthrough of terrifying archaic (cannibalistic, murderous) affect with the danger of the destruction of all psychic structure: the death of the self and the object world. To survive our infancy we need in some measure the power of emotional modulation—of establishing and reestablishing the *good-and-bad*. I am describing anal defensiveness so that it might be seen as a part contributed by the body ego to the mysterious but vital achievement of what Nunberg called the *synthetic* and Hartmann and his collaborators called the *integrative* functions of the psychic ego.

This achievement—to some measure made possible by what Freud calls our "life instinct," a metaphor for *healthy* animality—means partial triumph over, and transformation of, the murderous, narcissistic side of our animal nature. Attaining optimal transcendence is more difficult if nature deprives an individual child of necessary constitutional givens; or if Fate intervenes with loss of parents, environmental catastrophe, or with parental crime and neglect (soul murder).

We work as psychoanalysts to enable our patients to achieve integration, which is consummated if the patient (in the course of the repetition of the past in relation to the analyst) can acquire insight, and can bring into responsible consciousness and connect with emotional authenticity the past and the present; the bad and the good; the body and the soul; the anus and the halo in the sky. For those who need it and can bear it, psychoanalysis is our halting best (*i.e.*, good-and-bad) preparation for death-acknowledging, life-affirming psychosynthesis.[4]

I view the evolving functional panoply I call anal–narcissistic defense as having its beginnings in the body-ego system. Metaphorically, according to its somatic model, anal–narcissistic defense operates as a kind of sphincteric door—a door that must become able to close in order to control and to permit toleration of the unpleasure that results from the inevitable frustration of instinctual needs as well as from somatic pain. The power of controlling closure allows for the modulation of the powerful emotional and sensory intensities of our infancy. Shadows of these original intensities continue to develop beside and beneath modulating developmental economic transformations in the course of intrapsychic conflict. The sphincteric "door" can and must be able to open; that it is definitely closeable excludes us from the Eden of hallucinatory bliss derived from experiences of satisfaction at the breast (having it and being part of it), but compensatorily enables us to withstand the assault of the overstimulation of our senses that comes from within the body and from the world external to it. A range of compromise is permitted that grants us a range of humanity so that we can live, in varying degrees, with the good-and-bad, the pleasurable-and-painful, the anus–and–the halo in the sky.

Notes to Chapter Eight

1. Compare the defeated, abdicated, imprisoned Richard II (Act V, scene V) in his last minutes of life:

"I wasted time, and now doth Time waste me."

Richard is preconsciously anticipating (perhaps even longing for) the murderer who is about to cut short his time.

2. Wordsworth had the revolutionary proto-Freudian insight that adults have much to learn from children.

3. Compare Heimann (1962). Complementing my view that a burgeoning development of *defense* is the primary contribution of the anal phase, Heimann expresses the correlatable conviction that: "the significance of the anal phase lies in the fact that in this period the infant *experiences* the major clash between his narcissism and his object relations" (p. 408; the italics are mine, emphasizing how important it is that during this time the infant can *register* what is experienced).

4. Compare Freud (1941b) in one of his succinct last-recorded notes:

It is interesting that in connection with early experiences, as contrasted with later experiences, all the various reactions to them survive, of course including contradictory ones. Instead of a decision, which would have been the outcome later. Explanation: weakness of the power of synthesis, retention of the characteristic of the primary processes. (p. 299)

Appendix 1
Macbeth and Sphincter Defense

Shakespeare's *Macbeth* shows the defensive use of the "emotional sphincter" that results in deindividualization and dehumanization. The narcissistic regression is initiated by murder—a parricidal, oedipal crime, and as murder takes over Macbeth's mind, the need for nothingness gallops to keep pace with the acts of carnage.

At the start of the play Macbeth seems a decent-enough, feeling man, with ordinary loyalties and an active conscience. Once steeled (by the witches and Lady Macbeth) to murdering the king/father and taking his place, his regression (toward the preoedipal, archaic affect, and defensive devaluation) begins. By the end of the drama he has become the ruthless, indiscriminate killer of men, women, and children who cares for no one and nothing. His world has shrunk to the boundaries of his body, and only his own survival counts. In the last act of the play, he hears the shriek of the attending women who have witnessed the death of his wife, which he doesn't yet know about; he asks:

> Macbeth: What is that noise?
> Seyton: It is the cry of women, my good Lord.
> Macbeth: I have almost forgot the taste of fears.
>   The time has been, my senses would have cooled
>   To hear a night-shriek . . . I have supp'd full
>   with horrors;
>   Direness, familiar to my slaughterous thoughts,
>   Cannot once start me. (V/V/7-14)

Fear no longer has any meaning for this emotionally dead man. Earlier in his murderous course, at the feast after the killing of Banquo, Macbeth was terrified at seeing Banquo's ghost. But now he, the cannibal, has "supp'd full with horrors" and he can feel *nothing*—nothing about life, or death, or time, or loss. The scene continues:

> (re-enter Seyton)
> Macbeth: Wherefore was that cry?
> Seyton: The Queen, my Lord, is dead.

And there follows the famous soliloquy:

> Macbeth: She should have died hereafter;
>   There would have been a time for such a word—
>   To-morrow, and to-morrow, and to-morrow,
>   Creeps in this petty pace from day to day
>   To the last syllable of recorded time;

This is the meaningless "petty pace" of obsessive ritual, needed to contain the galloping "slaughterous thoughts" referred to above.

> And all our yesterdays have lighted fools
> The way to *dusty* death. (my italics; V/V/15-22)

"Dusty," a commentator notes (p. 150), refers to the "dust to dust" of the burial service; it is of course also an "anal" reduction of life and death to dirt. What follows is an allusion to life without values, and to *as-if, shadow* functioning.

> Out, out, brief candle!
> Life's but a walking *shadow*, a poor *player*,
> That struts and frets his hour *upon the stage*,
> And then is heard no more: it is a tale
> Told by an idiot, full of sound and fury,
> *Signifying nothing.* (my italics; V/V/23-27)

Life is not lived, but enacted; living is not being, but only signifying. Only his death, the culmination of a narcissistic regression, can bring Macbeth the nothingness of sleep his slaughter makes him crave but his conscience will not allow.

PARALLEL CLINICAL MATERIAL:
A LORD MACBETH OF MANHATTAN

I will simplify this man's history by stating that he had a witch-mother who cared little for him but gave him enemas and wiped his anus with compulsive zeal throughout his early childhood. He grew up to be capable of only "shadow" object relationships, and was currently living with a masochistic woman whom he abused; after mistreating her he would tearfully declaim about not being able to help himself and then she would feel sorry for him. Her initial tears of outrage, he later told me, gave him erections. In analysis, he continually offered his anus to be wiped and penetrated—but was unable to feel and to *own* that he was doing this. After a period of frightened compulsive promptness about paying his bill, he started to become provocatively tardy. He started this session by handing the analyst a check:

I almost forgot your check. I was afraid I would leave it in my coat outside. But I didn't want to put it in my pants pocket, not in my back pocket. I didn't want your check to be that close to my ass. I don't want it to be significant. It isn't significant! [Analyst]: Significant? [Patient]: The trouble is that despite my saying this kind of thing so many times, that stuff about my ass has for me the *significance of nothing*! [*cf.* Macbeth's soliloquy]. My life is nothing! [The patient was given to such "sound and fury" declamations.] My girl friend said to me that I never really talk to her and I never listen to her or remember what she says, as if she means nothing to me. I hated her for telling it to me—but it's true. I got so angry with her I almost fell asleep. [This "Macbeth" didn't "murder sleep" but used it (autohypnosis) as a defense.] It is true; she has no significance for me. I wouldn't care if she died. And your goddam check has no meaning either. Why can't you just change the way I am?

The patient, unable to feel the excitement and murderous hatred of his (largely anal-sadistic) impulses, had characteristically defended himself by dramatizing, and by degrading everything into meaninglessness. He was a Macbeth who had inhibited his ambitions and who had acted out murder only in a weakened, disguised, and disowned way—but its potentially terrifying presence in his consciousness made emotional sphincter control and autohypnosis imperative. The result was a kind of deindividualization and dehumanization.

In *The Three Sisters*, Chekhov has the denying cuckolded Andrei say of his wife, the ruthless Natalia Ivanovna (an attenuated, provincial Lady Macbeth):

A wife is a wife. She is honest, decent, well—kind, but along with all that there's something in her that reduces her to the level of some sort of petty, blind, coarse animal. In any case, she's not a human being (pp. 211–212).

Appendix 2
Freud and Rabelais

Freud's feelings about Rabelais are relevant to anal defensiveness. Freud refers to Rabelais at least five times in his published writings. One gathers (see 1900, p. 469) that at least the volume containing Garnier's illustrations to *Gargantua and Pantagruel* (which Freud tells of looking at) might at one time have been kept at Freud's bedside. Although Anna Freud (personal communication) has no awareness that Rabelais was a favorite writer of her father's and feels that she would have known if he had been, Freud characterizes Rabelais as "great" and "incomparable" (1900, p. 215). Two of Freud's own dreams in *The Interpretation of Dreams*, the "Count Thun dream" and the "dream of the open-air closet," lead to associations that involve Gargantua.[1] Freud's identification with the giant as a powerful superman who was able to do as he pleased centered on the episode of Gargantua's revenging himself on the people of Paris by urinating on them while he was *seated* (or so Freud says) on the cathedral of Notre Dame. Freud somehow derived the *sitting* from the book of Garnier illustrations to Rabelais that he mentions. Actually the illustration does not show the giant *sitting* (the word that set off my "goose" patient's associations). Grinstein (1968) reprints the illustration and says: "At no time does Rabelais mention that his hero Gargantua was 'sitting astride on Notre Dame and turning his stream of urine on the city' [this quote is from Freud on the open-air closet dream]. That detail comes from one of Jules Garnier's illustrations to Rabelais" (p. 430). Grinstein quotes the Le Clerq translation which doesn't mention either Notre Dame or sitting; but the church is there in the French original—here is Urquhart's more literal translation:

> and they prest so hard upon him that he was constrained to rest himself upon the towers of our Ladies Church; at which place, seeing so many about him . . . he untied his faire [codpiece] etc. (p. 50)

Neither the text nor the illustration by Garnier shows Gargantua *sitting*. The original text says *"soy reposer"*—resting himself—on the church; the illustration shows the giant *standing* astride Notre Dame.[2] Freud's fantasy supplied the sitting, undoubtedly through the connection with the "water closet." (Note the similarity to my "goose" patient whose toilet fantasy caused him to substitute *sitting* for *lying*, see page 52.) Freud's idea of Gargantua sitting on a symbol and appellation of the mother, and letting fly instinctively from that vantage point is truly Rabelaisian and is to be contrasted with my "goose" patient's subjection to the overstimulating, invasive mother when he was seated on the toilet.

Freud's dream thoughts (the associations of both dreams interconnect) lead to an antithesis between the megalomania connoted by the powerful giant and the helplessness of the small child; Freud relates this contrast with the developmental link between urination and the character trait of ambition. These two dreams about urination that express wishes for power and for revolution involve for Freud a specific reversal of past events and relationships condensed in his burning shameful memory of urinating in the parental bedroom at the age of seven—an action that occasioned his father's unforgettable response: "The boy will come to nothing" (1900, p. 216). The passive, weak potential-witness of the primal scene, the victim of this and perhaps other overstimulations (as my "goose" patient had been), attempted to discharge the overexcitement, anger, and longing with his phallic exhibitionistic urination. But the child's ambitious attempt could not succeed. The confrontation with his angry "giant" father simply augmented the boy's sense of inadequacy, his lack of sphincter control, and his fear of castration. But in the compensatory transformation of the dream fantasy, the dreamer is actively showing, instead of passively witnessing; *he* is the giant, and in his determined and forceful Gargantua-like use of his penis he discharges copiously and effectively through his urethra instead of becoming receptively overstimulated. The dreams reverse the involuntary incontinence that follows helpless lack of control of the "cloaca": urethra and/or anus. (In the "Count Thun" dream Freud hands a urinal to the potentially incontinent old father-figure.) In the dream of the open-air closet a powerful controlled flow of urine washes away encrusted piles of feces. Freud associated to the Augean stables that were cleansed by Hercules and says, "This Hercules was I" (1900, p. 469). The dream work transforms the little boy's inadequate management of his urinary stream into the power of the river Hercules diverted to sweep away the dung and pestilence of the Augean stables; the dream is a metaphor for urethro-phallic control banishing the dangers of anal erogeneity. The command and the discharge alluded to by the efficient grandiose washing away of the feces in the dream evokes the mutually interactive mastery of sphincters whereby satisfactory and reliable urethral and anal control are developmental prerequisites for the attainment of satisfactory and reliable phallic control.

But, as my "goose and rat" case history shows, what is needed is not only mastery of anal erogeneity and the anal sphincter, but of the aggression-laden oral and anal feelings ("archaic affect") involved with anal erogeneity. In a later paper (1930), Freud refers again to the linkage of ambition for power and urinary excitement. Here he points out the homosexual significance of this connection. In his description the urethral eroticism is primarily phallic rather than regressively anal, and destruction is relatively absent:

> Putting out a fire by micturating—a theme to which modern giants, Gulliver and Rabelais' Gargantua, still hark back—was therefore a kind of sexual act with a male, an enjoyment of sexual potency in a homosexual competition. (p. 90)

Freud makes another slip here; he has before in the dream book coupled the exhibitionistic urination of Gulliver and Gargantua. But although Gulliver does urinate to put out a fire in Lilliput, Gargantua's urination has nothing to do with a fire and does not have the predominantly competitive *libidinal* meaning Freud is referring to. Gargantua is urinating to vent destructive, revengeful anger. Annihilation rather than competition is evoked; and the offence of the Parisians alludes to overstimulation. The tone is comic, but the danger is deadly: in their curiosity, the Parisians "thronged so thick about him" that the giant became angry and:

> unfastened his noble codpiece and lugging out his great pleasure-rod, he so fiercely bepissed them that he drowned two hundred and sixty thousand four hundred and eighteen, exclusive of women and children. (p. 52)

Perhaps it is the need to block out this murderous urethral destructiveness that occasions Freud's slip. (See however Grinstein's convincing suggestion [1968, p. 232] that Freud may have unconsciously condensed two of Garnier's illustrations [both of which Grinstein reprints] to arrive at the coupling of Gargantua with Gulliver as urinating to put out the fire. The other illustration would increase the aggressive significance of urination. Gargantua is viewed from the rear; the castle at the Ford of Vede is burning. The text does not describe urination, but the picture does suggest it. The giant [*standing*, as the seven-year-old Freud had presumably done when he urinated in his parents' room, and *not sitting*] is shown destroying the castle with a club. Interweaving the two pictures would have provided a medium for the return of the repressed destructiveness.) At any rate, a deeper, more regressive and destructive level of homosexuality *was* involved for my "goose and rat" patient. Although his list of vanquished mistresses was meant to show him having bested his rivals in the urethral eroticism contest that Freud describes, my patient's competitive but hollow phallic athleticism actually masked the danger of the passive man's subjection to traumatic overstimulation and to cannibalistic rage, a danger that Rabelais indicates (an indication apparently suppressed by Freud), but was easily able to distance in the great book that so impressed Freud.

Notes to Appendix Two

1. The Count Thun dream (1900, pp. 208–218) is too long to be summarized. The first episode of the dream is characterized by Freud as leading to his associations about his boasting, and he says that this will be apparent to "anyone who will bear in mind the great Rabelais' incomparable account of the life and deeds of Gargantua and his son Pantagruel" (1900, p. 215). The dream is interpreted as stemming from Freud's ambition and his rebellious and revolutionary feelings. There are manifest dream elements (including a depiction of a plant to which Freud associates the French name *"pisse-en-lit"*) he links with urination and defecation; and also a dream image directly depicting an old man urinating.

The open-air (or water) closet dream:

> A hill, on which there was something like an open-air closet: a very long seat with a large hole at the end of it. Its back edge was thickly covered with small heaps of faeces of all sizes and degrees of freshness. There were bushes behind the seat. I micturated on the seat; a long stream of urine washed everything clean; the lumps of faeces came away easily and fell into the opening. It was as though at the end there was still some left. (1900, pp. 468–469)

2. Garnier's illustration shows the giant, his back to the viewer (so that his penis and urinating have to be inferred) standing astride Notre Dame; a billowing flood is pouring out from the front of the church and is rushing toward the foreground of the illustration.

References

Abend, S. (1981). Psychic conflict and the concept of defense. *Psychoanalytic Quarterly, 50,* 67–76.

Abraham, K. (1920). The narcissistic evaluation of excretory processes in dreams and neuroses. In *Selected Papers on Psycho-Analysis* (318–322). London: Hogarth Press, 1949.

—— (1921). Contributions to the theory of the anal character. In *Selected Papers on Psycho-Analysis* (370–392). London: Hogarth Press, 1949.

—— (1924). A short study of the development of the libido, viewed in the light of mental disorders. In *Selected Papers on Psycho-Analysis* (418–501). London: Hogarth Press, 1949.

Abrams, S. (1977). The genetic point of view: antecedents and transformations. *Journal of the American Psychoanalytic Association, 25,* 417–425.

American Psychiatric Association. (1987). *Diagnostic and statistical manual of mental disorders* (3rd ed., rev.). Washington, DC: American Psychiatric Association.

Auden, W. H. (1959). *About the House.* New York: Random House.

—— (1977). *The English Auden,* ed. E. Mendelson. New York: Random House.

——, & Kronenberger, L. (1962). *The Viking Book of Aphorisms.* New York: Viking Press.

Bakhtin, M. (1942/1968). *Rabelais and his World.* Cambridge: Massachusetts Institute of Technology Press.

Barnes, J. (1984). *Flaubert's Parrot.* London: Pan.

Bibring, E. (1941). The development and problem of the theory of the instincts. *International Journal of Psychoanalysis, 22,* 102–131.

Blake, W. (1793). The marriage of heaven and hell. In *William Blake,* ed. J. Bronowski. Baltimore: Penguin Books, 1958.

Blum, H. (1977). The prototype of preoedipal reconstruction. *Journal of the American Psychoanalytic Association, 25,* 757–785.

Brenner, C. (1974). On the nature and development of affects: a unified theory. *Psychoanalytic Quarterly, 43,* 532–556.

—— (1975). Affects and psychic conflict. *Psychoanalytic Quarterly, 44,* 5–28.

—— (1976). *Psychoanalytic Theory and Psychic Conflict.* New York: International Universities Press.

—— (1981). Defense and defense mechanisms. *Psychoanalytic Quarterly, 50,* 557–569.

Brown, N. O. (1959). *Life Against Death.* Middletown: Wesleyan University Press.

Calef, V., & Weinshel, E. (1981). Some clinical consequences of introjection: gaslighting. *Psychoanalytic Quarterly, 50,* 44–66.

Carpenter, H. (1981). *W. H. Auden: A Life.* Boston: Houghton, Mifflin.

Chasseguet-Smirgel, J. (1978). Reflections of the connexions between perversion and sadism. *International Journal of Psychoanalysis, 59,* 37–38.

—— (1984/1985). *Creativity and Perversion.* London: Free Association.

Chekhov, A. (1901). The three sisters. In *Best Plays,* ed. Stark Young. New York: Modern Library, 1956.

Curtis, H. (1985). Clinical perspectives on self-psychology. *Psychoanalytic Quarterly, 44,* 339–378.

Dahl, H. (1965). Observations on a 'natural experiment': Helen Keller. *Journal of the American Psychoanalytic Association, 13,* 533–550.

Dickes, R. (1965). The defensive function of an altered state of consciousness: a hypnoid state. *Journal of the American Psychoanalytic Association, 13,* 365–403.

Eisnitz, A. (1980). The organization of the self-representation and its influence on pathology. *Psychoanalytic Quarterly, 49,* 361–392.

Evans, E. (1892). *The Story of Caspar Hauser from Authentic Records.* London: Swan & Sonnenschein.

Fenichel, O. (1945). *The Psychoanalytic Theory of Neurosis.* New York: Norton.

Ferenczi, S. (1914). On the ontogenesis of an interest in money. In *Contributions to Psycho-Analysis* (319–333). New York: Basic Books, 1950.

—— (1925). Psycho-analysis of sexual habits. In *Further Contributions to the Theory and Technique of Psycho-Analysis* (259–297). London: Hogarth Press, 1950.

Flaubert, G. (1830–1857). *The Letters of Gustave Flaubert, Volume 1,* ed. F. Steegmuller. Cambridge: Harvard University Press, 1980.

—— (1857–1880). *The Letters of Gustave Flaubert, Volume 2,* ed. F. Steegmuller. Cambridge: Harvard University Press, 1982.

Fliess, R. (1953). The hypnotic evasion. *Psychoanalytic Quarterly, 22,* 497–511.

—— (1956). *Erogeneity and Libido.* New York: International Universities Press.

—— (1961). *Ego and Body Ego.* New York: International Universities Press.

—— (1973). *Symbol, Dream and Psychosis.* New York: International Universities Press.

Forster, E. M. (1921/1954). *Howard's End.* New York: Vintage Books.

—— (1927). *Aspects of the Novel.* New York: Harcourt & Brace.

Frame, D. P. (1977). *Rabelais. A Study.* New York: Harcourt Brace Jovano-vich.

Freedman, D. (1975). Congenital and perinatal sensory deprivations: their effect on the capacity to experience affect. *Psychoanalytic Quarterly, 44,* 62–80.

———, & Brown, S. L. (1968). On the role of coenesthetic stimulation in the development of psychic structure. *Psychoanalytic Quarterly, 37,* 418–438.

Freud, A. (1936/1966). *The ego and the mechanisms of defense.* New York: International Universities Press.

——— (1947). Emotional and instinctual development. In *Indications for Child Analysis and Other Papers, 1945–1956* (458–488). New York: International Universities Press, 1968.

——— (1949). Aggression in relation to emotional development, normal and pathological. In *Indications for Child Analysis and Other Papers, 1945–1956* (489–497). New York: International Universities Press, 1968.

——— (1952). The mutual influences in the development of the ego and the id: introduction to the discussion. In *Indications for Child Analysis and Other Papers, 1945–1956* (230–244). New York: International Universities Press, 1968.

——— (1965). *Normality and Pathology in childhood.* New York: International Universities Press.

——— (1966). Obsessional neurosis: a summary of psycho-analytic views as presented at the Congress. *International Journal of Psychoanalysis, 47,* 116–122.

Freud, S. (1886–1899). Extracts from the Fliess papers. *Standard Edition, 1.*

——— (1887–1902). *The Origins of Psychoanalysis.* eds. M. Bonaparte, A. Freud, & E. Kris. New York: Basic Books, 1954.

——— (1900). The interpretation of dreams. *Standard Edition, 4/5.*

——— (1905a). Fragment of an analysis of a case of hysteria. *Standard Edition, 7.*

——— (1905b). Three essays on the theory of sexuality. *Standard Edition, 7.*

——— (1907). Letter to C. G. Jung. In *The Freud/Jung Letters. The Correspondence between Sigmund Freud and C. G. Jung* (40), ed. W. McGuire. Princeton: Princeton University Press, 1974.

——— (1908). Character and anal erotism. *Standard Edition, 9.*

——— (1909). Notes upon a case of obsessional neurosis. *Standard Edition, 10.*

——— (1911a). Formulations on the two principles of mental functioning. *Standard Edition, 12.*

——— (1911b). Psycho-analytic notes on an autobiographical account of a case of paranoia (dementia paranoides). *Standard Edition, 12.*

——— (1912). On the universal tendency to debasement in the sphere of love. *Standard Edition, 11.*

——— (1913). The disposition to obsessional neurosis: a contribution to the problem of choice of neurosis. *Standard Edition, 12.*

——— (1914). On narcissism: an introduction. *Standard Edition, 14.*

——— (1915). Instincts and their vicissitudes. *Standard Edition, 14.*

—— (1917). Introductory lectures on psycho-analysis:XXVII. *Standard Edition*, 16.

—— (1917). On transformations of instinct as exemplified in anal erotism. *Standard Edition*, 17.

—— (1923). The ego and the id. *Standard Edition*, 19.

—— (1925). Negation. *Standard Edition*, 19.

—— (1926a). Inhibitions, symptoms and anxiety. *Standard Edition*, 20.

—— (1926b). The question of lay analysis. *Standard Edition*, 20.

—— (1926c). Die Frage der Laienanalyse. *Gesammelte Werke*. 14.

—— (1930). Civilization and its discontents. *Standard Edition*, 20.

—— (1933). New introductory lectures. *Standard Edition*, 22.

—— (1937). Analysis terminable and interminable. *Standard Edition*, 23.

—— (1940). An outline of psycho-analysis. *Standard Edition*, 23.

—— (1941a). Schriften aus dem Nachlass. *Gesammelte Werke*, 17.

—— (1941b). Findings, ideas, problems. *Standard Edition*, 23.

Friedman, L. (1982). The humanistic trend in recent psychoanalytic theory. *Psychoanalytic Quarterly*, *51*, 353–371.

Glover, E. (1935). A developmental study of the obsessional neurosis. *International Journal of Psychoanalysis*, *16*, 131–144.

—— (1938). A note on idealization. In *On the Early Development of Mind* (290–296). London: Imago, 1956.

Greenacre, P. (1957). The childhood of the artist: libidinal phase development and giftedness. *Psychoanalytic Study of the Child*, *12*, 47–72.

Grinstein, A. (1968). *On Sigmund Freud's Dreams*. Detroit: Wayne State Press.

Guttman, S. (1981). *Concordance to the Standard Edition of the Complete Psychological Works of Sigmund Freud*. New York: International Universities Press.

Hanly, C. (1982). Narcissism, defence and the positive transference. *International Journal of Psychoanalysis*, *63*, 427–44.

Heimann, P. (1962). Notes on the anal stage. *International Journal of Psychoanalysis*, *43*, 406–414.

Herzog, W. (1974). *Kaspar Hauser: Every Man for Himself and God Against All* (Film).

Hoffer, W. (1952). The mutual influences in the development of ego and id: earliest stage. *Psychoanalytic Study of the Child*, *7*, 31–41.

Jones, E. (1913). Hate and anal erotism. In *Papers on Psycho-Analysis*. London: Hogarth Press, 1923.

—— (1918). Anal-erotic character traits. In *Papers on Psychoanalysis* (413–437). Boston: Beacon Press, 1961.

Karlinsky, S., & Heim, M. (1973). *Anton Chekhov's Life and Thought*. Berkeley: University of California Press.

Kipling, R. (1937). Something of myself. In *Collected Works*, Volume *24*. New York: Doubleday, Doran, 1941.

Kris, E. (1956). On some vicissitudes of insight in psychoanalysis. In *Selected Papers* (252–271). New Haven: Yale University Press, 1975.

Kris, M. (1957). The use of prediction in a longitudinal study. *Psychoanalytic Study of the Child*, *12*, 175–189.

Kundera, M. (1984). *The Unbearable Lightness of Being*. New York: Harper & Row.

Lang, A. (1904). The mystery of Kaspar Hauser: the child of Europe. In *Historical Mysteries* (118–143). London: Smith & Elder.

Lorenz, K. (1963/1966). *On Aggression*. London: Methuen.

Mahler, M. (1968). *On Human Symbiosis and the Vicissitudes of Individuation*. New York: International Universities Press.

—— (1972a). On the first three subphases of the separation–individuation process. *International Journal of Psychoanalysis, 53*, 333–338.

—— (1972b). Rapprochement subphase of the separation–individuation process. *Psychoanalytic Quarterly*, 487–506.

——, Pine, F., & Bergman, A. (1975). *The Psychological Birth of the Human Infant*. New York: Basic Books.

McDougall, J. (1985). *Theaters of the Mind*. New York: Basic Books.

McGuire, W., ed. (1974). *The Freud/Jung Letters. The Correspondence between Sigmund Freud and C. G. Jung*. Princeton: Princeton University Press.

Neubauer, P. (1984). Anna Freud's concept of developmental lines. *Psychoanalytic Study of the Child, 39*, 15–39.

Orwell, G. (1949). *1984*. New York: Harcourt & Brace.

Painter, G. (1959). *Marcel Proust. A Biography. Volume 1*. London: Chatto & Windus.

—— (1965). *Marcel Proust. A Biography. Volume 2*. London: Chatto & Windus.

Partridge, E. (1937). *A Dictionary of the Underworld*. New York: Bonanza Books, 1949.

Peller, L. (1965). Comments on libidinal organization and child development. *Journal of the American Psychoanalytic Association, 13*, 732–747.

Prior, M. (1718). An epitaph. In *Oxford Book of Eighteenth Century Verse* (20–22), ed. D. Smith. Oxford University Press, 1926.

Proust, M. (1908–1909). Contre Sainte-Beuve. In *Marcel Proust on Art and Literature, 1896–1919* (19–278). New York: Carroll & Graf, 1984.

—— (1913). Swann's way. In *Remembrance of Things Past. Volume I* (3–464). New York: Random House, 1981.

—— (1921). Cities of the plain. In *Remembrance of Things Past. Volume II* (623–1170). New York: Random House, 1981.

—— (1927). Time regained. In *Remembrance of Things Past. Volume III* (709–1108). New York: Random House, 1981.

Rabelais, F. (1534/1973). *Gargantua*. Paris: Hachette.

—— (1534a). *The Lives, Heroic Deeds and Sayings of Gargantua and His Son Pantagruel*, tr. T. Urquhart & P. Le Motteux. New York: Simon & Schuster, 1929.

—— (1534b). *The Complete Works*, tr. J. Le Clercq. New York: Modern Library, 1944.

—— (1534c). *Gargantua and Pantagruel*, tr. J. Cohen. Baltimore: Penguin Books, 1955.

Rangell, L. (1955). On the psychoanalytic theory of anxiety: a statement of a unitary theory. *Journal of the American Psychoanalytic Association, 3,* 229-236.

—— (1961). The role of early psychic functioning in psychoanalysis. *Journal of the American Psychoanalytic Association, 9,* 595-609.

—— (1968). A further attempt to resolve the "problem of anxiety." *Journal of the American Psychoanalytic Association, 16,* 371-404.

—— (1978). On understanding and treating anxiety and its derivatives. *International Journal of Psychoanalysis, 59,* 229-236.

Rappaport, D. (1958). Quoted by Curtis, H. (1958). Clinical perspectives on self psychology. *Psychoanalytic Quarterly, 44,* 339-378.

Ritvo, S. (1984). The image and uses of the body in psychic conflict. *Psychoanalytic Study of the Child, 39,* 449-469.

Sacks, O. (1985). *The Man Who Mistook his Wife for a Hat.* London: Duckworth.

Sadger, I. (1910). Analerotik and analcharakter. *Die Heilkunde.*

Schreber, D. P. (1903/1955). *Memoirs of My Nervous Illness.* London: Dawson.

Schumann, R. (1840). Frauenliebe und Leben. *Samtliche Lieder* (84-105). New York: C. F. Peters, undated.

Schur, M. (1953). The ego in anxiety. In *Drives, Affects, Behavior,* ed. R. Loewenstein. New York: International Universities Press.

Shakespeare, W. (1595). *Richard II.* In *Shakespeare: Twenty-Three Plays,* ed. T. Parrott. New York: Scribners, 1938.

—— (1604). *Hamlet.* Boston: Atheneum Press, 1939.

—— (1608). *Macbeth.* Cambridge: Harvard University Press, 1951.

Shengold, L. (1966). The metaphor of the journey in "The Interpretation of Dreams." *American Imago, 23,* 316-331.

—— (1967). The effects of overstimulation: rat people. *International Journal of Psychoanalysis, 48,* 403-415.

—— (1971). More about rats and rat people. *International Journal of Psychoanalysis, 52,* 277-288.

—— (1975a). Soul murder. *International Journal of Psychoanalytic Psychotherapy, 3,* 366-373.

—— (1975b). An attempt at soul murder: Rudyard Kipling's early life and work. *Psychoanalytic Study of the Child, 30,* 683-724.

—— (1979). Child abuse and deprivation: soul murder. *Journal of the American Psychoanalytic Association, 27,* 533-559.

—— (1981). Insight as metaphor. *Psychoanalytic Study of the Child, 36,* 289-306.

—— (1982). Anal erogeneity: the goose and the rat. *International Journal of Psychoanalysis, 63,* 331-345.

—— (1985a). The effects of child abuse as seen in adults: George Orwell. *Psychoanalytic Quarterly, 54,* 20-45.

—— (1985b). Defensive anality and anal narcissism. *International Journal of Psychoanalysis, 66,* 47-73.

Singh, J., & Zinng, R. (1939). *Wolf Children and Feral Man.* New York: Harper.

Spence, D. (1982). *Narrative Truth and Historical Truth.* New York: Norton.

Spitz, R. (1945). Hospitalism: an inquiry into the genesis of psychiatric conditions in early childhood. *Psychoanalytic Study of the Child, 1*, 53-74.

—— (1946). Hospitalism: a follow-up report. *Psychoanalytic Study of the Child, 2*, 113-117.

—— (1957). *No and Yes: On the Genesis of Human Communication.* New York: International Universities Press.

—— (1965). *The First Year of Life.* New York: International Universities Press.

—— & Wolf, K. M. (1946). Anaclitic depression. *Psychoanalytic Study of the Child, 2*, 313-342.

Spruiell, V. (1976). *On Idealization.* (unpublished).

—— (1979). Freud's concepts of idealization. *Journal of the American Psychoanalytic Association, 27*, 777-792.

—— (1983). The self and the ego. *Psychoanalytic Quarterly, 50*, 219-244.

Steegmuller, F. (1972). *Flaubert in Egypt: A Sensibility on Tour.* Boston: Little, Brown.

Stoller, R. (1979). *Sexual Excitement: Dynamics of Erotic Life.* New York: Pantheon.

Swift, J. (1702). The problem, that my Lord Berkeley stinks when he is in love. In *The Poems of Jonathan Swift. Volume 1* (61-63). London: George Bell & Son, 1895.

—— (1731). Strephon and Chloe. In *The Poems of Jonathan Swift. Volume 2* (4-14). London: George Bell & Son, 1895.

Trilling, L. (1947). Freud and literature. In *The Liberal Imagination* (34-57). New York: Viking Press, 1950.

—— (1955). Freud: within and beyond culture. In *Beyond Culture* (89-118). New York: Viking Press, 1965.

Valenstein, A. (1973). On attachment to painful feelings and the negative therapeutic reaction. *Psychoanalytic Study of the Child, 28*, 365-392.

Von Feuerbach, A. (1832/1834). *Kaspar Hauser*, tr. H. Linberg. London: Simpkin & Marshall.

Wassermann, J. (1908). *Caspar Hauser*, tr. C. Newton. New York: Liveright, 1928.

Weinshel, E. (1970). The ego in health and normality. *Journal of the American Psychoanalytic Association, 18*, 682-735.

—— (1977). I didn't mean it: negation as a character trait. *Psychoanalytic Study of the Child, 32*, 387-419.

Wentworth, H., & Flexner, S. (1960). *Dictionary of American Slang.* New York: Crowell.

Whitman, W. (1856/1900). *Leaves of Grass.* Philadelphia: David McKay.

Wordsworth, W. (1803). Ode. Intimations of immortality from recollections of early childhood. In *Poetical Works* (403-406). New York: Thomas Y. Crowell. undated.

Yeats, W. B. (1914). Friends. In *Collected Poems* (122). New York: Macmillan, 1951.

—— (1933). Crazy Jane talks to the bishop. In *Collected Poems* (254-255). New York: Macmillan, 1951.

Index